Growing Up
With Literature

VielKa
PLATNER

Growing Up With Literature

Third Edition

Walter E. Sawyer, EdD
Russell Sage College

Foreword by Francis P. Hodge

Africa • Australia • Canada • Denmark • Japan • Mexico • New Zealand • Philippines
Puerto Rico • Singapore • Spain • United Kingdom • United States

NOTICE TO THE READER

Publisher does not warrant or guarantee any of the products described herein or perform any independent analysis in connection with any of the product information contained herein. Publisher does not assume, and expressly disclaims, any obligation to obtain and include information other than that provided to it by the manufacturer.

The reader is expressly warned to consider and adopt all safety precautions that might be indicated by the activities herein and to avoid all potential hazards. By following the instructions contained herein, the reader willingly assumes all risks in connection with such instructions.

The Publisher makes no representation or warranties of any kind, including but not limited to, the warranties of fitness for particular purpose or merchantability, nor are any such representations implied with respect to the material set forth herein, and the publisher takes no responsibility with respect to such material. The publisher shall not be liable for any special, consequential, or exemplary damages resulting, in whole or part, from the readers' use of, or reliance upon, this material.

Delmar Staff:

Business Unit Director: Susan Simpfenderfer
Executive Editor: Marlene McHugh Pratt
Acquisitions Editor: Erin O'Connor Traylor
Editorial Assistant: Alexis Ferraro
Executive Marketing Manager: Donna Lewis
Executive Production Manager: Wendy Troeger
Production Editor: Sandra Woods
Cover Illustrator: Sharon Barner

Printed in Canada
2 3 4 5 6 7 8 9 10 XXX 05 04 03 02 01 00

For more information, contact:
Delmar, 3 Columbia Circle, PO Box 15015, Albany, NY 12212-0515;
or find us on the World Wide Web at http://www.delmar.com

Library of Congress Cataloging-in-Publication Data

Sawyer, Walter.
  Growing up with literature/Walter E. Sawyer; foreword by
 Francis P. Hodge; illustrations by Sally Newcomb. — 3rd ed.
    p.   cm.
  Includes bibliographical references and indexes.
  ISBN 0-7668-0369-4
  1. Children's literature —Study and teaching (Preschool) —United
States. 2. Children—Books and reading. 3. Early childhood
education—United States—Curricula. I. Title.
LB1140.5.L3S28 2000
372.21'0973—dc21   99-21848
                                            CIP

Contents

Foreword by Francis P. Hodge

I am delighted to introduce the third edition of *Growing Up With Literature*. Many texts are available emphasizing classroom instruction in literature at all grade levels. Many texts also are on the market offering guidance to parents about the importance of books in the development of young children. This text, with over 100 newly added titles, takes the best of the aforementioned examples and treats the continuity of one to the other. This feature distinguishes *Growing Up With Literature* from many other contemporary literature-related texts.

Dr. Walter Sawyer, writing instructor at Russell Sage College, is eminently qualified to address this topic. I have known Dr. Sawyer, who is both a father and an educator, for over twenty years. He has worked diligently with his own children in their development as literate human beings. He has studied and guided school programs aimed at improving literary facility among school children, particularly at the elementary level.

Dr. Sawyer's approach is truly grassroots in origin. He starts with the WHYS and carefully leads the early childhood educator and the parent along the road to the WHAT, WITHS and the HOWS. His approach is a carefully conceived road map of operational ideas and suggestions. His points have been tested and have proven successful in numerous cases. He offers alternatives, suggesting titles that might be utilized; he indicates areas of concern; and, significantly, he advises caution and thoughtful planning by both parents and teachers.

Encouraging a love for literature, developing good readers, and making reading an integral part of everyday life are so important for young readers. Without a foundation from home and early childhood, children often experience difficulty in school, especially in mastery of reading skills. Working through the suggestions and recommendations offered by Dr. Sawyer in *Growing Up With Literature* can instill in young readers a love for and understanding of literature.

Dedication

To Jean C. Sawyer, who truly understands the beauty and power of literature.

W.S.

Preface to the Third Edition

The third edition of *Growing Up with Literature* is a book that celebrates the inter-action that can take place when quality children's literature is shared with young-sters. It is a comprehensive guide for the individual wishing to learn how to use children's books effectively in early childhood programs. Sections are included on selecting appropriate books, motivating children to participate in the experience, integrating literature into a program, and managing the process. Although the pri-mary audience for this text is practitioners in early childhood education programs, parents will find a wealth of information here as well.

The philosophy of the book is to present literature as an integrated part of an educational program rather than as an isolated feature used only at storytime. This approach is supported by much of the current thinking, theory, and research on the development of literacy. While the foundation of the book rests on firm con-ceptual ground, the practical aspects of working with children are at the forefront of the presentation. The book is a hands-on tool for both short- and long-range program planning. It explains such concepts as whole language, the role of com-puter technology, and emerging literacy in easily understood terms that are easi-ly translated into classroom practice.

- TIPS FOR TEACHERS is a new feature found in every chapter. It provides readers with practical suggestions related to the content of the chapter. The ideas can be easily and quickly used by early childhood teachers and caregivers.

- Over 100 new children's literature titles are suggested for use in activities outlined in the book. These new titles were selected for their relevance, interest, and beauty. Also included are strategies for locating virtually any picture book desired.

- New artwork has been included to depict children in literacy activities relat-ed to the focus of individual chapters.

- The chapter on media has been completely revised. It has been expand-ed to include the use of high-speed computers, literature-related CD-ROMs, and the internet. This chapter also describes the eleven websites that every parent and early childhood worker needs to know about.

- Included in this edition are hundreds of new ideas shared by readers, edi-tors, and reviewers who are dedicated to the literacy of young children.

- A new Appendix C outlines a thematic unit for preschoolers on the topic of bears. It identifies unit objectives, activities, children's books, poems, songs, hands-on activities, and parent activities.
- A new Appendix D identifies the author's most highly recommended children's books for reading aloud, theme development, and sharing with young children. The listing is organized by topic, making it a valuable resource for future use by readers.

The text, which focuses exclusively on picture books for young children, makes a valuable contribution to the field of early childhood education. Few practical books on using literature in early childhood programs are based upon the current thinking and theory on emerging literacy. *Growing Up With Literature* provides a wealth of practical ideas and strategies that can be implemented in the classroom. The clear, concise explanations describing the process of implementation ensure their transfer. In addition, hundreds of books appropriate for young readers are cited. A wide range of titles is used to familiarize the reader with the variety of books available. The citations range from classics to the latest contemporary publications. The third edition includes a listing of more than 100 additional children's book citations. They represent the best of children's titles published over the last few years.

Many special features are included. First, and most important, is the approach stressed within the book. The focus is on integrating literature as an integral part of education throughout all areas of the curriculum. This edition also includes expanded sections of nonfiction and multicultural titles for young children. Each chapter includes both references for further reading and a set of questions for thought and discussion. The questions tend not to seek rote types of answers. Rather, they require a more careful analysis of the material in the chapter in order to give a thoughtful and logical response. An instructor's guide is also available.

Walter Sawyer is a graduate of Siena College, Assumption College, and the State University of New York at Albany. He holds B.A., M.A., and EdD degrees. He is certified in and has worked at all levels of education from nursery school through graduate school. Currently he is an administrator for the Waterford-Halfmoon School District in upstate New York and teaches graduate courses in writing and reading at Russell Sage College. He has been an active member at all levels of the International Reading Association, and is past president of a local reading council. He was named "Educator of the Year" in 1994 by the School Administrators Association of New York State. He has a deep personal interest in storytelling and has published over 60 articles, books, papers, and chapters in the field of literacy. He is also author of *The Storm,* a children's picture book (Katonah, New York: Richard C. Owen, 1999).

The author would like to extend an acknowledgment to several key people in this endeavor: To Jean Sawyer who listened to and provided critical feedback on many of the chapters in addition to watching the children. To Andrew and Emily Sawyer who shared so many of the cited children's books in family read-aloud sessions. To the authors and storytellers who provided photographs for this book. To the publishers of children's books who generously granted permission to reprint covers of their books. To Frank Hodge for the Foreword to this book and for guiding us all down the right road. To our editor for all of her support and encouragement. To the following reviewers whose perceptive feedback and useful comments made *Growing Up With Literature* a better book:

Sally Curtis
Springfield Technical Community College
Springfield, MA

Doris Dunkleberger
Waterford-Halfmoon Elementary School
Waterford, NY

Veronica Getstow, Ph.D.
University of California, Los Angeles
Los Angeles, CA

Marian Leithead
Gardner College
Camrose, AB, Canada

Jeanne Mather, Ph.D.
University of Science and Arts of Oklahoma
Chickasha, OK

Nina Mazloff
Becker College
Worcester, MA

W.S.

A child's world is fresh and new and
beautiful, full of wonder and excitement.

– Rachel Carson

1 What's So Special about Literature?

Making reading a joyful experience for children lies at the heart of this book. Introduced correctly, literature can been seen throughout life as the friend and companion it deserves to be. In order for this to happen, the adults who work with young children need to foster this relationship with literature in their own lives. It is a mistake to think that one can teach children to love reading and literature without possessing that same love oneself. Children are quite perceptive; they can often spot false enthusiasm in a second.

Some of the best books written today are written for children. The books available for children are a wonderful place to begin or to extend a love for literature. The success of the strategies suggested in this book will depend on this love.

TIPS FOR TEACHERS

Appendix D lists a variety of children's books for reading aloud, theme development, and sharing with young children. The listing is organized by topic, making it a valuable resource for future use. Each of the books in the listing has been used many times, with children responding enthusiastically to the stories.

Literature has a special place in the development of the young child. Stories shared aloud in a warm atmosphere and at an appropriate pace can be the vehicle through which children learn about their world. The technology of television, telecommunications, and computer science sends information at us at an ever increasing speed and in greater abundance than ever before. However, people are not always capable of processing this information in any meaningful way. This is true for adults and it is true for children. When the amount of information is too great and the speed too rapid, the full meaning is lost. The nuances are not noticed. The subtle humor slips past. The message becomes devoid of emotion.

There has been an abundance of research over the past quarter of a century which stresses the importance of books and literature as part of a child's development. When children come to school already reading or with a deep interest in reading, certain critical facts can often be found in their preschool experiences. They usually had books in the home. They

1

observed adults reading. They were read to by adults. They had someone to talk to about books, reading, and literature.

While experience is a powerful teacher for a young child, books and literature can have a profound influence as well. Early in life, children strive for meaning. They try to find out how things work. They attempt to learn how people respond to them and what control they have over their environment. Young children need experiences with print that let them hear, tell, create, and explore the world around themselves as they seek to find meaning.[1] The purpose of literature and education is to help people arrive at this meaning. Given this, a broad exposure to literature is a critical component of child development.

Have education and family life succeeded in fulfilling the need to find meaning in life? The answer is partly yes. Despite the large amount of television viewing that young people engage in, sales of children's books are rapidly increasing. Most writers and many successful adults confirm the importance of books and of being read to in their early years. On the other hand, our nation has an alarmingly high secondary school dropout rate. Our level of adult illiteracy is high in comparison with other industrialized countries. More importantly, we tend to be a nation of people who choose not to read. Jim Trelease cites statistics that indicate that *TV Guide* is the most widely purchased weekly publication in the country. His work has uncovered the fact that our reading is both infrequent and lacking in quality.[2]

Young children need to be encouraged to develop interests and attitudes toward reading and literature that will stay with them throughout their lives. Such attributes can help children become competent students and thoughtful adults. Literature will enrich their lives and help them find meaning in their existence.

THE VALUE OF LITERATURE

Literature serves many needs and imparts many values. Although literature may not appear as spectacular as a computer game or television program, it provides something that neither of them can.

Children and adults often need time to reflect on their experiences. Allowing time to think results in deeper learning and understanding. One can always go back to a book to reread an enjoyable, confusing, or important part. This often cannot be done with other media. For example, a child's first experience with snow and playing in the snow can be thrilling. To make it even more meaningful and memorable, one might share Kim Lewis's touching tale, *First Snow,* set in the snowy whiteness of northern England. Other good choices include *Snowsong Whistling*, a nostalgic look at rural New England by Karen Lotz, *When Winter Comes* by Robert Maass, and Martin Waddell's *Little Mo.*

---

[1] Davis, J.K., & Williams, R.P. (1994, May). Lead sprightly into literacy, *Young Children,* 49, 41.

[2] Trelease, J. (1995). *The new read-aloud handbook,* New York: Viking Penguin.

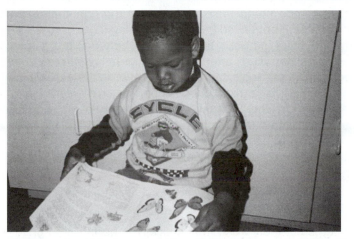

Children should feel comfortable with books. Courtesy Diana Comer.

TIPS FOR TEACHERS

Encourage children to relate their experiences to the story being read.
• Ask, "Can anyone tell us about a pet cat or dog?"
• Keep the child speaking by responding with, "What happened next?"
• Let children finish their explanations.

If a child seems reluctant about playing in the snow, one might read Emily Arnold McCully's *First Snow.* Told entirely in illustrations, it is the story of the smallest member of a mouse family who overcomes a hesitancy to play in the snow. Each of these books can be shared over and over again with a child.

The issue is not a matter of literature being positive and technology being negative. Rather, it is more a problem of balance. Both may be used for helping children develop in appropriate ways. There is certainly a need for children to be aware of the technology of their world. It will be an important part of their lives. However, it is equally important for books and literature to be an integral part of living. Literature can help children comprehend their world, build positive attitudes, and make a connection with their humanity.

Learning about the World

Through books, children can both learn about and make sense of their world. They learn about their world when books inform about or explain various parts of it. In so doing, books can also arouse the curiosity of children. After reading about something, youngsters will often seek to learn more about it. They may request similar books. They may recreate scenes from the book.

Children can understand their world better through the reinforcement of books. They may have experienced or seen something they do not fully understand. By learning more about it in books, they are often better able to achieve an accurate understanding. When plans are made for children to see or experience something new, books about the topic can be shared prior to the experience. If a trip to a fair or a zoo is planned, one might choose books such as *Is Your Mama a Llama* by Deborah Guarino or *The Pumpkin Fair* by Eve Bunting. Books will enable children to have more meaningful experiences. Learning is a process of relating new things to things that are already known. Since the pages of books can be studied, reread, and thought about over time, books are ideal tools for helping children learn and understand.

Building Positive Attitudes

Besides learning about their world, it is critically important that children develop positive attitudes about many things. They need to develop positive self-esteem and to see themselves as competent human beings capable of caring and of being loved. They need to develop tolerance for others who may not share their beliefs or who may be different from themselves in various ways. They need to develop a curiosity about learning and life. Books and literature can become primary tools for developing and satisfying that curiosity.

Self-Esteem. Literature can help children develop positive self-images in a stressful world. Economic hardships, crime, drugs, and conflicts in the world may be readily apparent even to young children. Family and health problems may be factors children are dealing with as well. Parental love is strong and usually exists even when there is tremendous hardship. The concept of parental love can be reinforced with books such as *The Mouse That Jack Built,* by Cyndy Szekere, *Another Mouse To Feed* by Robert Kraus, and *Koala Lou* by Mem Fox. In the latter story, Australian author/educator Mem Fox illustrates parental love in its purest form. Through books, children can identify with others like themselves. They can see how others deal with similar problems. By sharing a story with an adult, children can be encouraged to talk about some of these issues.

Literature can help children define their feelings and develop a sense of self. Stories that mirror the child's situation or are at least related to the situation can be chosen by a perceptive adult. Reading about others who are attempting to make sense of a similar situation can bring hope. Learning that some feelings are normal can enable children to understand that they themselves are normal. They can learn that there is no need for guilt.

Many books explore the idea of self-concept. Many address this as an issue of developing relationships among siblings and peers. Watty Piper's classic, *The Little Engine That Could,* has long been used in this way. A more recent story that deals with the problem with poetic humor is *Fathers, Mothers, Sisters, Brothers* by Mary Ann Hoberman. A book that relates to developing a sense of self within a set of siblings is *Jenny's Baby Brother* by Peter Smith.

Tolerance of Others. Literature can help children understand how they fit in and how important it is to relate to others. Adults who are successful in working well with others can provide good role models. They tend to know how to have their needs met in society while pleasing others at the same time. Besides providing a role model, adults work to set realistic goals and limits for group interaction. Providing appropriate role models is a powerful instructional tool.

Literature, through its art, imagery, humor, and empathetic characters, provides a teaching tool for developing tolerance. By learning how characters in stories develop solutions to social problems, children can begin to assume a role in goal and limit setting for their own behavior.

There are wonderful books that explore the nature of differences among people and the acceptance of others. *Watch Out for the Chicken Feet in Your Soup* by Tomie dePaola explores the acceptance by a young boy of his grandmother and her Old World habits. *Aunt Armadillo* by Robin Baird Lewis celebrates the relationship of a little girl and her eccentric aunt. *Bearsie Bear and the Surprise Sleepover* by Bernard Waber raises the potential for accommodation.

Curiosity about Life. Children possess a curiosity about the world around them. They want to know about things and places. They want to know about different people. They are proud of the things they have learned. Keeping this sense of wonder alive through a literacy program that includes a sound read-aloud program will help to encourage success in later schooling and in life. Books keep introducing new and fascinating topics. They encourage children to ask more questions and to seek more answers.

TIPS FOR TEACHERS

Praise children when they demonstrate a skill or ability.
- *Say, "That's right, Susan. That's the letter 'S,' just like in your name."*
- *Comment, "I like the way you told your story. You made it sound so funny."*
- *Smile, nod, and respond when children speak to you.*

If children are to succeed in later schooling, it is critical that they want to learn and succeed. While children can be forced to learn bits and pieces of isolated reading skills, no amount of pressure can force children beyond their capability. Exerting this kind of pressure on young children can be totally destructive to their desire to learn and read. Pressure cannot force them to be curious and enthusiastic about books and literature once they have decided that reading is tedious, dull, and boring. Once the desire to better understand oneself and life is lost, it is difficult to revive it. It is far better for adults to focus on sharing appropriate stories that foster self-esteem, a tolerance for others, and a curiosity about life.

Interest and pleasure in reading are often enhanced by the good feelings shared in reading a book together. Courtesy Diana Comer.

The Human Connection

Reading a book with a child can do many things for child and reader alike. The sharing that emerges from the relationship creates an important human connection. There is a personal interaction between the child and reader. There is time for the reader to react to the child's delight, confusion, anger, or fear. There is a feeling of warmth and safety for the child in the physical presence of the reader. The reader can assure the child that all is well and detect unasked questions. The book can be stopped or reread. Discussion can take place at any point without destroying the overall experience of the story.

The book becomes much more than a set of papers with markings and illustrations. The sound and rhythm of language can be slowed down, speeded up, made louder, or made to express emotions. The beauty of the language and the story can be developed in a manner appropriate to the children. The illustrations and photographs in the book can be touched, studied, discussed, and returned to as the story goes along. All of this is created within the relationship developed by the child and the reader.

EMERGING LITERACY AND LITERATURE

All adults want children to learn to read. However, there has been substantial debate as to when the teaching of reading should begin. Should reading skills be taught to preschool children? Should formal reading instruction be delayed until the child reaches seven years of age? Should the first-grade curriculum be pushed down into the kindergarten? Should children who have not mastered kindergarten readiness skills enter a transitional program between kindergarten and first grade until they have mastered the skills?

The answers to these questions depend on what is actually meant by the word "reading." Reading is the acquisition of meaning from a written text. The focus is on meaning. In view of this, children begin the process of learning to read from the moment of birth. They are engaged in learning to read when they first begin to listen for the voice of a parent, the rhythm of a story, or the soothing sounds of a lullaby. Some may argue that the very young child is using only listening skills, but this distinction between listening and reading is an artificial one. The two are inextricably related to each other; each supports the other.

Viewing grade levels as distinct is also an inadequate way of thinking about the way children learn to read. The grade levels in schools are for the convenience of adults rather than children. They enable adults to sort children based on age, ability, cultural awareness, and reading level. Children develop at widely varying rates and learn to read at different times in their development. Expecting all children to learn to read at a certain age or grade is hopelessly naive. Children tend to send signals when they are ready for new challenges. It is up to the adults to do a better job of reading these signals and responding appropriately to them.

There is a need to be aware of how literacy emerges long before formal schooling and to understand the role that literature can play in that emergence. To develop this awareness, one needs to develop a concept of what is contained in a real literacy curriculum and to couple this concept with a realistic understanding of how reading skills emerge. Based on this view, a set of realistic expectations for individual children can be formulated.

A Literacy Curriculum

Over the past few decades there has been an abundance of research on how young children develop literacy. Obviously, literacy develops best in a literate environment. Given the view taken in this book, a literate environment possesses certain features. These features are the experiences and materials that will best enhance the ability of children to derive meaning from their environment. Jerome Harste and Virginia Woodward have studied early literacy programs for many years. Their research identifies three key aspects of a literate environment:

1. Supporting the success of the learner;
2. Focusing on learning language; and
3. Allowing the learner to explore language.[3]

Each of their points needs to be considered.

---

[3] Harste, J., & Woodward, V. (1989). Fostering needed change in early literacy programs. In D. Stricklange & L. Morrow (Eds.) *Emerging literacy: Young children learning to read and write*, Chapter 12. Newark, DE. International Reading Association.

Supporting the Success of the Learner. This concept holds that children tend to learn best from first-hand experiences. The environment should be filled with a variety of printed material. Storytime should have a prominent role in a program. Many opportunities should be available for children to read, write, and draw. The physical area should have a variety of centers set up in such areas as housekeeping, art, music, mathematics, poetry, flannelboard, puppet stage, magnetic/chalkboard, writing/publishing, and literature. Finally, the program should make use of the community by both exploring it on field trips and by inviting members of the community to visit.

The National Association for the Education of Young Children (1997) identifies three key kinds of information that should always be used when working with young children in order to create developmentally appropriate practices. The first is a knowledge of child development and learning. This knowledge of age-related characteristics helps adults to develop materials and plan activities that will be healthy, engaging, and challenging to children. The second kind of knowledge is about the capabilities and interests of individual children, which is necessary in order to adapt and respond to those individual children. The third is a knowledge of the social and cultural environment of the lives of children. This information enables adults to develop meaningful learning experiences that are also respectful of the social and cultural environments of the children.

Focusing on Learning Language. Given the assumption that children develop literacy skills at different points in their development, one must be willing to invite them to read and write on their own level. Literature should be seen as a vehicle for exploring the world rather than as a tool for teaching reading skills. Reading and writing should be seen as playing, learning language, experimenting with words, sharing meaning, and clarifying thought.

Exploring Language. Language is a very complex thing, and mastering it can take a lifetime. Sophisticated strategies are required to fully master language and use it effectively. When there is an abundance of language opportunities and experiences, children learn to be more strategic in their attempts at reading and writing. Having parents, teachers, and visitors as models encourages children to attempt more complex language skills. By providing extensive opportunities for them to expand their communication through storytimes, play, pretending, and dramatizing, adults can help children develop a sense of authorship. *Authorship* is the idea of putting one's unique self into a story. Children may begin to do this by listening, creating, interpreting, reenacting, dramatizing, and discussing stories.

Reading Skills

Learning to read is important and necessary for all children. It occurs best after children have developed a love of stories and an interest in reading. A variety of reading skills are needed to be a competent reader. Some say that a phonetic approach in which children focus on learning the sounds of the letters is best. Others contend that a look-say approach that focuses on learning whole words is the superior approach. Advocates from each side largely ignore the more important issues. They tend to believe that their position represents the focus of reading. They ignore the fact that reading is more than sounding out words or identifying a list of words. Reading has to do with finding meaning in written text.

Children eventually need to develop both phonetic skills and a store of words that they can recognize on sight. However, they also need to understand other features of language such as semantics, syntactics, and pragmatics. *Semantics* refers to the meanings that words possess. Since the purpose of reading is to get meaning, understanding the meanings of words is critical to true reading. *Syntax* refers to the parts of speech. Nouns are different from verbs and verbs are different from adjectives. They each do something different in a sentence. What they do in combination is give a sentence meaning. *Pragmatics* refers to the practical functions of language. Such things as tone of voice, the degree of formality, and idioms might be grouped under this area. Each lends another key to the true meaning of the message.

The final point on reading skills concerns how and when they are taught to or learned by children. Traditionally, both word attack and comprehension skills have been taught in isolation. That is, the skills are taught through word lists, parts of words, sentences, and brief paragraphs developed to teach a particular skill. They may or may not then be tried out in an assigned piece of text. The belief is that if children are taught all of the little pieces of the "reading puzzle," they will then be able to put the puzzle together.

A contemporary wholistic approach to teaching beginning reading uses real words in real books written by real authors. The skills of reading are taught in the context of literature. There are no reading skills that were traditionally taught in isolation that cannot be meaningfully taught in the context of literature. Such an approach provides far more opportunities to also teach the semantics, syntactics, and pragmatics of language.

Realistic Expectations

Children need realistic expectations. Goals, when they are reached, can provide satisfaction and a sense of self-worth. If they are set too high they can lead to frustration, anger, and a sense of failure. If set too low they can encourage a lack of effort and a tendency to be satisfied with mediocrity.

Who sets the expectations? In education, it is generally the teachers and parents who set expectations. Perhaps this system should be questioned. Children may need to become more involved in developing expectations. When someone else sets the goals, there is a lack of emotional involvement by those who must strive to attain those goals. This does not mean that children should have total control. They need the security of knowing that adults can be depended on to provide appropriate guidance and to set reasonable limits.

A book that is interesting to a child can take on a magical quality for that child.

When expectations are set too uniformly or too high, serious problems can occur. This is already happening in education. It is probably impossible to determine exactly what happens first, but the net effect is often demoralizing to children. Accountability movements in education are an example. As the public demands improved education, legislatures respond with cost-effective devices. They tend to include such things as more rigorous standards for becoming a teacher and increased competency tests in reading, writing, and other basic skills for children. In order for children to be ready for the tests, the curriculum is pushed downward.

TIPS FOR TEACHERS

Make sure the program is ready for all children.
- *Prepare paint, crayon, clay, and pudding activities for children who need to continue to develop their fine motor skills.*
- *Remove all physical barriers that would prevent wheelchair access.*
- *Communicate with parents of children with disabilities to learn about their hopes, needs, and interests.*
- *Use screening test results to help change a program, not to deny access to a program.*
- *Make note of a variety of reactions to stories.*

Book display featuring author Cynthia Rylant. Courtesy Walter Sawyer.

Prospective kindergartners are now routinely screened for readiness to enter school. Kindergartners are frequently retained for a second year of kindergarten or placed in transitional first grades. Some school districts have two levels of kindergarten, one for those who are "ready," and one for those who supposedly need more time to become "ready." Various rationales are presented for each of these policies. They usually sound well-intentioned, often citing a need to give children more "time to be ready." Basically, however, this is a program designed to categorize children on the basis of such factors as intelligence, cultural background, and language skills. By separating more able children, it is likely that the expectations for them will be raised to an even more frustrating level. This separation also deprives them of the opportunity to share their skills with, and to develop an acceptance of, those who are less able. Separating less able children deprives them of a group of good language models and may also crush their sense of self-worth.

A true literacy program can accommodate nearly all children whether they are gifted, average, culturally deprived, or disabled. This is accomplished by providing a rich language environment, accepting children with the skills they possess, and countering some of the narrow views of literacy that still exist.

Organization of the Book

The chapters of this book are arranged in an order that provides a logical development to understanding an early childhood literature program. They may, however, be read in any order that suits the needs of the reader. Chapter 2 describes a variety of physical environments for enhancing the sharing of literature. Chapters 3 and 4 focus on literature itself. They describe criteria for selecting quality books and strategies for using various types of literature with children.

Chapters 5 and 6 describe a variety of procedures for the motivational and creative sharing of literature. Chapter 7 explores the critical aspect of integrating literature with all parts of the curriculum. It provides a variety of approaches and

Sketch by Dick Bruna. A visit with an author or illustrator can be a most exciting time. Courtesy Dick Bruna.

TIPS FOR TEACHERS

Borrow library tapes of authors reading their own books.
- *Always read the book aloud to children before using a tape.*
- *Give children something to listen for or discover in the tape, such as how the author reads certain lines of dialogue.*
- *Have children act out the roles of the characters in the story as the author reads it.*

suggestions for developing units. Chapter 8 addresses ways of using books to assist children with their emotional understanding of the world through bibliotherapy. Chapter 9 discusses the influence of television, media, and technology on literature and how they can be used effectively with children. Finally, Chapter 10 summarizes the concept of using the community in conjunction with a literature program for children.

Authors and Illustrators

The people who write and illustrate books for children often rely heavily on their own childhood for ideas. They tend to be careful observers of youngsters they see around them. As such, they are quite in tune with much of childhood. Learning about the personal life and thoughts of an author or illustrator can be a powerful motivation for reading that author's book. The knowledge can be shared with children at various points surrounding the reading of a book. Some books even allow readers to see how authors develop their books. *The Art Lesson* by Tomie dePaola is an autobiographical depiction of a young child who later becomes an author/illustrator of children's books. *How a Book Is Made* by Aliki clearly and accurately depicts the creation of a children's book. Information about authors can be found on book jackets, in reference books in the children's sections of libraries, in the stories themselves, in magazines about children's literature, and by writing to publishers. If resources are available, sponsoring a day with an author can be a tremendously rewarding experience for children and adults alike. Author visits to bookstores are a low-cost option.

SUMMARY

Literature should be a joyful experience. It is really about the wonders of life. The basic assumption of this book is that literature has tremendous value for young children. Literature is different from other informational media in that it usually includes another human being with whom the story is being shared. Literature derives its value from three things: First, it informs and excites children about the world in which they live. Second, it contributes to developing a positive self-image and the acceptance of others. Finally, literature serves to help children connect to both the people sharing a story with them and the people within the story.

Literature has a definite place within a literacy program. It serves as the material in which children explore language. Children do this through such things as listening to, reenacting, and interpreting the story. Within the literacy curriculum one must determine the appropriate place of reading skills and how they will be learned. Realistic expectations must be formed with each individual child's needs in mind.

One of the ways literature can be made more meaningful is to help children make the connection between the people who write and illustrate children's books and themselves.

QUESTIONS FOR THOUGHT AND DISCUSSION

1. How does the transfer of information from a book differ from the transfer of information from a television program?
2. Defend or refute: The United States is a "nation that reads."
3. How can literature help young children learn about their world?
4. How can a child's self-esteem be addressed through literature?
5. Defend or refute: Preschool children who are capable of learning the alphabet and word lists should learn them at that time.
6. What does the term "reading" really mean?

7. How can reading competency tests for elementary school have a negative effect on the preschool or kindergarten child?

8. According to Harste and Woodward, what three key features should be present in a literacy curriculum?

9. Why aren't phonics enough to help a child learn to read?

10. How do traditional and wholistic approaches to teaching beginning reading differ?

CHILDREN'S BOOKS CITED

Aliki (Brandenberg). (1986). *How a book is made.* New York: Harper and Row.

Bunting, E. (1997). *The pumpkin fair.* Boston: Houghton Mifflin.

DePaola, T. (1989). *The art lesson.* New York: G. P. Putnam's Sons.

DePaola, T. (1974). *Watch out for the chicken feet in your soup.* New York: Simon and Schuster.

Fox, M. (1988). *Koala Lou.* San Diego, CA: Harcourt Brace Jovanovich.

Guarino, D. (1997). *Is your mama a llama?* New York: Scholastic.

Hoberman, M.A. (1993). *Fathers, mothers, sisters, brothers.* New York: Puffin.

Kraus, R. (1987). *Another mouse to feed.* Englewood Cliffs, NJ: Prentice Hall.

Lewis, K. (1996). *First snow.* Cambridge, MA: Candlewick.

Lewis, R.B. (1985). *Aunt armadillo.* Scarborough, Ontario, Canada: Annick Press.

Lotz, K.E. (1993). *Snowsong whistling.* New York: Dutton.

Maass, R. (1993). *When winter comes.* New York: Holt.

McCully, E.A. (1985). *First snow.* New York: Harper and Row.

Piper, W. (1930). *The little engine that could.* New York: Platt and Munk.

Smith, P. (1988). *Jenny's baby brother.* New York: Viking Penguin.

Szekere, C. (1997). *The mouse that Jack built.* New York: Scholastic.

Waber, B. (1997). *Bearsie Bear and the surprise sleepover.* Boston, MA: Houghton Mifflin.

Waddell, M. (1993). *Little Mo.* Cambridge, MA: Candlewick.

SELECTED REFERENCES

Brazelton, T.B. (1988). *What every baby knows.* New York: Ballentine.

Browne, K.W. & Gordon, A. (1985). *Beginnings and beyond—Foundations in early childhood education.* Albany, NY: Delmar Publishers.

Cambourne, B. (1988). *The whole story: Natural learning and the acquisition of literacy.* Auckland, New Zealand: Scholastic.

Charlesworth, R. (1987). *Understanding child development—For adults who work with children.* Albany, NY: Delmar Publishers.

Clay, M. (1991). *Becoming literate: The construction of inner control.* Portsmouth, NH: Heinemann.

Dopyera, J. & Lay-Dropera, M. (1989). *Becoming a teacher of young children.* New York: Random House.

McClure, A. & Kristo, J. (1996). *Books that invite talk, wonder, and play.* Urbana, IL: National Council of Teachers of English.

National Association for the Education of Young Children (1997). *Developmentally appropriate practice in early childhood programs serving children from birth through age 8.* Washington, DC: National Association for the Education of Young Children.

Wells, G. (1986). *The meaning makers: Children making language and using language to learn.* Portsmouth, NH: Heinemann.

There are no problems –
only opportunities to be creative.

– Dorye Roettger

2 Planning for Success

The experience of reading to young children is enhanced when planning has taken place. A place for reading is more than just ambiance. It sets the tone for the entire reading experience. The reader must develop understandings, patterns, and plans for a successful reading encounter. Each age has different needs, interests, and preferences that can be used to encourage children to interact with the story. There are several questions a teacher might ask when planning a reading:

- Is the material age appropriate?
- Did I read the story first so that I am familiar with it?
- How will I motivate the children to want to be involved with the story?
- Where and when will we read the story?
- Why am I reading this particular story?
- How can I make this story most meaningful to the children?
- Is the story understandable to children from all cultures?

A great deal of material needs to be considered before these questions can be answered. Knowing the answers will benefit both the reader and the children each time a story is planned.

There are several key principles of child development to keep in mind in planning literacy activities. These principles are derived from those identified by the National Association for the Education of Young Children (NAEYC) as particularly relevant for informing developmentally appropriate practices. While all of the NAEYC principles are important, four are especially applicable to planning successful literacy activities for young children. The first principle is that the physical, social, emotional, and cognitive domains of child development are closely related. Activities should therefore be planned that foster the integration of these domains. A second relevant principle is that development proceeds at different rates from child to child. Children should not be expected to all be interested in or respond to a single activity in the same way. A third principle that is particularly relevant is that development and learning take place in multiple social and cultural contexts. Adults need to plan activities such that bridges to understanding can occur. A fourth principle is that play is an important vehicle for learning. It constitutes an opportunity for practicing new capabilities and allows children to demonstrate their learning in a safe context.

CREATING A GOOD ENVIRONMENT FOR INFANTS

There are many theories and sources of information concerning how infants grow and develop. It is not necessary to review all of the research here. However, it is necessary to review some of the general concepts. This review will form a foundation for understanding the relationship between child development and emerging literacy.

The most important factor in the language acquisition process is the interaction of adult with child. It is the sound of soft soothing words that helps the infant respond when frightened or upset. These sounds may be a parent's voice, the sounds and rhythm of a lullaby, or the words of a pleasant rhyme.

While there are rival theories about just how children develop language, there is substantial agreement that even very young infants listen to and respond to the sounds of language. Infants respond by making sounds of their own. The sounds help them make their needs known and express emotions. For example, during the first three months infants learn to cry in different ways to indicate hunger, discomfort, and other feelings. This behavior is quickly followed by more complex forms of sounds, such as cooing at three months, babbling at six months, and forming articulated sounds such as "Ma-ma" and Da-da" at nine months. Words are acquired slowly at first, and then at an ever increasing rate.

Emerging Language

At about the age of one year words become meaningful to the child. For some advanced children, this experience can occur at eight months. After age two, children acquire language at an extremely rapid rate. By age three, the typical child uses up to 200 words in simple questions and statements.[1]

Throughout this period, there is a need for adults to provide language to children through talk and through contact with the environment. Adults should provide encouragement and opportunities for infants to experience their environment. Part of this exploration will be the investigation of language and its uses. Children will explore how it sounds, what it does, and how it can be used.

Linking Language to Literature

Singing songs, reading stories, doing simple fingerplays, and playing games with a high amount of adult-child interaction are the best ways to initiate a connection with literature. Traditional rhymes, Mother Goose stories, and poetry are easy to memorize and recite. Infants enjoy hearing these types of literature whether they are being cuddled, rocked, or just resting in a crib.

Holding an object in front of an infant and telling a story about it is pleasurable for an infant from birth. For example, one might hold a small stuffed kitten up to the child and recite the "Three Little Kittens" rhyme while for child touches or

---

[1] Watt, M.R., Roberts, J.E., & Ziesel, SA. (1993, November). Ear Infections in Young Children: The Role of the Early Childhood Educator. *Young Children*, 49, 71.

pets the toy. With infants of eight to fifteen months of age, learning the sounds that things make is a great motivation. As they develop, babies enjoy making the sounds of an object. They do this well before they are able to name the object. Familiar objects to use for this activity include a car, truck, airplane, train, animal, and boat. One can further encourage children's language acquisition and understanding of the words by reinforcing and accepting their approximations of the sounds. This lets children know that others understand their developing language patterns.

Reading to Infants

Each month that books are not read to infants is a month that is lost forever. Books can be read to infants from the moment they are born. The books should, of course, be durable if the child is going to handle them. Hardcover books, board books, and plastic books are good beginning books. The pictures used in the books should be simple and bright, as very young children are not able to focus on busy pictures.

TIPS FOR TEACHERS
Children are never too young to hear a story.
* *Read stories aloud at naptime, during feeding, and at snack time.*
* *Recite rhymes and fingerplays as stories for very young children.*
* *Talk about what you are doing, in the form of a story, to infants.*

Books should be treated as something special. They are not something one eats. The concept of respecting books can be constantly modeled. Paperback books are more difficult to use with infants as they do not hold up well with the touching that most infants do with books. This does not mean to avoid such books. Rather, the adult must maintain more control over the book itself. There is nothing wrong with saying that the book is going to be kept by the caregiver. It can always be shared again. This approach allows the use of many books with children.

When reading books with infants, include the use of props such as toys with the reading. Effective utilization of puppets, toy cars, and other objects featured in the story can enhance the reading experience. The object connects the infant with the story in a positive, hands-on manner.

Reading Areas for Infants

In setting up a reading area for infants, the caregiver must remember that infants sit on laps, crawl about, and listen in various positions and in various places. Ideally, the reading area should be on the floor. Colorful pillows, quilts, and mats are inviting and comfortable. Adding a few stuffed toys makes it a special place.

Mobiles, wall hangings, and soft sculptures can also be added to enhance the setting. Cardboard boxes can be used to make story-related cars, boats, and trains. This will help to stimulate the children's imaginations by creating a concrete representation of the story. Re-creating parts of the story in play is an important part of language development. Through re-creating the story, children are dealing with and making sense of language. In this case, they are replicating the language of the author and the reader.

Dorothy Kunhardt's *Pat the Bunny* is great fun to read with infants. As the book progresses, the reader has the opportunity to touch the cottontail of the bunny, smell some flowers, look in a mirror, play peek-a-boo, and engage in other similar activities. Re-create the reading and language experience by using the ideas from the book within the reading area. For example, include in the reading area a peek-a-boo game, a mirror activity, and scented flowers. The book is most interesting for infants, but both older children and adults may enjoy reading it over and over again.

Enjoyable books should be read as often as infants respond to them. Children will usually point to their favorites even before they can ask for them verbally. It is important to remember to continuously share the beauty of the language through repeated readings of favorite stories. Language should be shared in a warm, pleasant environment. Books will naturally become an important part of children's lives if shared from birth.

Creating an Environment for Toddlers

Picture a lovely summer day with an occasional tornado roaring through, making touchdowns of mayhem every few miles. This provides some idea of a toddler's day. Ever curious, toddlers seem determined to fit years of exploration and discovery into each day. The attention of toddlers may quickly jump from object to object. On the other hand, they can sustain attention in a particular pursuit if motivated and involved. Most toddlers do enjoy completing tasks. However, the tasks must be age appropriate in order for toddlers to achieve success without becoming frustrated.

Toddlers are more able to assert themselves and their independence than younger children. The word "no" is more than a word for many of them; sometimes it seems to be a creed. For this reason, care must be taken when encouraging toddlers to stay on a task when they feel they have completed it. "Me done!" is rarely spoken by a toddler without the exclamation mark at the end.

Motivation is important in planning environments for toddlers. They want to hear stories and look at books if they feel the activity is exciting. The storyteller or reader must provide effective presentations of the tale and show enjoyment in the activity. The closeness and warmth of the reading experience is still a major part of the setting. Toddlers like to point to and touch books as they are read. They like to feel a part of the experience. Caregivers need to plan for this when choosing books. To enhance the environment for toddlers, be patient, provide pictures and language, and create language together through stories and storytelling.

Using Language. Toddlers make many attempts to use language. They use it to satisfy their needs, to make themselves understood, and to understand their world. It has been known for many years that children understand much language before they are able to say those same words, sentences, and paragraphs.[2] They make intelligent generalizations with language based on whatever language rules they already know. For example, a child might say, "I hurt-ed myself," or "Me go."

The beginning stages of writing emerge at this stage. From the first time a child touches a crayon to a paper, or even thinks about doing it, writing has begun. It will take several years to develop, but all of the pictures and attempts to put something meaningful in a visual form are part of the child's developing writing ability.

During this period of life, adults must provide time, opportunities, models, encouragement, and acceptance. Children are drawn to whatever language is available. They like its sounds and rhythm. Language models and a wide variety of experiences should be provided. On the other hand, this is not the time for correction of incorrect language structures by children. The same is true for drawing and writing attempts. Children need acceptance of their honest attempts to create meaning. They need someone to listen to them and someone to tell about their drawings.

Toddler Humor. During this time, children develop a sense of humor. This humor begins with simple substitution in which the toddler is aware that the substitution has been made. For example, a child knows that "Mama" is the sound for mother and "Gaga" is the sound for daddy. When mother asks in the name game "Who Am I?" the child responds with "Gaga" while looking at mother, and then bursts out laughing. The child has made a joke. More jokes will be attempted, especially if they are encouraged by the laughter of the child's audience.

Toddlers love zany humor, and there are many books to satisfy this craving. Using the idea of a rooster waking up the other animals, Denys Cazet creates a rollicking story with a surprise ending in *Nothing at All.* Toddlers will respond knowingly to the mischievous antics of Billy in Pat Hutchins' *Three Star Billy.* Using nine multi-ethnic children, Margaret Miller sets up a series of logical questions and preposterous answers in *Can You Guess?* Stories in which animals act out of character are sure to get a response. Good choices in this area include Paul Brett Johnson's *The Cow Who Wouldn't Come Down* about a flying cow, David McPhail's *Pigs Aplenty, Pigs Galore,* Laura Numeroff's *Dogs Don't Wear Sneakers,* and Elizabeth Winthrop's bathtime story, *Asleep in a Heap.*

More subtle forms of humor for toddlers are available as well. Good beginning choices include *Baby Rock, Baby Roll* by Stella Blackstone, *Where's the Bear?* by Byron Barton, and Dave Ross's two books, *A Book of Hugs* and *More Hugs.* Mem Fox creates a tale that allows the reader to make full use of voice to

[2] Carroll, J.B. (1964, Spring). Words, Meanings and Concepts. *Harvard Educational Review* 34, 178-202.

create a mental picture in *Night Noises.* Two fanciful choices for more able children include *Dear Mr. Blueberry* by Simon James and *Chester the Worldly Pig* by Bill Peet.

Many nursery rhymes also provide humor. For example, have you ever really seen a dish run away with a spoon? Have you ever seen kittens washing mittens? Do people really live in pumpkins? Picturing the absurdity is half the fun of listening or reciting these rhymes. Nursery rhymes also lend themselves to wonderful art activities and dramatic presentations that toddlers can easily enjoy. For example, children can engage in dramatizing dishes running away with spoons and creating such items as bags of wool, golden eggs, and spiders on tuffets. Barbara Reid has selected, and illustrated with clay relief, a number of Mother Goose nursery rhymes in *Sing a Song of Mother Goose.* Another good choice, Zena Sutherland's *The Orchard Book of Nursery Rhymes,* combines Mother Goose with familiar short verses, tongue twisters, and nonsense poems. The illustrations are effective and the books are sturdy. The repetitive parts of stories are easy for toddlers to repeat. They can often join in reciting some of the repeated lines. Careful selection of nursery rhymes will help to eliminate those that are violent or sexist.

Toddler Interests. Toddlers have an interest in the objects and events around them. They want to know the sounds, the "whats," and the "whys" of everything. They want to know who everyone is and what they do.

One way to respond to this need is to provide appropriate books for children to explore. Board books and other smaller-sized books are just right for toddlers. They often provide basic terms and ideas that toddlers see and do each day. Examples of such books include *Little Bear's Bedtime* and *Little Bear's Day,* both by Jane Hissey, *Let's Go* and *Let's Pretend,* both by Amy MacDonald, *Everyday Garden* and *Everyday Children,* both by Cynthia Rylant, and Juan Wijngaard's

Author/illustrator Dave Ross.
Courtesy Dave Ross.

Australian author Mem Fox.
Courtesy Mem Fox.

series with titles such as *Bear, Cat, Dog,* and *Duck.* Each of Wijngaard's board books contains five short stories that develop descriptions, actions, and cause-and-effect relationships.

Toddlers can explore their emerging vocabularies in books such as *Early Morning in the Barn* by Nancy Tafuri, *Hiding* by Shirley Hughes, and *Everyday Pets* by Cynthia Rylant. The activities and accomplishments of toddlers are presented in *Toddlers* by Catherine and Laurence Anholt, *Rosy's Pool* by Lucy Dickens, *While I Am Little* by Heidi Goennel, *My Bike* by Donna Jakob, *Jump Along* by Neil Morris, and *Joe Joe* by Mary Serfozo. As toddlers begin to reflect on their own existence as individuals, they can begin to appreciate stories such as *Bear and Baby* by Catherine and Laurence Anholt, *Tom and Pippo on the Beach* by Helen Oxenbury, international best-seller *The Rainbow Fish* by Marcus Pfister, *A Teeny Tiny Baby* by Amy Schwartz, and *Oh, Baby!* by Sara Stein.

Jump Along: A Fun Book of Movement *by Neil Morris.* Reprinted by permission of Carolrhoda Books.

British author Neil Morris.
Courtesy Neil Morris.

Other books and authors have specifically addressed the interests of toddlers as well. Helen Oxenbury's books can be used to demonstrate many basic concepts. The illustrations are clear and simple, telling the story without any text. *Good Night, Good Morning,* for example, tells the story of the day's cycle for a toddler. The child character goes through the book doing all of the same things that the toddler reader might do on a typical day. Jan Ormerod's *Making Friends* is a delightful book with large print text. It is brief, contains age-appropriate sentences, and includes appealing illustrations. Jan Ormerod has addressed the topics of exercise, sunshine, and babies in other books. The First Little Golden Book series of books develops many concepts. For example, Stephanie Calmenson's *My Book of Seasons* helps the reader come to know the seasons by using the five senses to experience each one. These bright, colorful books are endearing and full of fun.

Eric Carle's writing is exceptional for toddlers. The illustrations are excitingly colorful. They possess a visual texture not often found elsewhere. Each book has a special attraction. For example, *The Very Hungry Caterpillar* shows caterpillars and what they might eat. In fact, the caterpillar eats right through the illustrations. This book is always a favorite.

Reading Areas for Toddlers. A reading area for toddlers must be engaging and interesting. The area should be on the floor, but a low loft-type structure might also be used. Toddlers love to climb. To add comfort and fun, place large pillows and stuffed toys in the area. A large stuffed toy for the toddlers to sit on can be a creative addition. Rocking chairs are a nice touch in any reading area. The motion is soothing, and a rocker is usually large enough for a reader and a couple of toddlers to sit together to share a story. Carpeting should be used with any wooden loft or stairway loft.

Decorated walls and mobiles are an easy accent that can be changed often. They keep the interest level high. Visibility is important with toddlers. Objects and

The Rainbow Fish *by Marcus Pfister.*
Copyright (c) 1992 by Nord-Sud. Verlag AG,
Gossau Zurich, Switzerland. Used by
permission of North-South Books, New York.

furniture should not interfere with the adult's ability to maintain eye contact with
the children.

Boxes and large climbing structures with pillow centers also make a reading
area a special place. Many windows should be cut in the large boxes if they are
used. The boxes can be decorated with white paint to make an igloo. Windows
can be cut to suggest a spaceship. Boxes can be painted brown to make a jungle

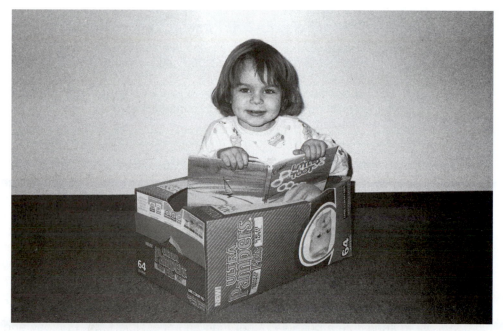

Reading is special anywhere. If the story is captivating, any place can be the
right place for reading. Courtesy Diana Comer.

hut. Books that represent the topic can be placed inside the box. The children's interest is heightened when they participate in creating and changing the reading area and its props.

Creating an Environment for Preschoolers

Children of three to four years of age never seems to stop asking why. Their questions are both the bane and the bonus of parents and caregivers. Preschool children are very interested in themselves and their families. They are fascinated by the world around them, and are beginning to realize that it includes others outside their immediate environment. It is a time of incredible stretching and growth of knowledge. Preschoolers seem to be sponges for information, always wanting to know how, why, and where.

Using Language. At the preschool level, children continue their rapid development of language skills and vocabulary growth. They are now able to use language as a tool for understanding themselves and their surroundings.

The writings of preschoolers consist of drawings, attempts at writing, and dictated stories. Whether or not adults can tell what the child has drawn, the artwork does have definite meanings to the child. The role of the adult is to provide much interaction for the child in the form of listening, answering questions, asking questions, providing language models, and sharing experiences.

TIPS FOR TEACHERS

Use books that contain new and interesting words in them.
* *Tell children the meaning of the new words they will be hearing in the story.*
* *Use new words from a story in your own speech after the story.*
* *Respond positively to children attempting to use new words they have learned in a story.*

Preschool Humor. The child's sense of humor is beyond simple word substitutions. Preschoolers are more sophisticated than toddlers and don't laugh as readily at dishes running away with spoons. The preschool child's humor requires a semblance of possibility. *Curious George* by H.A. Rey appeals to this more sophisticated humor. George, a well-loved character, gets into all sorts of mischief by circumstances rather than by design. The humorous aspects of the plot are possible, yet highly improbable. Therein lies the humor. For example, when George plays with the telephone, he mistakenly rings the fire department. This causes a hilarious chain of events.

Three- and four-year-olds still laugh at certain words, but they are more likely to substitute a possible rather than an impossible term. Fantasy and dramatic play is still important for these children. Preschoolers love to "play house" and act

Canadian author Robert Munsch.
Photo credit Whitman Golden Canada Ltd.

out roles as well. At this age, "Little Red Riding Hood" is no longer just a story. It is an event that can be acted out both seriously and humorously with only a few props.

Preschooler Interests. Values are often included in many of the stories intended for preschoolers. Children at this age are concerned with themselves and their feelings. Don Freeman's *Corduroy* tells of a teddy bear that is rejected by children because it is missing a button. Eventually it is acquired by a little girl who loves it anyway. The story is reassuring to preschoolers because it demonstrates the value of love over perfection.

Dr. Seuss's books often reinforce values while providing great fun through illustrations and language. Horton the elephant makes difficult decisions which, in the end, reinforce the correctness of the honest choices made. The Grinch shows how love can change people. The Lorax challenges children to think about the environment. Each book has a special style. In *Horton Hatches the Egg,* Horton sits on a bird's egg through terrible trials and tribulations. The egg hatches eventually, and the reader is treated to an amazing conclusion. Children will sit through this lengthy book over and over again. They do so because they can empathize with the story from beginning to end.

Preschoolers are fascinated with differences. They notice differences of sex, size, disability, houses, and so forth. As might be expected, they want to know why these differences exist. Betty Jean Lifton's *Tell Me a Real Adoption Story,* Roslyn Banish's *A Forever Family,* Connie White Pirner's *Even Little Kids Get Diabetes,* Caroline Bucknall's *One Bear in the Hospital,* and Stan and Jan Berenstain's *He Bear, She Bear* are books that address some of these differences in positive and reassuring ways. Their tone is quite appropriate for preschoolers.

Preschoolers also have fears which should not be ignored. Realizing that others have similar fears can alleviate much of the stress created by these fears.

Fears can include being alone, dealing with an older sibling, anger, frustration, the darkness, and so on. Some titles and authors on these topics include Bernard Waber's *Ira Sleeps Over,* Judith Viorst's *Alexander and the Terrible, Horrible, No Good, Very Bad Day,* Maurice Sendak's *Where the Wild Things Are,* and Allen Say's *Allison.* In Say's book, a young girl comes to an awareness and acceptance of her adoption by befriending a stray cat.

Reading Areas for Preschoolers. The reading area should be more adventurous for preschoolers than for toddlers. Lofts, mattress tents, and truck tires with pillows are good choices. Lighting is important with this age group because the children will be looking more closely at the words, and some may be beginning to read. Daylight should be used when possible. Therefore, locating the reading area near a window is recommended.

Recognizing the need of this age group to understand the "why" of things makes good sense in creating a reading area. One might include informative mobiles of seasons, planets, and stars. Posters illustrating what is inside such things as bodies, mountains, and the earth are good choices for walls. Locating real animals near the reading area is a fine idea, particularly when focusing on animal stories.

TIPS FOR TEACHERS

Encourage children to respond to each other's questions.
• Reinforce children's responses to each other.
• Say, "That was a very good answer to Billy's question."
• When children don't respond to each other, help them do so by repeating or rephrasing the question raised.

Obviously, these ideas take careful planning. However, including them as part of the lesson helps motivate the children. The availability of props after the book is read will encourage the children to re-create or reconstruct the book through talk and play. For example, after reading Jimmy Kennedy's *The Teddy Bear Picnic,* place a teddy bear and the book in the reading area on a rocking chair. In most cases, one will soon see children in the chair, leafing through the book and hugging the teddy bear. Making the reading area easy to change will help both the adult and the children to continue to have creative interactions with books.

Creating an Environment for Kindergarten

Kindergarten children are successful in many tasks. Their skills often show a good deal of self-reliance. Supervision by adults need not be as direct as it is for the earlier age groups. Kindergarten children are active and enjoy outdoor play. They show more cooperative play both at home and in school. On the other hand, the mix of five- and six-year-olds can present a wide range of skills and abilities, and children this age take note of what their friends say and do. The result can be a concern for what others think that may lead to a reluctance to join in activities unless others are involved first. Adults must sometimes initiate the involvement of children in activities. The activities and stories must be chosen to engage the active interests of these children.

The Power of Language. During the ages of five and six, children experience the power of language. They come to understand how language can express ideas and emotions, create stories and meanings, and be used to experience life. For some time now, they have been aware that they are surrounded by print. At this stage, children use complex sentence structures, compare words with greater ease, tell stories, and recognize words in print.[3] They read some words in print, and they attempt to include words within their drawings.

The role of adults at this stage of a child's language development is to take advantage of the many opportunities that arise for helping the child experiment with and enjoy language. One can encourage children to understand that the printed word can represent all of the meanings and feelings that oral language can contain. The focus should be on meaning rather than on the correct form. A child's invented spellings (e.g., "I lik mi kat." for "I like my cat.") should be accepted without negative comment. The child will come in contact with correct spellings over and over again. The discovery of the correct forms will occur naturally and be incorporated into the child's original writing.

Kindergarten Interests. The powerful and the mystical are of great interest to kindergarten children. New editions of the classic stories of "Cinderella," "Sleeping Beauty," and "Rapunzel" are wonderful for reading aloud to five- and six-year-olds. They respond to epic adventures where, through enchantment and strength, the hero overcomes evil. The more overwhelming the odds, the better the story is for them. There are many lesser known fairy tales and stories that can be used to both keep children's interest and to compare with more popular versions. For example, children can discover that Snow White had a sister named Rose Red in older tales. Reading several versions of the same story can be used to help children compare stories. Kindergarten children enjoy giving their opinions.

Fairy Tales From Hans Christian Anderson by the author of the same name and *Household Stories* by the Grimm Brothers are good sources for classic tales. The texts of both books, however, may be challenging for some young readers. Many classic tales are also told in single books with wonderful illustrations. A favorite is *Beauty and the Beast* illustrated by Karen Milone. The jealous sisters in this book are so ugly that the beast is not so scary in comparison. The ending is pure fairy tale. Care should be taken to avoid violent fairy tales.

---

3 Dale, P.S. (1976). *Language Development.* New York: Holt, Rinehart and Winston.

Kindergarten children are very involved with learning about their bodies and social interactions. At times they may find it difficult to play and interact because of the increased need to fit in with their peers. It is healthy for them to discover that these mixed feelings occur with other children as well. In *Little Bobo Saves the Day* by Serena Romanelli, a young orangutan experiences fear and uncertainty about human beings. By coming to know them, Bobo loses his fears and gains a friend.

Troubling issues greatly affect the kindergarten child. The same issues that cause conflict for adults can be agonizing to a child. When the adults in a child's life are going through the emotional stress of a death, divorce, separation, unemployment, or other personal difficulties, they often seek to protect the children from the hurt. Unfortunately, this seldom works. Children feel the pain anyway, and when adults try to protect them from it, they may feel excluded. Being isolated or feeling isolated rarely helps anyone through a difficult time. Reading books on the topic that is causing distress can help the child understand what is happening.

Other issues that kindergarten children are concerned with include adoption and disabilities. Youngsters can be cruel to other children who are different. Yet most children will act kindly and supportively to such children when given the opportunity to learn about the differences. Fear and ignorance provoke unkind behaviors. Adoption is presented in a reassuringly perceptive manner by using the character of a cat in *Horace* by Holly Keller. A similar approach is used by Maggie Glen in *Ruby,* the story of a teddy bear with physical disabilities. Readers will cheer for Ruby right through to her triumphant victory over the prejudice and ignorance of others. Additional books that present disabilities with clarity and sensitivity include *Charlie's Chuckle* by Clara Berkus and Margaret Dodd, *My Buddy* by Audrey Osofsky, *Arnie and the New Kid* by Nancy Carlson, and *Jooka Saves the Day* by Giles Eduar. Such books put to rest fears and beliefs such as, "I'll get adopted if I misbehave . . . This is catching . . . He's just trying to get attention." Dealing with these concepts honestly through literature can replace ignorance with truth and understanding. Understanding often leads to caring and acceptance.

TIPS FOR TEACHERS

Invite many different people to share a book at storytime.
* *A nurse or doctor could read a book about a sick child.*
* *A social worker could read a book involving adoption.*
* *A grocer could read a book in which food plays a role.*

Our world is undergoing an information explosion, and kindergarten children are involved in this phenomenon. They can acquire knowledge, concepts, and ideas from both fiction and nonfiction titles that address things such as calendars, dinosaurs, and aboriginal life in the Australian outback. Titles worth a reading include *Going for Oysters* by Jeanie Adams, *Belinda* by Pamela Allen, *Elephants Aloft* by Kathi Appelt, *The Shape of Things* by Doyle Ann Dodds, *Alligators and*

Chester the Worldly Pig *by Bill Peet.*
Reprinted by permission of Houghton
Mifflin.

Others All Year Long: A Book of Months by Crescent Dragonwagon, *A Picture Book of Thurgood Marshall* by David A. Adler, *Gulls...Gulls...Gulls* by Gail Gibbons, *The Glow-in-the-Dark Book of Dinosaur Skeletons* by Annie Ingle, and *When This Box Is Full* by Patricia Lillie. Lillie's book is not just for reading. Everyone can have a box to truly experience the book. Content books can provide much information for children who thirst for knowing the what, why, and how of things.

Interest in reading grows for kindergarten children. ABC books and I Can Read books have an increasing attraction as the year progresses. Whether one is a proponent of early reading instructional programs or not, ABC books can be delightful. There are a great many available, each different, with a variety of illustration styles. Norman Bridwell's *Clifford's ABC,* Steven Kellogg's *Aster Aardvark's Alphabet Adventures,* Sylvia Cassedy's *Zoomrimes,* Bill Martin, Jr. and John Archambault's *Chicka Chicka Boom Boom,* Betty Root's *My First Dictionary,* and Richard Scarry's *Find Your ABC's* are just a few of the favorites.

Reading Areas for Kindergarten Children. Setting up a reading area for kindergarten children should be a group project. Involve the children in the planning, constructing, and changing of the area. Start the year with just the space set aside in the room. Bring in materials, and discuss how the reading area can be created. The more children are involved in the planning, the greater their emotional commitment will be to the reading area and to reading. Most ideas, even if they initially seem impossible, can become a reality to some extent. With some imagination, one can create gardens, planets, caves, jungles, or treehouses for a classroom reading area.

Practical Considerations for Reading Areas

The reading area is for reading, sharing, and interacting with books. It may also be referred to as the reading corner, reading nook, or reading center. The reading area and the time spent there with children both need to reflect the caregiver's

Children enjoy picture books even if they are not yet able to read all of the words. Courtesy Diana Comer.

attitude toward books, reading, literacy, and children. The best attitude is a relaxed one toward all four. Children need to experience, listen to, interact with, and enjoy the ideas in books and children's magazines. A reading area should give the feeling that books are an open invitation. They are to be enjoyed. The size of the space set aside for the reading area is not particularly important as long as it can comfortably contain the people using it at one time. What is important is the effective use of the space by the children. The visual and aesthetic appeal of the reading area promotes its effective use. This is achieved by making the space appropriate for the age of the children and warmly inviting.

Where to Put a Reading Area. Every room is set up differently. Any room arrangement has both strengths and weaknesses. A reading area may be set up in a corner, along a wall, or in a loft. When initially planning an area, keep in mind traffic patterns and lighting.

Traffic patterns are important in a classroom. Move tables and screens to create large and small spaces within the room. Large spaces encourage movement. They can be distracting and chaotic. Small spaces are useful for separating children into interest areas for smaller projects. However, small spaces used to channel children through a room can be busy and noisy. The reading area, therefore, is best located off the beaten path, away from both large and small traffic areas. One may locate a reading area near a dress-up or music area. In this way, books and ideas can spill over into play in these other areas. Try a variety of arrangements to see which works best with a particular class and program.

Lighting is an important consideration for a reading area. Poor lighting or inappropriate lighting can cause problems that are easily avoided. Since it is soft and easy on the eyes, natural lighting is preferred. This means that the reading area must be near a window. A location near the window allows for such reading-related activities as daydreaming, bird watching, and cloud gazing.

It is not always possible to use natural lighting. There should be a backup plan for cloudy days, dark mornings, and late afternoon hours. Many schools have fluorescent lighting for the whole room. However, some situations might call for a darkened room with only a small lamp for reading. Incandescent lamps are preferred to overhead fluorescent lights for the softer glow they emit. In addition, some find fluorescent light hard on the eyes. This is especially true when it creates a glare on glossy pages and chalkboards. Lamp bulbs should be a minimum of 100 watts when used for reading. Soft white bulbs are superior to regular lamp bulbs as they reduce the glare.

What kind of lamps should be used? Heavy lamps sitting on tables should be avoided. They can tip over too easily, resulting in injury to children. Hanging lamps, wall lamps, and undercounter lamps avoid these tipping dangers. Cords are a hazard in areas that encourage lounging, crawling, and snuggling. They can be chewed on and tripped over. Lamps that are securely attached to walls or ceilings are not in the way. They cannot be knocked over, and their cords can be covered or discreetly tucked out of the way.

For those difficult spots such as lofts, cubby areas, and cloakrooms, undercounter lights are inexpensive, safe, and easily installed. They offer a good source of light. Any lamp used should be properly installed, carry the Underwriters Laboratory stamp of approval, and have no frayed or uncovered wires.

After space and lighting have been selected, consider the furnishings of the reading area. Will a couch or carpeting be used? Will it be a theme space? A loft? These decisions depend on size, creativity, and materials. The possibilities are endless.

Costs of a Reading Area. Cost is a factor in any planning. For day-care centers and schools, a reading area is a necessity. Although schools and centers should include the cost of reading areas in their budgets, alternative funding and sources of supplies can also be considered. Sources of free materials include stores, families, friends, yard sales, and social service agencies. Once the reading area is planned, one should make a list of materials needed. The list can be shared with all of the potential sources of free materials. Thank you notes set up a friendly contact for future classroom endeavors. Positive public relations are provided for both the school and the donor when the school or town newspaper publishes a story about the donations.

Kinds of Materials Needed

The most important need is for many, many books. A reading area also needs places to shelve books and places for people. It needs dividers, props, and decorations. Audiovisual equipment such as tape players, VCRs, videotapes, and computers may be used in the reading area but kept elsewhere. These audiovisual items are generally shared with other areas within the school or center, and are borrowed or loaned only for specific activities.

Places to Display Books. Display books on wire racks or front-facing bookcases that allow the book covers to be seen. These are generally constructed of sturdy metal or hardwood. They are long-term investments that will give many years of use. The two sizes ordinarily used are shorter tabletop models and taller floor models. Both types can be costly, however. Someone with basic carpentry skills may be able to provide a comparable display at a more reasonable cost.

Second-hand bookcases are also a source for book storage and display furniture. Stores that are refurbishing or going out of business may be able to provide display units that are appropriate for books. One center used this approach to purchase a sturdy case with four lower drawers and a pegboard on the back. The five-foot unit, costing fifteen dollars, now serves as a pegboard, room divider, storage unit, and shelving area for children's books and other materials.

Retail stores can also provide displays made of heavy cardboard. Most often these displays are discarded after they are used for a limited amount of time. When stores are finished using displays, they are often willing to give them away. They work fine for most children's books. One such display, a styrofoam turkey from a liquor store, was used for several years in a center for a variety of purposes. Think creatively to see the possibilities in these store displays.

Other unconventional items may also be used for book storage and display. These include plastic dishpans, apple baskets, laundry baskets, milk crates, wicker baskets, metal laundry tubs, kitchen cabinets, and plastic wastebaskets. With some construction skills, one can create inexpensive and sturdy shelving with pine boards and concrete blocks from a lumber yard.

Whatever is used, it should showcase the books. The books should be placed in such a way that they almost ask to be picked up and read.

Places for People. "A gentle rain pattering on the window . . . a warm quilt wrapped around you . . . nestled in a lap for a story." This is an image of a great place to be for a story. It is cozy, warm, and comfortable. Comfort is a key word for a reading area. Keep in mind the age and size of the children when planning the space for a reading area. Children love to snuggle into reading. They move around. They wriggle. They sometimes sit perfectly still. The seating in a reading area should be on the floor or a mattress for the greatest protection against falls.

Small beanbag chairs as well as regular size stuffed chairs might be used. Care should be taken when using furniture with hard wooden arm rests. Furniture legs can be cut off or removed to make the size more appropriate for children. Sofa cushions and mattresses can be used on the floor as seating areas. Tent covers for a mattress can turn the area into a boat, automobile, or a cave. A child's swimming pool can be filled with pillows and stuffed toys as a seating area. Small chairs, rocking chairs, and stools might also be used in a reading area.

A loft makes a wonderful reading area for young children. Have a knowledgeable person construct or prepare the loft. It should be carpeted, no higher than four feet from the floor, and sturdily built. Protective slats or railings should have spaces no larger than two inches wide so that children will not become stuck between the rails. Avoid pillows and other items that could cause a fall from the loft. When using carpeting as a seating surface, inspect the best carpets before making a decision on which to use. Wool carpets can be hot and itchy. Indoor-outdoor carpet is very durable. Nylon carpet cleans easily. Remnants from carpet distributors can be bound for a minimal price, eliminating any ragged edges. With large needles and upholstery thread, create a patchwork carpet out of carpet samples. An advantage of the patchwork carpet is that the finished rug contains various patterns, textures, and types of carpeting. It can become a tactile masterpiece and define each child's space. Be aware, however, that use of the area by those with allergies may make carpeting a poor choice of material.

Wall Dividers. A reading area should be apart from the flow of traffic. Room dividers can help create a space where there seems to be none available. Dividers that allow for maximum flexibility include wide bookcases, bulletin boards, pegboards, stand-up flannelboards, and chalkboards. Furniture can form part of the boundary of the reading area. The back of a sofa, a row of chairs, and a row of cushions can all serve as dividers. While one can purchase room dividers and supports from commercial supply companies, they can also be constructed from large cardboard boxes or four-foot by eight-foot sheets of plywood. Dividers need be only three feet in height to provide reading privacy. This height allows the adult to retain visibility of all of the room.

Reading can be done almost anywhere.
Courtesy Diana Comer.

Creating a Reading Area

It is the extras that often make a difference in almost anything. Attention to details can make a good thing better. So it is with reading areas. Think of the reading area as an expressive part of the room. It should include items that reflect children's work and creativity. Part of the wall can include a bulletin board that changes as the seasons pass. Various themes can be reflected. Puppets or stuffed toys can reflect favorite stories.

During "Dinosaur Week" books such as Betty Birney's *Tyrannosaurus Tex,* Diane Dawson Hearn's *Dad's Dinosaur Day,* and Bob Kolar's *Stomp, Stomp* could be read. A mobile of children's renderings of favorite dinosaurs could be hung up. A stuffed dinosaur or an inflatable dinosaur could be added to the other animals in the reading area. A dinosaur chart might be placed on the wall. Place red vinyl balls in the area as dinosaur eggs. Sources for these items include educational supply companies, yard sales, relatives, and friends. In addition, bookstores increasingly stock stuffed characters from books.

TIPS FOR TEACHERS

Invite parental participation in the creation of reading environments.
- *Ask a team of parents to create a themed area for holidays of the season.*
- *Plan a unit with parental input, including ideas for extension at home.*

Other innovative ideas for decorating include using large boxes to create special environments from telephone booths to ships. Add a branch of a tree for an aesthetically pleasing feature in a reading area. It can be decorated for the season. Decorations could range from crepe paper leaves to cotton balls to cutout snowflakes. The children can add these to reflect the seasonal change. Nontoxic live plants are always pleasing and popular in reading areas. They should be kept out of reach of small infants and toddlers.

Children can and should contribute to the aesthetic surroundings of the reading area. Constructing books and posters is personally rewarding to children. When displayed, these items surround the area with an aura of positive self-esteem. The children become aware that their contributions are as important as the other books and materials in the reading area.

PUTTING IT ALL TOGETHER

In order to see the "big picture" of a reading area, sketch out all of the parts of the area on paper. Seeing all of these components together in an illustration gives a feel for the total package. Figure 2–1 illustrates a few ideas for a reading area. Figure 2–2 illustrates an actual classroom reading area.

Figure 2–1. Although reading areas can vary in size and furnishings, they should always provide a feeling of closeness and wlecome. Courtesy Diana Comer.

Keep in mind that the more involved children are in the design and makeup of the area, the more comfortable they will be in the exciting world of books and stories.

Holding a Book for Storytime

Note the significance of the small details in successfully reading a story to children. Reading to children is more than picking up a book and reading it aloud. The setting is important. The choice of materials is important. The way the book is held is important. The book should be firmly grasped by the reader and held at eye level for the children.

After or during the reading of each page, the book should be moved from side to side. This will ensure that all of the children will see the pictures and the text. If the children cannot see the illustrations, they may become bored or frustrated. If this happens, they will likely lose interest in the story.

If the adult is familiar with the story text, holding the book in this fashion will cause no problems in the flow of the narrative. If the children are seated, the easiest way to hold the book is to keep the thumb in the center of the pages and the book open in front of the group. One need not move the book, as the children should be able to see quite well from their seated position.

Figure 2–2. A successful reading area is one in which children feel comfortable and safe. Courtesy Diana Comer.

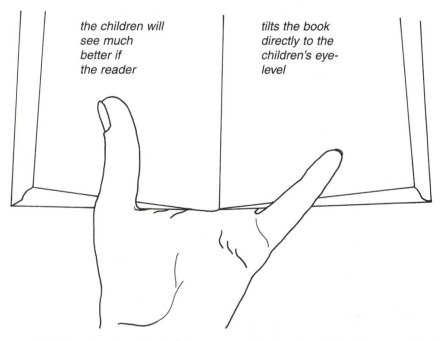

the children will see much better if the reader

tilts the book directly to the children's eye-level

Holding a book so that children can see the words and pictures may take a little practice, but it is an important skill for story sharing. Courtesy Diana Comer.

Everyone can see the book being shared.

Choosing a Place

The place chosen for reading a book depends on the size of the group and the space used to accommodate the group. With larger groups of children, the reader will generally select a circle-time area. With smaller groups, the reading area of a small corner will work well. Naptime is a good opportunity for reading aloud. A story at that time provides a soothing listening experience for the children as they begin their quiet time.

Several factors contribute to a positive reading experience. Always select a comfortable spot where the lighting is adequate but not in anyone's eyes. Make certain there is plenty of room for wriggling so the children will not be bumping into each other. Figure 2-3 illustrates several successful seating patterns.

Choose a place without immediate distractions. The housekeeping corner of the room or a spot next to the class gerbil may be too busy for a reading spot. When reading out of doors, check for anthills, damp ground, and insects that could turn reading time into first-aid time. Children warm up for the story with a related fingerplay or song. This will provide both motivation and personal involvement in the story. Make sure all of the children will be able to see the illustrations. Finally, always know the story before attempting to read or share it with others.

Discovering Great Books

Books are a key part of any classroom's inventory. Adding to the classroom library within a budget can be a difficult problem. Once the teacher has decided which books are needed for the classroom library, the challenge becomes one of finding the books.

a.

b.

e.

c.

d.

Figure 2–3. Successful seating patterns can take a variety of formats. Shown clockwise from upper left are (a) single line, (b) children on lap, (c) semicircle for a small group, (d) floor-and-chair combination for larger groups, and (e) risers for larger groups. Courtesy Diana Comer.

Libraries. If the room is housed in a public or private school, the school library is the first source for borrowing needed books. Most librarians welcome suggestions concerning book selections for the school library. Librarians are terrific at finding the right books to complement themes, units, and special classroom projects. The public library is an additional source of books. Every classroom should have its own permanent collection as well. To find these books, search in yard sales, book stores, catalogs, book clubs, library discard sales, book fairs, estate sales, and moving sales.

A question that should be addressed is whether or not paperback books should be part of the classroom library. For reading aloud, a paperback offers the same story as a hardcover edition, but at a lower cost. Some disagree over whether paperback books are viable for classroom use. There are valid points to each side of the argument.

Paperback Books. There are many excellent editions of both classic and contemporary award-winning books available in paperback. Technology has improved the quality and durability of many paperbacks.

For the price of one hardcover book, one can purchase several paperback books. With the cost so much lower, a teacher can buy more books now rather than buying only a few copies each year. In this way, the variety of books found in the classroom library increases more rapidly.

Hardcover Books. These are more expensive, but they stand up better to the wear and tear of everyday use. Although the initial cost is higher, the books need not be replaced as often. Since most books are printed initially in hardcover, a wider variety of titles is usually available.

Children need access to a wide range of books. Courtesy Diana Comer.

The answer to the paperback versus hardcover argument is probably that both have a legitimate place. The caregiver can take advantage of both kinds by buying some paperbacks to increase the variety and some hardcover books to enhance the durability of the collection. If necessary, paperback books can be limited to short-term use so that their life can be lengthened.

Since infants and toddlers need a hands-on experience with books, one might wish to limit their paperback book use. On the other hand, literacy development demands that books get into the hands of children as soon as it can be done meaningfully. Plastic books with rounded edges and posterboard books are best for babies and very young children.

Book clubs can offer an inexpensive way to purchase good quality contemporary and classic books. The regular offerings are usually in paperback, but bonus points can be earned. The bonus points can be used to purchase hardcover editions, cassettes, and posters. Each month free posters, books, and stickers are usually sent as well. Caldecott Award winners are often offered by the clubs. In addition, the clubs can be used by parents as a convenient way to increase home libraries.

The club offerings should always be optional so that neither parents nor children feel obligated to buy. Clubs that offer books appropriate for young children include Scholastic's Firefly and SeeSaw Book Clubs, Troll Book Club, Weekly Reader Children's Book Club, Parents Magazine Read-Aloud Book Club, Grolier's Dr. Seuss and His Friends Book Club, Trumpet Book Club, Walt Disney Music Company, and Western Publishing's Sesame Street Book Club. (See Appendix A.)

Publishers' book catalogs often offer excellent starter sets of books for libraries. Sets may be purchased by subject area.

Big books are large size editions that enable children to more easily share the reading experience. Some big books are trade book stories reprinted in a larger format. Others are stories made specifically for a big book. These latter stories tend to be predictable in terms of repeated phrases and sentences throughout. This predictability allows children to recognize some of the print and join in the actual reading. Publishers that distribute big book editions include Random House, Houghton Mifflin, Scott Foresman, Scholastic, Harcourt Brace Jovanovich, McGraw-Hill, Sundance, Troll, and The Wright Group. (See Appendix A.) When writing to publishers, it is usually helpful to indicate the age or grade level you are interested in.

Adults and Children as Storytellers

Clara Thompson, a turn of the century educator, said that nothing in human nature had changed in education since she first taught in a one-room schoolhouse. Education is only as good as the individuals working within it. Children learn when one is able to reach them and bring them into the process of education. This is still true.

TIPS FOR TEACHERS

Show children how to use their faces and body language to help tell a story.
* *Create a "copy me" game to show children how it feels when they make a happy, sad, surprised, or scared face.*
* *Use a mirror to help children create facial and body movements relevant to a story.*

Adults must remember that body language and preparation impart nuances that young children perceive. When one is prepared to share a story or teach a lesson, there is an air of confidence. Children notice this and respond to it. The enthusiasm is increased when the reader feels confident and at ease. One becomes natural and less inhibited in the telling of the tale when this confidence is present. Children can build on this modeling, using their terrific imaginations to do some storytelling of their own.

Communicating a Message. Telling a story involves more than reading it. Share the message and the emotion that exists between the lines and within the illustrations. In planning a reading, know the story well. It is impossible to plan a story experience if the plot and the story are unknown to the teller.

When reading or retelling, don't start until the children are listening. Use a transition activity and a motivation to bring the children into a story mood.

The reader must speak clearly and maintain eye contact. It helps to speak a little slower and more distinctly than when using a normal speaking voice. This helps all to understand the words.

Use of Voice. Use the voice effectively. A powerful and adaptive tool in storytelling, the reader's voice can be soft, loud, teasing, brash, or soothing. Different voices for different characters and varied pitches and tones of voice all help create and maintain interest in the story.

Maintain the rhythm of the story. This means reading louder and faster for some parts of the story, while other parts of the story may require a slow or whispering voice.

Body Language. Body language is a part of storytelling. To eliminate the need to shift and move, get into a comfortable position before beginning the tale. With just a bit of exaggeration, one's face can be used as a mirror of the story's action. Subtlety is necessary here. Maintaining eye contact is important for keeping the children's attention on the story. Pausing before plot shifts adds to the excitement. One might even pause at a suspenseful point and ask an open-ended question about what might happen next. Finally, demonstrate enjoyment in the telling of the story. Choose a wide range of good books that both the teacher and children will enjoy. Be discriminating. Never use a book just because it's available or because it was used last year. Make each book a special memory.

SUMMARY

In this chapter, it was found that the environment in which literature is shared with children is critical. Planning the setting for storytelling and sharing books is an important part of any early education program. Children respond to setting. They also respond to the opportunity to be involved in the planning of the setting.

The reading environment should be carefully designed to reflect age-appropriate approaches to the children. Therefore, it is necessary to have some understanding of various aspects of literacy development in infants, toddlers, preschoolers, and kindergarten-age children. This information will assist in designing reading areas.

The reading area sends many messages to children about the importance of reading, the joy of reading, and the role of the child in reading and literature. Children come to understand that they are active participants rather than passive recipients.

The adult is the primary tool needed to transfer the information from the book to the child. Storytelling skills may not be natural to everyone, but they can be developed with practice and forethought. The effective use of body language and voice can greatly enhance the reading process. Planning the storytelling experience is an absolutely essential part of sharing a story with children.

QUESTIONS FOR THOUGHT AND DISCUSSION

1. What concerns should one have when planning a story?
2. When do infants begin to associate sounds with meaning?
3. Describe a possible reading area for children.
4. What are some of the characteristics of a toddler that a story reader might want to take into consideration?
5. What should one look for in an illustration designed for infants and toddlers?
6. How does humor seem to manifest itself in a preschooler?
7. What changes might one make in converting a toddler reading area into one suitable for preschoolers?
8. What social changes seem to occur as children go from the preschool stage to the kindergarten years?
9. Kindergarten children are too young to be involved in contemporary social issues. Defend or refute this statement.
10. How might one change a preschool reading area into one that is suitable for kindergarten children?
11. What should one consider when choosing a site for a reading area?
12. Discuss various ways to display books so that children will be encouraged to use them.
13. Describe various ways of seating children for reading, and identify the circumstances under which each would be used.

CHILDREN'S BOOKS CITED

Adams, J. (1993). *Going for oysters.* Morton Grove, IL: Albert Whitman.

Adler, D.A. (1997). *A picture book of Thurgood Marshall.* New York: Holiday House.

Allen, P. (1992). *Belinda.* New York: Viking.

Anderson, H.C. (1993). *Fairy tales from Hans Christian Anderson.* New York: Chronicle.

Anholt, C., & Anholt, L. (1993). *Bear and baby.* Cambridge, MA: Candlewick.

Anholt, C., & Anholt, L. (1993). *Toddlers.* Cambridge, MA: Candlewick.

Appelt, K. (1993). *Elephants aloft.* San Diego, CA: Harcourt Brace Jovanovich.

Banish, R. (1992). *A forever family.* New York: Harper Collins.

Barton, B. (1997). *Where's the bear?* New York: Mulberry.

Berenstain, S. & J. (1974). *He bear, she bear.* New York: Random House.

Berkus, C., & Dodd, M. (1992). *Charlie's chuckle.* Rockville, MD: Woodbine House.

Birney, B. (1994). *Tyrannosaurus Tex.* Boston: Houghton Mifflin.

Blackstone, S. (1997). *Baby rock, baby roll.* New York: Holiday House.

Bridwell, N. (1986). *Clifford's ABC.* New York: Scholastic.

Bucknall, C. (1991). *One bear in the hospital.* New York: Dial.

Calmenson, S. (1982). *My book of seasons.* Racine, WI: Western.

Carle, E. (1981). *The Very Hungry Caterpillar.* New York: Philomel.

Carlson, N. (1992). *Arnie and the new kid.* New York: Puffin.

Cassedy, S. (1993). *Zoomrimes.* New York: HarperCollins.

Cazet, D. (1994). *Nothing at all.* New York: Orchard.

Dickens, L. (1991). *Rosy's pool.* New York: Viking.

Dodds, D.A. (1994). *The shape of things.* Cambridge, MA: Candlewick.

Dragonwagon, C. (1993). *Alligators and others all year: A book of months.* New York: Macmillan.

Eduar, G. (1997). *Jooka saves the day.* New York: Orchard.

Fox, M. (1989). *Night noises.* San Diego, CA: Harcourt Brace Jovanovich.

Freeman, D. (1968). *Corduroy.* New York: Viking.

Gibbons, G. (1997). *Gulls...Gulls...Gulls.* New York: Holiday House.

Glen, M. (1991). *Ruby.* New York: G. P. Putnam's Sons.

Goennel, H. (1993). *While I am little.* New York: Tambourine.

Grimm Brothers, *Household Stories.* New York: McGraw-Hill.

Hearn, D.D. (1993). *Dad's dinosaur day.* New York: Macmillan.

Hissey, J. (1993). *Little Bear's bedtime.* New York: Random House.

Hissey, J. (1993). *Little Bear's day.* New York: Random House.

Hughes, S. (1994). *Hiding.* Cambridge, MA: Candlewick.

Hutchins, P. (1994). *Three Star Billy.* New York: Greenwillow.

Ingle, A. (1993). *The glow-in-the-dark book of dinosaur skeletons.* New York: Random House.

Jakob, D. (1994). *My bike.* New York: Hyperion.

James, S. (1991). *Dear Mr. Blueberry.* New York: Macmillan.

Johnson, P.B. (1993). *The cow who wouldn't come down.* New York: Orchard.

Keller, H. (1991). *Horace.* New York: Greenwillow.

Kellogg, S. (1997). *Aster Aardvark's alphabet adventures.* New York: Mulberry.

Kennedy, J. (1983). *The teddy bear picnic.* LaJolla, CA: Green Tiger.

Kolar, B. (1997). *Stomp, stomp.* New York: North-South.

Kunhardt, D. (1962). *Pat the bunny.* Racine, WI: Western.

Lifton, B.J. (1994). *Tell me a real adoption story*. New York: Knopf.

Lillie, P. (1993). *When this box is full.* New York: Greenwillow.

MacDonald, A. (1994). *Let's go.* Cambridge, MA: Candlewick.

MacDonald, A. (1994). *Let's pretend.* Cambridge, MA: Candlewick.

Martin, B., Jr., & Archambault, J. (1989). *Chicka chicka boom boom.* New York: Simon and Schuster.

McPhail, D. (1993). *Pigs aplenty.* New York: E.P. Dutton.

Miller, M. (1993). *Can you guess?* New York: Greenwillow.

Milone (illus.), K. (1981). *Beauty and the beast.* Mahwah, NJ: Troll.

Morris, N. (1991). *Jump along.* Minneapolis, MN: Carolrhoda.

Numeroff, L. (1993). *Dogs don't wear sneakers.* New York: Simon and Schuster.

Ormerod, J. (1987). *Making friends.* New York: Lothrop, Lee & Shepard.

Osofsky, A. (1992). *My buddy.* New York: Holt.

Oxenbury, H. (1982). *Good night, good morning.* New York: Dial.

Oxenbury, H. (1993). *Tom and Pippo on the beach.* Cambridge, MA: Candlewick.

Peet, B. (1965). *Chester the worldly pig.* Boston: Houghton Mifflin.

Pfister, M. (1992). *The rainbow fish.* New York: North-South.

Pirner, C.H. (1994). *Even little kids get diabetes.* Morton Grove, IL: Albert Whitman.

Reid, B (1994). *Sing a song of Mother Goose.* New York: Scholastic.

Rey, H.A. (1963). *Curious George.* Boston: Houghton Mifflin.

Romanelli, S. (1997). *Little Bobo saves the day.* New York: North-South.

Root, B. (1993). *My first dictionary.* New York: Dorling Kindersley.

Ross, D. (1980). *A book of hugs.* New York: Crowell.

Ross, D. (1983). *More hugs.* New York: Crowell.

Rylant, C. (1993). E*veryday children.* New York: Bradbury.

Rylant, C. (1993). *Everyday garden.* New York: Bradbury.

Rylant, C. (1993). *Everyday pets.* New York: Bradbury.

Say, A. (1997). *Allison.* Boston, MA: Houghton Mifflin.

Scarry, R. (1973). *Find your ABC's.* New York: Random House.

Schwartz, A. (1994). *A teeny tiny baby.* New York: Orchard.

Sendak, M. (1963). *Where the wild things are.* New York: Harper and Row.

Serfozo, M. (1993). *Joe Joe.* New York: McElderry.

Dr. Seuss (pseud. for T. Geisel) (1940). *Horton hatches the egg.* New York: Random House.

Stein, S. (1993). *Oh, baby!* New York: Walker.

Sutherland, Z. (1990). *The orchard book of nursery rhymes.* New York: Orchard.

Tafuri, N. (1997). *Early morning in the barn.* New York: Mulberry.

Viorst, J. (1972). *Alexander and the terrible, horrible, no good, very bad day.* New York: Atheneum.

Waber, B. (1972). *Ira sleeps over.* Boston: Houghton Mifflin.

Wijngaard, J. (1991). *Bear.* New York: Crown.

Wijngaard, J. (1991). *Cat.* New York: Crown.

Wijngaard, J. (1991). *Dog.* New York: Crown.

Wijngaard, J. (1991). *Duck.* New York: Crown.

Winthrop, E. (1993). *Asleep in a heap.* New York: Holiday House.

SELECTED REFERENCES

Berk, L.E. (1997). *Child development.* Boston: Allyn and Bacon.

Brazelton, T.B. (1983). *Infants and mothers: Differences in development.* New York: Delacorte Press.

Elkind, D. (1989). *The hurried child.* Reading, MA: Addison Wesley.

Morrison, G.S. (1990). *The world of child development.* Albany, NY: Delmar Publishers.

National Association for the Education of Young Children (1997). *Developmentally appropriate practice in early childhood programs serving children from birth through age 8.* Washington, DC: National Association for the Education of Young Children.

Salkind, N.J. (1985). *Theories of human development.* New York: John Wiley.

Two roads diverged in the woods,
and I took the one less traveled by.
And that has made all the difference.

– Robert Frost

3 Choosing the Best Literature

This is an age of tremendous choice for consumers. Nearly everything purchased or selected requires decisions about the model, color, style, or type. This is true for cars, jewelry, food, stereos, and even the tools used to write this sentence. Choosing books for young children is no different. Every year over 4,000 new books for children are published. A kindergarten teacher who might use two books per day over a 180-day school year would need 360 books per year.

Making a selection from the tens of thousands of books available is not a simple task. The right choices require sensitivity and thought. The teacher must consider both the curriculum and the needs of the children, then match those considerations to the books available. A book of great quality might not be right for a particular group. A book of poor quality, even if it fits the curriculum perfectly, is of little value to the teacher or the children.

In addition, one needs to consider the purpose of using a particular book with children. Is it for the sake of the illustrations and photographs? Is it to help children understand the topic being studied? If children are motivated to learn more about a specific topic, such as knights, dragons, or dinosaurs, the high interest these topics generate will help children increase their attention span while a longer piece is read. For this reason, it is not unusual for young children to have an amazing knowledge of the names and characteristics of several different dinosaurs.

This chapter examines the way to begin, by discussing aspects of good literature and the manner in which books are presented or put together. A summary is included of the various types of literature and some of the honors awarded to them.

HOW TO BEGIN

The best way to get started is to become an expert observer of children. This is not meant in the psychological sense of coding children's activities on a chart or checklist. Rather, the teacher must actively attend to the actions, language, and social interactions of children. One must always wonder what a child means by saying or doing a particular thing, as well as why the child said it or did it in that way. By becoming a child-watcher, the teacher will enter the world of children and learn what has meaning for them. This is critical because the most important characteristic about language is that it carries meaning. A book by a famous author, full of dazzling illustrations and gorgeous print, is useless unless or until it has meaning to the child.

By understanding individual children, the teacher can select books that are meaningful to most children in general. This is more difficult than it may seem. It is important for the teacher to consider books that go beyond his or her personal interests and preferences. While everyone has such preferences, it is important to not act on this personal bias in selecting children's books. Books that reflect the interests of the children will help both the teacher and the children to grow.

TIPS FOR TEACHERS

Always read a book by yourself before reading it to children.
- *Write post-it notes to yourself as cues to use a different tone of voice or a specific movement in the story.*
- *Make sure the book does not contain content that would greatly upset children.*
- *Note places to pause and talk with the children about the story.*
- *Identify places to stop and ask, "What do you think might happen next?"*

Children will often listen with understanding to books they cannot read by themselves. Lists of books grouped according to developmental levels are often distributed by libraries. These lists may provide a starting point for the new teacher or supply additional titles for the experienced teacher.

Mother Goose stories and fairy tales, *when chosen with care,* can be used with very young children along with a variety of other materials. Books with large text, colorful print, simple subjects, touchable surfaces, and rhythmic language are quite pleasing. Young children are also interested in books about themselves, self-help skills, their families, and objects from their surroundings. The teacher should be sensitive to individual problems and concerns within the class. Some characters and topics can be frightening to some children. On the other hand, a child who has experienced the death of a pet might find consolation in a book on that topic.

Betsy Hearne[1] has stated, "Children's books are the place for powerful emotions, powerful language, powerful art. If the book you're reading seems boring, toss it. The book probably is boring, and there are thousands that aren't." As drastic as this approach may seem, it does have validity. Children should not be bored by the books and stories read to them. The teacher's role is to instill a desire to know, to imagine, and to read. A child who is wiggling and bored by the third page of a thirty-two-page book is not inspired to do anything but escape.

The teacher must take into account the interests of the class when making a selection. Even if the book meets all selection criteria, it may not capture the

[1] Hearne, B. (1990). *Choosing books for children: A common sense guide.* New York: Delacorte Press.

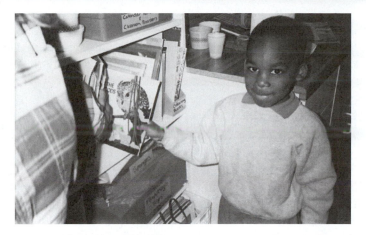

Children enjoy the independence of choosing their own books. Courtesy Diana Comer.

attention of a specific group of children. If this happens, it should be put aside, or perhaps presented again at a later time.

After knowing the children, think about the books themselves. With bookstores, libraries, and children's book clubs available in most communities, access to books is not usually a major problem. Talking to librarians, educators, and others associated with children is a good beginning source of information to develop a listing of potential books. They may also suggest additional sources such as *School Library Journal, The Horn Book Magazine,* and its parent newsletter *Why Children's Books?*

Hundreds of recent titles are cited in this book, but they may not all be readily available in an area. Books can and do go out of print. Moreover, bookstores and libraries can carry only a fraction of the thousands of books that are available. If you can't find a title cited in this text, ask your librarian to acquire a copy through the inter-library loan process. If you want to purchase a copy of a certain book, most bookstores will obtain the book for you from their book service company. It is important to keep reading and reviewing as many books as you can.

ASPECTS OF GOOD CHILDREN'S LITERATURE

Are the things that make a book good for children different from the things that make a book a good piece of literature for adults? Probably not. Of course with adults authors can write longer pieces with more complex topics, but these are differences in quantity. The quality of literature can and should be similar for both children and adults. Those who spend time reading literature written for children will soon discover that people who write successfully for children possess much talent. They are every bit as competent as those who write for adults. This does not mean that all children's books are good. There are both good and poor books written for children just as there are good and poor books written for adults.

The aspects of literature that make a book good, for children or for adults, include characterization, setting, plot, and theme. The adequate development of these elements is found in nearly all high-quality literature. Depending on the piece, one element might be emphasized more than the others, but all are important.

Characterization

Every story has at least one character, and usually there are more. Characters may be animals, people, objects, or imaginary beings. There should not be more characters than are necessary to tell the story. Above all, they must be real to children. The characters from literature who stand the test of time are those act realistically and have real emotions. They give a glimpse of the reader's own self. The reader has a sense of "Yes, I know that feeling or that situation." In short, the reader cares about the character because of an emotional bond.

Characters Must Be Credible. Characters must talk and act true to their role or nature. A good author will let the reader know the personality and motivations of the character through the individual's thoughts, words, actions, language, and expressions. The author must be accurate with each of these in order for the reader to believe in the character. In *My Great Aunt Arizona*, Gloria Houston masterfully presents a character portrait who possesses believability and depth. Based on a real-life individual from Houston's family in early twentieth-century Appalachia, Aunt Arizona is a credible character because the author helps the reader to believe in what she does and who she is. Going back another hundred years, David McPhail presents a New England farm boy in the early nineteenth century through brief diary entries in *Farm Boy's Year.* Returning to Revolutionary War times, Ann Turner presents a credible young Tory girl in *Katie's Trunk* who learns through the kindness of a patriot enemy that there are good people on both sides of the war.

In their series of books about the Stupid Family *(The Stupids Die, The Stupids Step Out, The Stupids Have a Ball)*, the writer/illustrator team of Harry Allard and James Marshall creates characters who are credible in spite of their incredibleness. The Stupids are a family who do everything . . . well, stupidly. The children mow the rug with a lawn mower and water the house plants with a garden sprinkler. Mrs. Stupid makes a dress out of live chickens, while Mr. Stupid eats eggs in the shower. Only the cat and dog seem to have any common sense. It is the fact that these characters are accurate to themselves that endears them to readers. Also, readers relate to the Stupids because everybody has done something foolish, though perhaps not quite as foolish as what the Stupids do. James Marshall explores this foolishness still further in his series of books beginning with the wonderful *George and Martha*.

Characters Must Be Consistent. The character may change and grow, but the basic portrayal must remain intact. That is, the character should not become a totally different character as a result of the experience in the story. In Munro

Sister Bear and Brother Bear. Courtesy Stan and Jan Berenstain.

Leaf's *The Story of Ferdinand,* circumstances change about the famous bull, but Ferdinand remains a pacifist. In *Curious George,* H. A. and Margaret Rey's monkey character learns from his mistakes but doesn't lose his personality or monkey qualities. Sometimes characters don't grow or learn from their mistakes. In Norman Bridwell's books about Clifford, the big red dog, the dog is always consistent in his ability to cause problems with his size. Readers can count on that.

Characters can grow in several ways at once while remaining consistent. Such is the case of the main character in Robert Munsch's *Love You Forever.* In this touching story, a newborn baby and his mother grow over time to where the child becomes a young man with a child of his own while the mother becomes old and frail. The reader follows the child as he grows both physically and emotionally

Author/illustrator Norman Bridwell, creator of the much loved Clifford books. Courtesy Norman Bridwell.

Author Tom Birdseye.
Courtesy Tom Birdseye.

through childhood, adolescence, and adulthood. The underlying goodness and love that the two share triumph at the end, showing the consistency of the love the generations share. Continuing with this topic, several related books present wonderfully consistent portrayals of babies and children to share with toddlers and preschoolers. These include *Here Come the Babies* by Catherine and Laurence Anholt, *Waiting for Baby* by Tom Birdseye, *Our Teacher Is Having a Baby* by Eve Bunting, and *Chatterbox Jamie* by Nancy Evans Cooney.

TIPS FOR TEACHERS

Ask children to tell why they like certain storybook characters.
• *Validate children's attempts to identify with a character.*
• *Ask "why" and "how" questions in response to children's statements about the characters.*

Memorable characters from literature possess personalities that render them unique. Their personalities do not necessarily have to be overpowering. Rather, they are based on real aspects of humanity that make them special. Perhaps the character acts or speaks in a way that reminds readers of themselves. Perhaps the character does these things in a way readers wish they could. Few children are unaware of Dr. Seuss and Mercer Mayer characters, even though most don't know exactly what the characters are. The strong interaction between the reader and the personality is based on the strength of the personality and the believability of the character. Virginia Lee Burton draws the reader into the personality and emotional feelings of a building in *The Little House,* while Shel Silverstein does the same thing with a tree in *The Giving Tree.* Silverstein brings readers into the heart of the tree, feeling the changing seasons and the sensitivity of the relationship between the tree and the boy.

Child characters who are not stereotypical are frequently found in books for young children. In *William's Doll* by Charlotte Zolotow, readers meet a boy who, more than anything else in the world, wants a doll of his own. Others in the story don't understand why a boy would want a doll until his grandmother skillfully shows how natural a toy a doll can be for any child. In Tomie dePaola's autobiographical story *The Art Lesson,* the main character's personality and creativity continually shine through as he struggles with the rigid requirements of the school art curriculum.

The characters of Madeline by Ludwig Bemelmans, Little Tim by Edward Ardizzone, Max by Rosemary Wells, Amelia Bedelia by Peggy Parish, and Frog and Toad by Arnold Lobel stay with the reader for a lifetime. These characters touch the reader personally with whimsy, humor, empathy, and the stirrings of the need for independence.

Animal Characters. Animal characterizations are an important part of children's literature. Beatrix Potter gave her animals personality, but kept them in their delightful animal roles. She allowed them to continue to follow their natural instincts. Her drawings depicted them with clothing and human aspects as they went about stealing vegetables from a garden and living in a mouse hole. Each character is believable, yet retains the charm of its animal nature. Else Holmelund Minarik accomplishes the same thing with her Little Bear books as do Jan and Stan Berenstain in their Berenstain Bears series. In the latter series, the actions, emotions, and situations are all human, and the bears do not appear to have just stepped out of the woods. Instead, they have a humanlike home in the form of a tailored tree house.

Stories combining humans and animals provide a unique bridge between the two types of characters. In *Chestnut Cove* by Tim Egan, the hippolike generic animals of a village learn about the danger of greed. During the competition of a watermelon-growing contest, the villagers are caught off guard by an unexpected crisis. The problem brings the villagers to their senses and the community back together. Taking off from the ending of a familiar fairy tale, Teresa Celsi presents a childlike look at fear in *The Fourth Little Pig.* Having been traumatized by the big bad wolf, it takes the sister of the three little pigs to coax them out of their house and back into the world. Still another view of animals is found in nonfiction books such as *Bears, Bears, and More Bears* by Jackie Morris.

Portraying animals in a variety of character roles is quite valid and can be a positive and enjoyable experience for the reader. Difficult topics can be approached through animal characters causing less traumatic reactions from children who may see themselves living or feeling the situation in the book. Topics such as new babies, moving, hospitals, divorce, and death are distanced through the use of animal characters. The safety that such an approach affords can help a child deal with the stressful topic.

Children often learn about animals and their habits from animal characters in books. They will sometimes correct or question a story when an animal character is not true to its animal roots. Even when this occurs, it does not lessen enjoyment of fantasy or humanlike animals. It demonstrates the great interest in animals that most children have during their early years. The best authors demonstrate a skillful blending of true animal characteristics and human behaviors in their animal characters.

Setting

The term "setting" usually makes the reader think about where and when a story takes place. This is partly correct, but a setting is often much more. Besides the actual location and time period of the story, the setting may include the way the characters live and the cultural aspects of the environment. Suppose a story takes place in a small town at the time of the Civil War; it would make a difference if the town were located in the North or the South. The geography might not have much of an effect, but the moral tone would be quite different. A story is also affected by whether the characters are living in poverty or wealth.

The possibilities of setting are numerous, and each possibility has the potential to change the moral, ethical, and social tone of the story. This is true because the characters are closely connected to the setting. Characters do not act in a vacuum; they act in a specific place, time, and social environment. Just as people in real life do, characters in stories act in certain ways depending on their setting. For example, people who are very hungry will behave differently depending on whether they are in a classroom, church, or restaurant. That is the expectation; but, of course, in stories and in real life, individuals who don't quite conform to expectations can create interest and excitement.

The setting in children's books varies widely. It can be a current setting, such as Boston Gardens in Robert McCloskey's *Make Way for Ducklings.* Or it can be a historical setting, as provided in historical fiction stories like *Barefoot—Escape on the Underground Railroad* by Pamela Duncan Edwards. Using a narrative format, this story shares an important piece of history taking place in the nineteenth-century countryside, with fields, swamps, and forest clearings. The visual effect of white-lettered text on the dark, night-time illustrations sets the mood as the main character seeks the shelter of the next safe house.

Settings from around the world are presented in *When Grandma Came* by Jill Paton Walsh. In this story, Grandma recalls her travels in words and illustration to Mt. Desert Island, the Arctic, Africa, Australia, India, and the Nile River. Another example of a book presenting different settings is Barbara Cooney's *Miss Rumphius.* In this touching story, also illustrated by the author, a young girl begins and ends her life on the coast of Maine. In the middle of the story, however, the setting shifts as she travels around the world. Cooney uses the reason for the girl's travels to neatly tie the various settings into a unified tale.

A setting can be implied rather than specifically described in the text or depicted in the illustrations. Jungle animals and descriptions of their homes would enable the reader to detect that the setting is a jungle or zoo.

Setting can reinforce the underlying theme of a story. In *Goodnight Moon* by Margaret Wise Brown, the setting of the bunny's moonlit bedroom reinforces the theme of the warmth, safety, and security that a child finds when settling down for a good night's sleep. In another story that takes place in a child's bedroom, *Where the Wild Things Are* by Maurice Sendak, the author cleverly confines the entire action to the room. Through the child's and the reader's imagination, the setting changes to the sea and finally to a faraway island where the wild things live. The reader is carried along with the dream. The child's anger at being sent to his room in the first place is balanced by the love symbolized by the hot dinner found upon returning from the imaginary, anger-filled journey. The dinner, left there by his mother, demonstrates that he is cherished. The setting changes enhance the character's feelings as the story proceeds.

Home Settings. The setting of a home can also be used to create a sense of anxiety, humor, or sadness when the unexpected happens. Gentle anxiety prevails in Lynn Gordon's *Lights Out! The Witch's Revenge* as the home of Audrey and Andrew is invaded by a witch. The acetate windows in the book fit a standard

Some books are read and enjoyed by generations of young readers.
Courtesy Diana Comer.

size flashlight. This allows the reader to project some of the story on the wall of a darkened room as the tale is read. In Tomie dePaola's *Nana Upstairs and Nana Downstairs,* a child's familiar world is made bewildering and sad when he experiences the death of a grandparent. It is only through the interaction of the child's creative character and the setting that the problem of the story is resolved. A wonderful home setting story for younger children is *So Much* by Trish Cooke, illustrated in gouache by Helen Oxenbury. The repeating action is the arrival of various family members in anticipation of a surprise party for Daddy. As the guests arrive, they pass the time by kissing, cuddling, and hugging the baby because they love him SO MUCH! The anticipated arrival of a new member of the household is the subject of *Will There be a Lap for Me?* by Dorothy Corey, illustrated by Nancy Poydar. As the birth of baby draws near, Kyle's mother's lap disappears. As things settle down after the arrival of the new baby, however, Kyle's special place returns.

School Settings. Stories set in schools are popular because children easily relate to them. Patricia Reilly Giff's Ronald Morgan series *(Today Was a Terrible Day; Watch Out, Ronald Morgan; Happy Birthday, Ronald Morgan)* has a wide audience. Ronald always seems to have problems in the school setting. He has a poor self-concept and is often unaware of things going on around him. His teacher, in the best teacher tradition, helps Ronald by encouraging him and helping him to discover by himself that he really can do many things. In *Chrysanthemum* by Kevin Henkes, an all too common problem is confronted. Chrysanthemum can't wait until her first day of school. She is quickly disappointed as others make fun of her first name. The story leads naturally into a discussion about self-esteem, respect, and pride. Listeners and readers will roll with laughter at the originality of Andrew Clements' story, *Billy and the Bad Teacher.* Elivia Savadier's accompanying wacky illustrations are a treasure to behold as well.

Nature Settings. Romantic settings such as the mountains and the ocean are popular as well. In *Dogteam* by Gary Paulsen, a man takes his dogsled for a run in the winter forest on the night of a full moon. Ruth Wright Paulsen's watercolor illustrations present the beauty and majesty of the great north woods. Another gorgeous night setting is presented in June Crebbin's *Fly By Night.* Stephen Lambert's illustrations reflect the coming of night as a young owl eagerly anticipates its first flight. A beautiful book about living near the ocean is Alvin Tresselt's *Hide and Seek Fog.* While the fog creates problems for the adults, the children make superb use of this change in their usual setting. Roger Duvoisin's illustrations of the fog-enshrouded town are so vivid the reader almost feels the moisture hanging in the air.

Plot

The plot can be seen as a kind of road map to a story. An author plans a plot to help the reader make sense out of the story. Usually the plot unfolds in chronological order, but not always.

Plot is an artificial rather than a natural element, with the purpose of simplifying life. The author does this by selecting some events, some characters, and some emotions. There are a limited number of episodes, and only those that are necessary to the story are included. By presenting the action, excitement, and suspense that allows conflict to develop, a good plot allows children to become personally involved in the story.[2] When this happens in conjunction with effective character development, children become hooked on the tale simply because they care about the characters as the situations unfold.

A plot is created with characters and settings in mind. That is, the author asks himself or herself, given the characters in a certain setting, what would tend to occur naturally? Writers Holman and Harmon[3] state that from this viewpoint, the function of plot is to translate character into action. In Aliki's *We Are Best Friends,* Peter and Robert are pals who are suddenly faced with the fact that Peter must move away. The reader is taken with wit and humor through a range of emotions and adjustments from anger, loneliness, and boredom to happiness and new friendships.

One might view plot as containing a beginning, middle, and end. The beginning should quickly set up interest for the reader. Younger children have shorter attention spans, so this point is even more important for them. Interest is established by using characters and a conflict that the reader can relate to and care about. The conflict should grab the attention of the reader and create a desire to find out what happens. In *Lizzy's Invitation* by Holly Keller, Lizzy is faced with the fact that she is not invited to another child's birthday party. Keller sets up another serious childhood problem, the death of a pet, in another of her books, *Goodbye, Max.* In *Ira Sleeps Over* by Bernard Waber, Ira's happiness at being invited to sleep over at a friend's house is shaken when his big sister asks him if he will be bringing his teddy bear along. He must then deal with the contrasting problems of wanting to be more grown up, yet still desiring the security of childhood comfort objects. Finally, Robert Munsch's witty book, *I Have to Go,* begins on page one with the parents and child involved in the problems of toilet training.

In the middle of the plot, the conflict or problem may become more defined. The rising action created by the interaction of the characters helps the reader become more emotionally involved with the plot. The resolution of the conflict or even the recognition of who or what is the cause of the conflict should not be too obvious at this point. If the reader knows what happens now, there is little point to

2 Norton, D.E. (1995). *Through the eyes of a child: An introduction to children's literature.* New York: Macmillan.

3 Holman, H.C., & Harmon, W. (1992). *A handbook to literature* (6th ed). New York: Macmillan.

finishing the story. Rather, the reader should feel more and more drawn into the story. The quickening pace and the building of tension should continue as the reader approaches the ending. By creating twists in the plot through new problems and by suggesting false endings, the author intrigues and motivates the reader to reach the ending. Barbara Shook Hazen includes such plot twists in *Tight Times,* her story of a child and his already impoverished family who spend much time dealing with the desire to have a pet at a time when the father has just lost his job. Author/illustrator Kevin Henkes provides a clever plot twist that young children will understand in *A Weekend With Wendell.* Sophie, dreading the idea of spending a weekend with bossy Wendell, solves the problem by turning the tables on him.

The ending contains the climax and the resolution of the plot. The climax is the highest point in dramatic tension, the point where everyone is quiet and sitting on the edge of his or her seat. The resolution is the final outcome of the problem or conflict. Even if the ending is happy, it can have an unexpected twist. In Dr. Seuss's *Horton Hatches the Egg,* children delight in the elephant-bird who hatches for the faithful Horton. In Dr. Seuss's *The Lorax,* children are given an unexpected last-minute reprieve from the pollution mess.

When the plot includes a child attempting to resolve a conflict, it is most appropriate if the child solves the problem without interference from adults in the story. In Nancy Evans Cooney's book, *The Blanket That Had to Go,* the child develops a satisfying solution concerning her fear of going to her first day at kindergarten without her security blanket.

Sometimes the plot presents a problem in which there is no satisfactory solution, such as in Eve Bunting's *The Wall.* A boy and his father experience the ongoing feeling of the loss of the boy's grandfather as they visit the Vietnam Memorial. Ronald Himler's illustrations perfectly capture the melancholy mood on this cold winter day.

The plot should be clear and believable even if the author asks the reader to travel into a world of fantasy. It should move from part to part with ease and consistency in order to maintain understanding and interest. Plots that are transparent or confusing will be boring to the young child. If the teacher can tell the final outcome on page one, chances are good that the child will be able to do this as well. If a child is confused, it will be difficult to maintain his or her interest. Books with believable, understandable, and creative plots should be selected.

Theme

The theme of a story is an abstract concept the author has embedded in the story. The theme may include such ideas as the strength of friendship, the fragility of life, family life, or becoming independent. It is made concrete through other parts of the story such as characterization, setting, and plot. The theme often teaches a lesson or persuades the reader of something.

Illustrations can enhance the theme. In *The Polar Express,* Chris Van Allsburg sets the tone of the theme with the bleak, gray snow scenes of the home

THE POLAR EXPRESS

The Polar Express *by Chris Van Allsburg is a holiday season favorite.* Reprinted by permission of Houghton Mifflin Co.

and the child. The full-color illustrations fit perfectly with the theme of Verna Aardema's *Why Mosquitoes Buzz in People's Ears,* illustrated by Leo and Diane Dillon. Good illustrators find a way to reflect the theme in their illustrations.

Identifying Themes. The theme can be an overview or an underlying part of the book. There can be one or several themes or subthemes in a story. The theme often reveals the author's purpose in writing the book; for example, the author may use the story to help children understand or develop sensitivity to some issue or event. Even simple books for toddlers have underlying themes, such as pride in self and independence in a book about getting dressed. The concept of civilization versus nature is an integral theme in *Little Brother Moose* by James Kasperson, as a young bewildered moose wanders in and out of a town. A story from the humorous George and Martha series by James Marshall tells of an awful meal that Martha prepares for George. Through the telling of the tale, the underlying themes of friendship and honesty become clear to the young reader. As the story proceeds, George's dilemma is handled in a positive and humorous way.

The theme of siblings, with all of the joys and difficulties those relationships may entail, is frequently found in children's literature. Jean Little tells the story of how two sisters learn an important lesson on the meaning of bravery in *Jess Was the Brave One.* In *Brothers and Sisters* Maxine Rosenberg presents three very different children to make the point that sibling joys and challenges transcend the position of the sibling, sex, age, and cultural background. The themes of teasing, suffering from teasing, and the need for peace among siblings all emerge.

A theme should not be too obvious; it should unfold for the reader. Most well-written stories have layers of reasons or themes that add depth and dimension to the plot. *Mufaro's Beautiful Daughters* by John Steptoe is an African tale that can be read as a simple story in which the virtuous daughter is rewarded. It can also be read for its themes of showing kindness, bravery, dealing with jealousy, acting with and accepting   consequences for one's actions. Many lessons can be learned from this one story about life and human nature. The illustrations, which won the Caldecott Honor Medal, provide a refreshing complement to the story.

The four areas of character, plot, setting, and theme are integrated in a successful story. Keeping a file of books that meet the criteria for each characteristic is an effective organizational tool. A one-page or half-page summary could be developed for each book, including the following items:

> Title
> Author
> Concepts in book
> Short narrative of story
> Does it meet the criteria for characterization?
> Does it meet the criteria for setting?
> Does it meet the criteria for plot?
> Does it meet the criteria for theme?

The file of books can grow over the years as new titles are published, increasing its value with each passing year.

Censorship. The American Library Association and its Office for Intellectual Freedom have noted an increase in censorship over the past few decades. Books written for young children, some of them winners of prestigious awards, are not immune to this problem. Censorship ordinarily occurs when parents object to material their children are being exposed to in school. Parents do have a right to hold and discuss their views about materials. Teachers should make every attempt to accommodate concerns by providing alternate materials for those children whose parents have expressed concerns. Censorship occurs when parents, teachers, or members of the community attempt to restrict the rights of others by banning the use of objectionable materials. The major themes related to censorship include violence, negative depictions of parents, devils, witches, sexuality, homosexuality, and low self-esteem. While teachers should be able to use whatever materials they feel best meet the needs of the program, they need to be ready to address censorship attempts as they arise. Figure 3–1 contains a list of books that are most frequently the targets of censorship.

Educator Rick Traw (1996) describes a South Dakota censorship incident that received national attention and in which he was involved. The schools in Sioux Falls had adopted an anthology of children's literature containing traditional folk tales, holiday stories, and multi-cultural stories. Most of the literature had previously been published in the form of single-volume picture books. According to Traw, within the first month of use of the literature, a group of fundamentalist activists launched a censorship campaign to have the material removed on the grounds that stories involving Halloween, mythology, and non-Christian multi-cultural settings were teaching the children Satanism and witchcraft. The superintendent of schools appointed a citizen's committee to review the literature and

---

Banned Children's Books

Allard, Harry and Marshall, James. *The Stupids Have a Ball.*

Allard, Harry and Marshall, James. *The Stupids Step Out.*

The Bible.

Dahl, Roald. *Matilda.*

Dahl, Roald. *The Witches.*

Grimm Brothers. *The Complete Fairy Tales of the Brothers Grimm.*

Handford, Martin. *Where's Waldo?*

McDermott, Beverly Brodsky. *The Golem: A Jewish Legend.*

Merriam, Eve. *Halloween ABC.*

Newman, Leslea. *Heather Has Two Mommies.*

Prelutsky, Jack. *Nightmares: Poems to Trouble Your Sleep.*

Sendak, Maurice. *In the Night Kitchen.*

Silverstein, Shel. *A Light in the Attic.*

Silverstein, Shel. *Where the Sidewalk Ends.*

Steig, William. *The Amazing Bone.*

Steig, William. *Caleb and Kate.*

Wallace, Daisy, ed. *Witch Poems.*

Willhoite, Michael. *Daddy's Roommate.*

Adapted from a general listing in Doyle, R.P. (ed.) (1994). Banned books 1994 resource guide. Chicago, IL: American Library Association.

Figure 3–1. Frequently banned books.

make recommendations for its use. After a year of hearings and discussions, it was decided that the literature was quite innocent and its use should be continued. Traw notes that although the censorship battle was won in Sioux Falls, the censors may have ultimately won the war. The same censorship arguments were repeated across the land, and the book's publisher eventually withdrew it from the U.S. market.

PRESENTATION

The presentation of the story involves those factors that relate to the plot, setting, characterization, and theme. It is difficult to separate the aspects of presentation since a good book will integrate them into a whole work that is greater than the sum of the individual parts. They are separated here for discussion purposes only. The four parts of the presentation discussed include

1. Text style used in the printing;
2. Narrative style;
3. The illustrations or photographs used; and
4. Anti-bias factors within the book.

TIPS FOR TEACHERS

Anticipate the visual impact an illustration will have on children.
* *Build up suspense by saying, "Wait until you see the picture on the next page."*
* *Ask, "Why do we laugh at the character in this picture?"*
* *Invite children to tell how they feel when looking at an illustration.*

Text Style

The style of print used in the text is important to the effect of the story. Text style also contributes to the success of the unity between the text and the illustrations. Hundreds of type settings are available. The style, size, color, and location of the print must fit the purpose of and feeling created by the narrative.

Print Size. Roger Duvoisin's *Veronica* uses tiny standard print set against humorously huge illustrations of the hippopotamus, making her look even more gigantic. Jean de Brunhoff's *Babar and the King* is set with a script that appears similar to a child's early cursive penmanship. The illustrations are at the bottom of the page, or fill the entire page. Sometimes the text is placed between the boxed-off illustrations where it fits the story best. The simple, expressive illustrations blend with the cursive style of print without conflict.

Dr. Seuss's *Hop on Pop* is meant to help beginning readers. He has chosen a standard script found in many reading books, but the size is much larger. Standard print is about one-quarter of a centimeter tall. In Dr. Seuss's book, emphasized words are a full centimeter tall, while the words in the rest of the sentence are three-quarters of a centimeter tall. This print fits the purpose and style of the book and is a good contrast with the zany pictures.

Dorothy Kunhardt's *Pat the Bunny* has very little print. What print there is, however, is a half centimeter tall and done in a child's manuscript. In *Yo! Yes!* author/illustrator Chris Raschka, using only thirty-four words, provides a multi-cultural look at friendship. Each huge charcoal word with its accompanying illustration jumps off the page to tell a story.

In *The Grouchy Ladybug* by Eric Carle, the print starts as one size and grows with the story. Carle's use of small pages building to larger and larger

Once upon a time....

Once upon a time....

Once upon a time....

ONCE UPON A TIME....

ONCE UPON A TIME....

Once upon a time....

Once upon a time....

Once upon a time....

Types of print

pages as the ladybug encounters ever bigger animals is enhanced by the effective use of print size. The print reaches whale size at the conclusion of the book. Virginia Lee Burton also uses this change of type size in her book, *Choo Choo: The Story of a Little Engine Who Ran Away.* Throughout the story, the train's name continues to appear in print. Every time it appears, it does so in larger print, standing out clearly within the text. The frequency of the large printed name grows along with the rising action of the story.

Print Color. Color is another key choice for print. Pamela Duncan uses large white typed lettering on dark backgrounds to tell the story of *Four Famished Foxes and Fosdyke* as the young foxes get a lesson in using their heads during a series of night-time raids on a nearby henhouse. Robert McCloskey chooses a standard print in the same sepia color as the illustrations in *Make Way for Ducklings.* Other books have used color in additional creative ways depending on the needs and purpose of the story.

Print Location. Print can be placed in various locations on the page. It may be spaced as in poetry. Although words are usually placed in paragraphs, variations can also be used.

In summary, the choice and placement of print can enhance or diminish the effect of the narrative and its illustrations. In a quality book, the choice of print is always a consideration that shows.

Narrative Style

Each author has an individual style for telling his or her tale. This style is reflected in the choice of words, the figures of speech, the rhythmic pattern of the language, the structure of sentences, and the use of rhetorical devices. Style differences create a wide diversity in children's books. In *The Painter,* author/illustrator Peter Catalanotto uses an autobiographical style as the basis of a story in which a young child is not allowed to accompany her artist-father as he works each day in his home studio. Dr. Seuss uses a poetic style to tell a narrative.

Poetic Style. A. A. Milne uses poetry in the Christopher Robin stories to bring the reader into the world of Christopher and Pooh. The rhythm is bouncy and fun, hinting to the reader that the stories will be likewise.

The Brothers Grimm alternate narrative with poetry in a character's dialogue for a special effect that is well remembered: "Queen, you are full fair, 'tis true, But Snow White fairer is than you," from "Snow White and the Seven Dwarfs"; and, "Little tree, little tree, shake over me, That silver and gold may come down and cover me," from "Aschenputtel."

The Night Before Christmas by Clement Moore is a classic poetic tale that has enchanted generations of young children. This new edition, with charming watercolor illustrations by Tasha Tudor, is a feast for the eyes and the ears.

Repetitive Style. Repetition is used to create a delightful tale in *Millions of Cats* by Wanda Gag. By the time the reader gets to "trillions of cats," children are eagerly anticipating and joining in the repetition.

Ludwig Bemelmans's short, rhyming narrative fits well with the stories of the twelve little girls in the ever popular *Madeline.* The adventures in the Madeline series always begin with the same opening lines which, for hundreds of children, have come to mean that enjoyment will surely follow.

Margaret Wise Brown has a natural touch with her books for children. *Goodnight Moon* is one of the most popular bedtime stories with preschoolers because the simple script reflects a reassuring ritual played out in almost every child's house each night.

Judith Viorst uses a running narrative with a repetition that exposes the thoughts and the focus in *Alexander and the Terrible, Horrible, No Good, Very Bad Day.* The title itself is the repetition line. The illustrations aptly show just how the events of the narrative are making Alexander feel. This book causes laughter because all readers can empathize with the story. The descriptive language includes words such as "scrunched," "smushed," and the therapeutic "I'm going to Australia." Many adults love this book as much as children do.

Point of View. No matter what the style, good literary narratives include all the components of good fiction. Besides such technical aspects as plot and setting, point of view is involved as well.

Today's stories, more so than those of yesterday, are frequently told from the child's perspective, rather than from the perspective of an adult. Think of how a child might describe a kitchen. In the past, the adult perspective would have determined the words, even though they might be ascribed to a child. For example, "My kitchen has four big chairs with shiny red seats. The cookie jar looks like a big fat doll and it's always full of yummy things to eat." Contemporary literature, using a more realistic child's point of view, might describe the same kitchen as, "The kitchen has lots of legs and a blue floor with crumbs and a sticky Kool-Aid patch that the cat licked almost clean." The latter description was by a three-and-one-half-year-old girl who described the kitchen not as an adult would see the kitchen, but as she actually did see it. The difference is important. The perceptive writer of children's books has the ability to see life or events from the child's perspective. It is this special ability that creates a child-loved classic. These are often the books children want to read again and again.

A good narrative style has several ingredients. First, the flow of language should be appropriate to the story. The use of words should enhance the story and the understandings it is attempting to convey. The narrative style should hold the reader's interest and contain a bit of intrigue, mystery, or surprise. The conflicts and conflict resolutions should make sense and feel right to the reader. They should draw the reader into the story enough to care about them both. Finally, the print choices should mesh with the author's purposes.

Topics and themes in children's literature have greatly expanded over the past several years, but the artistry of a good storyteller is still the cornerstone of a memorable book. The narrative style is a major part of the story that will be remembered, repeated, and enjoyed even when the book has long been misplaced or lost. A good narrative is real, touching the child as well as the child still hiding in every adult.

Good children's literature is good literature. It is difficult to resist its beauty, simplicity, and comedy. A good children's story gives adults the chance to remember, to dream again, and to find joy in the sense of wonder that was once theirs as children.

Illustrations and Photographs

The illustrations and photographs used in children's literature are as important for young children as the narrative. Children should be provided with high-quality artwork as they begin their lives, because exposure to fine artwork and photography builds an appreciation and love for art. Children have an openness of mind and imagination to appreciate a wide variety of art. They are not opinionated or biased about one type of art or another.

The criteria that should be used for making judgments about the illustrations and photographs in children's books include integration with the story, attention to detail, texture, and color.

TIPS FOR TEACHERS

Take children on short field trips to museums and galleries to develop an appreciation for art.
- *Create an art show and reception for the parents and siblings to see the art created by the children.*
- *When several children are drawing similar pictures (e.g. pets), have some use crayon, others use colored pencils, and still others use pastel markers.*
- *Seek donations of cameras and film to include photographs by children as part of an art display.*

Artistic Modes. The criteria used for judging the quality of illustrations can be applied to a variety of artistic modes. In using color, artists may choose crayon, oil pastels, chalk, water crayon, and so forth. Shading, detailing, and smudging are techniques that are used as part of this medium. Each gives a different expression to an illustration. These tools are used to create a soft feeling, a bold expression, or other emotion. Feodor Rojankovsky, Raymond Briggs, Thomas Locker, and Nancy Ekhorn Burkert are artists who display exceptional talent with the use of color.

Pen and ink is a traditional medium used quite often in children's books. It may be used as an outline or with various sketchings to enhance detail. Shel Silverstein, Nonny Hogrogian, E. H. Shepard, Robert Lawson, and Leonard Weisgard are masters of this technique.

Artist's illustration of a cat in three media: charcoal (top), colored markers (middle), and pastel (bottom). Courtesy Emily Sawyer.

Woodcuts and linocuts are used by several illustrators to create a broad range of finished products. They can yield very detailed results or bold and dramatic images. The colors can be brown, black, or other darker colors and may be used with or without a lighter wash. Each color can also be painted separately onto the woodcut and printed by hand. Superb examples of the technique can be seen in the works of Wanda Gag, Evaline Ness, Marcia Brown, Don Freeman, Antonio Frasconi, Ed Emberly, and Marie Hall Ets.

Colored pencils or charcoal yield a different texture and feel than crayon or paint. This is a very painstaking process to use for an entire book, but it can create an effect that other techniques cannot duplicate. Artists Susan Jeffers, Taro Yashima, and Chris Van Allsburg (conte pen) have produced outstanding examples of this process.

Photographers for children's literature are special people. They must be able to visualize as a child and also possess the technical skill to capture the picture that precisely meets the needs of the narrative. Tana Hoban, Roger Bester, Bruce McMillan, and Thomas Mattieson provide dazzling examples of this type of photography.

Artists who choose collage must have a bit of the collector within themselves. Ezra Jack Keats pinned his fabric bits on his wall to keep them visible. The textures and feel that collage can offer are limitless. Materials can come from anywhere and anything. Tissue paper, as used by Eric Carle, and fabric and wallpaper, as used by Keats, are the more common materials. A spectacular example of the use of collage is found in author/illustrator Stephen Kroninger's *If I Crossed the Road.* This story, told from the point of view of a young child, shares the dreams of possibilities that are just across the road.

Painted Illustrations. Paint is by far the most common medium for artwork in children's books. It is often used with other media to give a contrasting texture and color. Paint can be the thin, soft wash of tempera or watercolor, the bold, brash reds and purples of oil, or the thick, textured look of acrylics. This diversity and richness of color and texture makes it a popular medium. Maurice Sendak, Mitsamasa Anno, Gyo Fujikawa, Chris Soentpiet, Stephen Gammell, James Ransome, Susan Jeffers, Brian Wildsmith, Dick Bruna, Tasha Tudor, Tomie dePaola, Steven Kellogg, Arnold Lobel, and Donald Carrick are but a few of the fine painters whose illustrations appear in children's literature.

The most difficult part of the painter's job is to create a series of illustrations that satisfy the painter as well as his or her audience. Some artists prefer to work in one medium and perfect their craft while others prefer to use several types of media. Marcia Brown is a multitalented illustrator who has successfully tried almost every medium. For example, *Dick Whittington and His Cat* uses woodcut in black and white. Brown's book, *Cinderella,* a Caldecott Medal winner, is done in subtle pastels.

Several artists use historical, master, and contemporary styles in their work. Leo and Diane Dillon, in *Ashanti to Zulu* by Margaret Musgrove, use tribal motifs. Native American motifs are used by illustrator Charles Reasoner throughout Terry Cohlene's retelling of a Cheyenne legend in *Quillworker.* Paul Goble uses beautifully expressive native American symbols in *The Girl Who Loved Wild Horses.* Cheryl Harness combines elements of romanticism, impressionism, and the Hudson River school of painting in *The Amazing Impossible Erie Canal.* In this gorgeous nonfiction book, the watercolor, gouache, and colored pencil illustrations can be used to tell the story with or without the text. Barbara Cooney uses an old master style in *Ox-Cart Man* by Donald Hall. This book is reminiscent of a visit to an art museum's Americana collection. These styles require much research and attention to detail.

Effective use of light and dark is another tool of the skilled artist. Chris Van Allsburg paints with dramatic use of light in *The Polar Express* and *Jumanji. Owl Moon* by Jane Yolen incorporates a powerful use of light as the storyline progresses through the owl hunt. John Schoenherr's expansive style makes readers feel like they are walking through the woods themselves.

Rosemary Wells humorously uses type and illustration in a style all her own. For example, when she uses the word "between" in the text, it is actually placed between two objects in the illustrations. When Morris, in *Morris's Disappearing Bag,* uses a bag to hide in, children identify with him. They see themselves hiding in the bag as well.

All of these artists, and new artists such as Mark Teague, Robin Ballard, Chris Raschka, Thor Wickstrom, and Timothy Bush, will keep children's literature exciting for years to come. They follow the path of Randolph Caldecott, William Mulready, Kate Greenaway, Sir John Tenniel, and Leslie Brooke of the nineteenth century. New artists, like new writers, are emerging each year to both continue tradition and explore new possibilities.

When selecting books, ask if the choices you are making will stand the test of time and love. Every book used with children should be a quality book in both narrative and illustration. Additional in-depth information on children's book illustration can be found in the works of Judith Saltman,[4] John W. Griffith and Charles H. Frey,[5] Charles Panati,[6] May Hill Arbuthnot and Zena Sutherland,[7] L.E. Lacy,[8] J.H. and C. Schwartz,[9] and Helen Williams.[10]

Integration with Text. The integration of the illustrations and photographs with the text refers to whether or not they fit all aspects of the narrative. One reason that Leo and Diane Dillon are so successful with their two Caldecott-winning African tales is their ability to transport the reader to Africa. They do so with the effective use and integration of color, design, and text.

Illustrations must be integrated with each other as well as with the text. Leo Lionni is a master of illustration-to-illustration unity. In *Swimmy,* he creates the feeling of enormity by allowing the reader to see the fish swimming in the entire ocean. The detail even includes a fish flowing off the page as if it is continuing to swim there. Donald Crews also shares this talent for integration. In *Freight Train,* the reader sees the train move from page to page at increasing speed.

An example of good integration of text and illustrations is Pamela Duncan Edwards's *Four Famished Foxes and Fosdyke,* in which the dark background reinforces the bold white lettering. In Aliki's, *We Are Best Friends,* the print is similar to a primer print. It is located throughout the book at the page bottoms, apart from the illustrations. The dramatic sadness of the tale is increased tenfold when the text shifts to the heartwrenching letter that is part of the story. The letter, written in a child's beginning handwriting, is expertly integrated into the narrative. Dr. Seuss is also most adept at effective and creative integration of text and illustration. In *The Shape of Me and Other Stuff,* he successfully integrates bright colors, large bold print, and shadow shapes. The words are clearly and enjoyably emphasized without distracting from the game of guessing the shadows.

Works of lesser quality do not include this thoughtful integration. They often use gimmicks that attempt to be clever. In actuality, such gimmicks detract from and disrupt the story flow. In previewing children's books, look at the type of print

---

4 Saltman, J. (1985). *The Riverside Anthology of children's literature.* Boston: Houghton Mifflin.

5 Griffith, J.W., & Frey, C.H. (eds.). *Classics of children's literature.* New York: MacMillan.

6 Panati, C. (1987). *Extraordinary origins of everyday things.* New York: Harper & Row.

7 Arbuthot, M.H., & Sutherland, Z. (1985). *Children and books.* Chicago: Scott Foresman.

8 Lacy, L.E. (1986). *Art and design in children's picture books.* Chicago: American Library Association.

9 Schwartz, J.H., & Schwartz, C. (1991). *The picture book comes of age.* Chicago: American Library Association.

10 Williams, H.E. (1991). *Books by African-American authors and illustrators.* Chicago: American Library Association.

Talking about covers and illustrations found in books is an important part of the picture book experience.

to see if it is appropriate for the type of book and age level of the children. It should be checked to see if the words are clear and easy to find, rather than hidden throughout the page. The type should not be crowded, allowing the child's eye to pick up on the spacing between the words.

Attention to Detail. Quality illustrations and photographs stand out from mediocre art because of attention to detail. Illustrations need to accurately reflect the narrative. For example, if a story calls for a monkey to wear a red hat, it must be the same shade of red and the same hat throughout the story. Poor quality books may vary these details. Children demand truth from their stories. They will count every object on a page to be certain that the twenty cats are there, just as the story said they would be.

The 1988 Caldecott winner, *Owl Moon* by Jane Yolen, illustrated by John Schoenherr, demonstrates a keen attention to detail. The owl seems to lift off the page and stand eye-to-eye with the reader. The illustrations in this book each provide a breathless moment and are unencumbered by text except for a few words on the following page. Good illustration such as this draws the reader into the page. It offers something to be discovered. As is the case with good paintings, more is found each time one looks at the pictures.

TIPS FOR TEACHERS

Encourage children to respond to stories through their artwork.
* *Tell children about a character or activity that you liked in the book while you draw it.*
* *Provide clay to make sculptures of storybook characters.*
* *Involve children in the creation of a mural or diorama of a book's setting using leaves, paper, crayons, glue, and other relevant materials.*

The exemplary photographer does not merely provide a picture of a boat. Rather, a moment or a time of day is captured so that the photograph of the boat is something special. The backdrop of the shot is carefully chosen. The type of film and the speed of the film are considered. Perhaps hundreds of shots are taken in order to achieve the one best photograph. These details show in the final outcome and account for the quality difference found in better pictures.

Texture. Distinctive illustration provides a sense of texture that is three-dimensional. Some artists use paint, some use collage, and some use woodcuts. In each case, the best work joins the picture, the text, and the reader. The skillful use of space and art should expand the text. An artist may outline figures in black to clarify shape, or use colors to define boundaries or special words. Whatever techniques are used, they should tie the art to the text and further the purpose of the story.

Author/illustrator Ezra Jack Keats. Courtesy Beverly Hall.

Eric Carle and Ezra Jack Keats are illustrators who work with collage. The appearance of textures in their work effectively invites children to touch the pages. Indeed, some of Carle's books have a three-dimensional component that provides an actual texture to the touch. The illustrations and text blend so well that they seem to be one.

Color. Color can lend a dramatic effect to good artwork and add beauty, but there are many books without color, or with limited use of color, that are truly memorable. Just as some movies are meant to be seen in black and white, some books are meant to use color sparingly.

Harold and the Purple Crayon by Crockett Johnson is illustrated entirely with a purple crayon line drawing. The book is a favorite of young children and inspires them to create their own purple drawings. They readily respond to the humor and novelty of the book. *Little Bear's Friend* by Else Holmelund Minarik, illustrated by Maurice Sendak, is another superb example. It is wistfully and delicately illustrated in black line sketching with a soft wash of browns and greens. The effect visually enhances the text narration and is appealing to children. Alvin Tresselt's book, *I Saw the Sea Come In,* is deftly illustrated by Roger Duvoisin. The pages of black ink sketches, washed with blues and touched with black shading, emphasize the lonely beach scenes. When he uses full color as a contrast, the effect is riveting. These illustrations are also visually dramatic in terms of the story narrative. The bold use of color makes *Around Town* by Chris Soentpiet come alive. Concepts, moods, and feelings are reinforced as a young girl and her mother go strolling on a warm, sunny Saturday, taking in the sights, sounds, smells, and tastes of the city.

Make Way for Ducklings by Robert McCloskey, on the other hand, is still one of the most popular books for youngsters, yet the entire book is etched in soft brown sepia. The realism in the details of the illustrations make the pages come alive without the use of color.

The illustrations and photographs used in children's literature should not only be integrated, but should possess a pleasing design, color usage, and, where appropriate, a suggestion of texture. The reader should find the illustrations interesting and involving. These criteria are demanding, which is one of the reasons one must search for quality works among the large number of books published each year.

There are many other talented artists who are worthy of being known as children's book artists. Young people everywhere, and adults as well, applaud their efforts. If the artist awakens in the developing child an awareness and love of art, this love will remain long after the child has become an adult. The artist will have opened a world of aesthetic joy forever. Children often attempt to re-create images from the story in a variety of ways. Figure 3–2 illustrates the range of possible images children may create after listening to a story about foxes.

⌾ Anti-bias Factors

Respectable companies publishing children's books today do not accept works with open bias toward race, sex, religion, age, or disability. However, there are still many books from years gone by in libraries and school collections that do contain

Illustration by John Schoenherr. Reprinted by permission of Philomel Books. From *Owl Moon* by Jane Yolen, illustrations © 1987 by John Schoenherr.

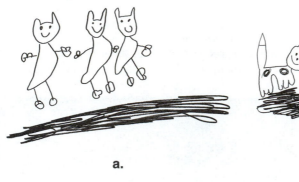

a.   **b.**

c.   **d.**

Figure 3–2. Young children used art to respond to the book Four Famished Foxes and Fosdyke *by Pamela Edwards, illustrated by Henry Cole. The illustrations depict the foxes on their way to raid a henhouse (3–2a); covered with eggs thrown at them by the chickens (3–2b); returning to their foxhole in failure (3–2c); and eating the meal prepared for them by Fosdyke (3–2d).* Courtesy Walter Sawyer.

The interests of children cross gender lines. Courtesy Diana Comer.

both subtle and overt negative bias. Anyone planning to use literature with children should preview the books for signs of bias.

Many young adults do not remember the Dick and Jane reading books. In these stories, Jane wore a dress and passively watched as Dick did all the exciting childhood activities. One might wish to share books of this type to appreciate the changes that have occurred in both our society and in children's literature. This activity can help to raise the consciousness of all against such bias.

Another less obvious prejudice is the lack of multi-cultural characters. This is bias by omission, and is still prevalent in some classroom collections.

Sensitivity to bias by those who care for children ensures that collections of books reflect a realistic picture of society. Multicultural books should be included whether or not the student group includes minority children.

Identifying Bias. It is not difficult to determine if a book collection is biased by omission. First, count the number of books in the collection. Next, determine how many of the books contain animal characters, white children as characters, Hispanic children as characters, black children as characters, and other minority children as characters. Finally, look at the numbers and make your own decision. There is no magic number or percentage, but if the size of the numbers and percentages surprises you, action probably needs to be taken.

A good collection need not have all minority-based or multicultural books, but it should have a representative number of such books. The stories should appeal to all children, and not just be there because they include characters of certain race, sex, or age or with a disability. Characters must fit into the story without artificial dynamics. The story should be the main element, and the inclusion of the minority group characters should mesh with the story. The fit should be so good that the children are left with the feeling that it is a great story, rather than the feeling that it is a great black story or great Hispanic story. *Abuela's Weave* by Omar Castaneda is a wonderful story from a Hispanic culture, but it is wonderful primarily because of its warm characters and important themes, not because it is about Hispanics. Many themes of tales from Africa or the inner city touch all children. Many ethnic fairy tales or farm stories make all children share a common response and feeling. These are the books to add to a collection, books that broaden the sensitivity and understanding of all children.

This same basic idea holds true for sexism in books. Characters such as Ramona Quimby in Beverly Cleary's books and Emily Arrow in Patricia Reilly Giff's stories are strong female models. They are not perfect children, but they share a common humanity that is appreciated by all children. Bring the subject of sexism out into the open and discuss it with children by using books such as *Old Turtle* by Douglas Wood. It is the story of a wise old female turtle who helps those around her understand that everything on earth needs to be in harmony. Cheng-Khee Chee's watercolor illustrations lend a majestic and finely detailed sense of authority to the story. The issue of boy-jobs and girl-jobs can be effectively dealt with through stories such as *Mama Is a Miner* by George Ella Lyon. The child in the story is both proud and fearful of her mother's hard and dangerous occupation. Peter Catalanotto's large luminous watercolors of mother and daughter shimmer with energy. Subtle sexism is prejudice that often dissipates when teachers and parents become aware of its existence.

Other biases exist against individuals with disabilities and those with religious or regional class differences. Inclusion of books such as Judith Caseley's *Harry and Willy and Carrothead* and Carol Carrick's *Stay Away from Simon* can

Little friends in jungle deep

Illustration by Gyo Fujikawa. Reprinted by permission of Grosset and Dunlap. From *Faraway Friends,* © 1981 by Gyo Fujikawa.

Mama Is a Miner *by George Ella Lyon.* Used by permission of Orchard Books, New York.

Author George Ella Lyon. Used by permission of Orchard Books, New York.

help teachers and students become sensitive to such realities of our world. If approached in the same manner as with the others, these biases by omission can also be remedied.

SUMMARY

Choosing the best books available for use with young children is critically important. Since children are forming their thoughts and opinions about almost everything, one must help and encourage them with useful, sensitive, and thought-provoking ideas. Exposure to the best possible stories and illustrations will help them in this area while giving them an appreciation for quality literature

Author Carol Carrick. Courtesy Carol Carrick.
Photo credit: Jules Worthington.

as well. The criteria for choosing literature may seem involved. However, once a teacher or parent gains these critical skills, it becomes second nature to apply them.

The criteria combine judging aspects of literature and assessing how stories are presented. Good literature will motivate children to want to hear stories and to learn to read. The illustrations will help children comprehend the story while encouraging them to develop an appreciation for line, shape, and color. Teacher sensitivity allows children to learn to be careful, thoughtful readers who have already started to develop critical thinking skills about facts and information.

QUESTIONS FOR THOUGHT AND DISCUSSION

1. How should a teacher approach the task of choosing good literature?
2. Why can an understanding of the aspects of literature and a knowledge of presentation be helpful in choosing quality literature?
3. How can a list of Caldecott Medal winners be helpful in selecting books?
4. What are the limitations of using only books that have won Caldecott Medals?
5. How can one determine if the illustrations in a book are appropriate?
6. What are some general goals for using literature with children?
7. Why is it important to consider plot, character, setting, and theme when selecting books?
8. Why is it important to look for bias in children's books?
9. What are some of the different media used in book illustration?

CHILDREN'S BOOKS CITED

Aardema, V. (1985). *Why mosquitoes buzz in people's ears.* New York: Scholastic.

Aliki (Brandenberg) (1982). *We are best friends.* New York: Greenwillow.

Allard, H. (1981). *The Stupids die.* Boston: Houghton Mifflin.

Allard, H. (1978). *The Stupids have a ball.* Boston: Houghton Mifflin.

Allard, H. (1974). *The Stupids step out.* Boston: Houghton Mifflin.

Anholt, C., & L. (1993). *Here come the babies.* Cambridge, MA: Candlewick.

Bemelmans, L. (1939). *Madeline.* New York: Viking.

Birdseye, T. (1991). *Waiting for baby.* New York: Holiday House.

Brown, M. (1939). *Cinderella.* New York: Scribner.

Brown, M. (1950). *Dick Whittington and his cat.* New York: Scribner.

Brown, M.W. (1947). *Goodnight moon.* New York: Harper & Row.

Bunting, E. (1992). *Our teacher is having a baby.* New York: Clarion.

Bunting, E. (1990). *The wall.* New York: Clarion.

Burton, V.L. (1937). *Choo Choo: The story of a little engine who ran away.* Boston: Houghton Mifflin.

Burton, V.L. (1937). *The little house.* Boston: Houghton Mifflin.

Carle, E. (1977). *The grouchy ladybug.* New York: Crowell.

Carrick, C. (1985). *Stay away from Simon.* New York: Clarion.

Caseley, J. (1991). *Harry and Willy and Carrothead.* New York: Greenwillow.

Castaneda, O. (1993). *Abuela's weave.* New York: Lee and Low.

Catalanotto, P. (1995). *The painter.* New York: Orchard.

Celsi, T. (1992). *The fourth little pig.* Austin, TX: Steck Vaughn.

Clements, A. (1993). *Billy and the bad teacher.* New York: Picture Book Studio.

Cohlene, T. (1990). *Quillworker.* Mahwah, NJ: Troll.

Cooke, T. (1994). *So much.* Cambridge, MA: Candlewick.

Cooney, B. (1982). *Miss Rumphius.* New York: Viking Penguin.

Cooney, N.E. (1981). *The blanket that had to go.* New York: Putnam.

Cooney, N.E. (1993). *Chatterbox Jamie.* New York: G.P. Putnam's Sons.

Corey, D. (1992). *Will there be a lap for me?* Morton Grove, IL: Albert Whitman.

Crebbin, J. (1993). *Fly by night.* Cambridge, MA: Candlewick.

Crews, D. (1978). *Freight train.* New York: Greenwillow.

De Brunhoff, J. (1963). *Babar and the king.* New York: Random House.

DePaola, T. (1989). *The art lesson.* New York: Putnam.

DePaola, T. (1973). *Nana upstairs and Nana downstairs.* New York: Putnam.

Duvoisin, R. (1969). *Veronica.* New York: Knopf.

Edwards, P.D. (1997). *Barefoot—Escape on the underground railroad.* New York: Harper Collins.

Edwards, P.D. (1997). *Four famished foxes and Fosdyke.* New York: Harper Collins.

Egan, T. (1995). *Chestnut Cove.* New York: Houghton Mifflin.

Gag, W. (1928). *Millions of cats.* New York: Coward McCann.

Giff, P.R. (1986). *Happy birthday, Ronald Morgan.* New York: Viking Kestral.

Giff, P.R. (1980). *Today was a terrible day.* New York: Viking Penguin.

Giff, P.R. (1985). *Watch out, Ronald Morgan.* New York: Viking Penguin.

Goble, P. (1978). *The girl who loved wild horses.* New York: Macmillan.

Gordon, L. (1997). *Lights out! The witch's revenge.* New York: Little Simon.

Hall, D. (1979). *Ox-cart man.* New York: Viking Penguin.

Harness, C. (1995). *The amazing impossible Erie Canal.* New York: Macmillan.

Hazen, B.S. (1979). *Tight times.* New York: Viking.

Henkes, K. (1996). *Chrysanthemum.* New York: Mulberry.

Henkes, K. (1995). *A weekend with Wendell.* New York: Mulberry.

Houston, G. (1992). *My Great Aunt Arizona.* New York: HarperCollins.

Johnson, C. (1955). *Harold and the purple crayon.* New York: Harper & Row.

Kasperson, J. (1995). *Little Brother Moose.* Nevada City, CA: Dawn.

Keller, H. (1987). *Goodbye, Max.* New York: Greenwillow.

Keller, H. (1987). *Lizzy's invitation.* New York: Greenwillow.

Kroninger, S. (1997). *If I crossed the road.* New York: Simon and Schuster.

Kunhardt, D. (1962). *Pat the bunny.* Racine, WI: Western.

Leaf, M. (1936). *The story of Ferdinand.* New York: Viking.

Lionni, L. (1963). *Swimmy.* New York: Pantheon.

Little, J. (1991). *Jess was the brave one.* New York: Viking.

Lyon, G.E. (1994). *Mama is a miner.* New York: Orchard.

Marshall, J. (1972). *George and Martha.* Boston: Houghton Mifflin.

McCloskey, R. (1941). *Make way for ducklings.* New York: Viking.

McPhail, D. (1992). *Farm boy's year.* New York: Atheneum.

Minarik, E.H. (1960). *Little Bear's friend.* New York: Harper & Row.

Moore, C. (1997). *The night before Christmas.* New York: Simon and Schuster.

Morris, J. (1995). *Bears, bears, and more bears.* Hauppague, NY: Barrows.

Munsch, R. (1987). *I have to go.* Toronto, Ontario, Canada: Annick.

Munsch, R. (1986). *Love you forever.* Scarborough, Ontario, Canada: Firefly.

Musgrove, M. (1977). *Ashanti to Zulu: African traditions.* New York: Dial.

Paulsen, G. (1993). *Dogteam.* New York: Dell.

Raschka, C. (1993). *Yo! Yes?* New York: Orchard.

Rey, H.A., & Rey, M. (1941). *Curious George.* New York: Houghton Mifflin.

Rosenberg, M. (1991). *Brothers and sisters.* New York: Clarion.

Sendak, M. (1963). *Where the wild things are.* New York: Harper & Row.

Seuss (pseud. for T. Geisel) (1963). *Hop on Pop.* New York: Random House.

Seuss (1940). *Horton hatches the egg.* New York: Random House.

Seuss (1971). *The lorax.* New York: Random House.

Seuss (1973). *The shape of me and other stuff.* New York: Random House.

Silverstein, S. (1964). *The giving tree.* New York: Harper & Row.

Soentpiet, C. (1994). *Around town.* New York: Lothrop, Lee and Shepard.

Steptoe, J. (1987). *Mufaro's beautiful daughters.* New York: Lothrop, Lee & Shepard.

Tresselt, A. (1965). *Hide and seek fog.* New York: Mulberry.

Tresselt, A. (1954). *I saw the sea come in.* New York: Lothrop, Lee & Shepard.

Turner, A. (1992). *Katie's trunk.* New York: Macmillan.

Van Allsburg, C. (1982). *Jumanji.* Boston: Houghton Mifflin.

Van Allsburg, C. (1985). *The Polar Express.* Boston: Houghton Mifflin.

Viorst, J. (1972). *Alexander and the terrible, horrible, no good, very bad day.* New York: Atheneum.

Waber, B. (1972). *Ira sleeps over.* Boston: Houghton Mifflin.

Walsh, J.P. (1992). *When Grandma came.* New York: Penguin.

Wells, R. (1975). *Morris's disappearing bag.* New York: Dutton.

Wood, D. (1992). *Old turtle.* Duluth, Minnesota: Pfeifer-Hamilton.

Yolen, J. (1987). *Owl Moon.* New York: Philomel.

Zolotow, C. (1982). *William's doll.* New York: Harper and Row.

SELECTED REFERENCES

Butler, D. (1997). *Babies need books.* Portsmouth, NH: Heinemann.

Cullinan, B. (1989). *Literature and the child.* San Diego, California: Harcourt Brace Jovanovich.

Cullinan, B. (1992). *Read to me: Raising kids who love to read.* New York: Scholastic.

Derman-Sparks, L. (1989). *Anti-biased curriculum.* Washington, DC: National Association for the Education of Young Children.

Lipson, G.B., & Romatowski, J.A. (1983). *Ethnic pride—Explorations into your ethnic heritage, cultural information—Activities and student research.* Chicago: Good Apple.

Stewig, J.W. (1988). *Children and literature.* Boston: Houghton Mifflin.

Traw, R. (1996). *"Beware! Here there be beasties: Responding to fundamentalist censors.* The New Advocate, 9, (1), 35–56.

Trelease, J. (1995). *The new read-aloud handbook.* New York: Viking Penguin.

I touch the future–I teach.

– Christa McAuliffe

4 Using Various Types of Literature

In addition to having books on the children's level, it is also important to surround children with books at several levels to motivate and inspire them to want to read "all by themselves." Books used in beginning reading programs are known as *basal readers*. These books are part of an integrated set of textbooks, workbooks, teacher's manuals, and related materials used to provide developmental reading instruction. Basal readers usually contain a selection of short pieces written for that particular text. The vocabulary of the selections is usually carefully controlled to use only certain words at different levels. Basals might be included in programs for young children, but they are not necessary. They tend to neither contain sufficient quality literature nor take advantage of a child's natural curiosity and language.

Because of all that must be considered, much time is needed to make the right choices. Since time is not what most early childhood educators possess in large quantities, it is imperative that the teacher use time effectively. If good matches are to be made between children and books, caregivers need a deep understanding of the children, a solid knowledge of how to select appropriate books, and a broad knowledge of the children's books available. The purpose of this chapter is to expand the reader's knowledge of traditional and current children's literature. Accordingly, summaries are offered of the wide range of literature available for young people.

The categories used to classify books may vary. The categories used here are broad ones and could be broken down into further subcategories. The depth of knowledge of each category can be increased by studying book reviews or, better yet, reading and discussing the actual books.

FINGERPLAYS/CHANTS/RHYMES

Young children benefit from the rhythm and sounds of language. Through adult modeling of fingerplays, chants, and rhymes, children can learn these rhythms and sounds. Perhaps this is why such literary forms are found in almost every culture, country, and language. The songlike quality of these language forms makes them easy to listen to, respond to, and learn. Since these forms are often short, they are easily remembered after being repeated several times. Repetition can help children learn to speak words as they are needed. Fingerplays allow children to coordinate hand motions with words in a manner that facilitates small muscle development and eye-hand coordination.

Adults should always support children's development of self-esteem. The fact that these literary forms enable children to experience success is an important reason to use them. The successful acquisition of fingerplays and rhymes makes children feel competent about their learning ability while providing a language skill achievement that will enhance their literacy development.

Fingerplays and Chants

A fingerplay is a short poem put to rhyme or beat. A fingerplay has hand motions; a chant does not. Any fingerplay can be chanted in a singsong fashion, and many chants can be made into fingerplays. A teacher can make up and sing a chant such as, "It's clean-up time, it's clean-up time. Let's all cooperate," to help children with the transition from free play to circle time. Chants and fingerplays are positive ways to help children learn about social expectations and concept development in an informal manner. An example of a rectangle concept fingerplay is, "Long–short, long–short. The rectangle is long–short, long–short." As the fingerplay is sung, children trace the rectangle shape in the air. As the word "rectangle" is reached, the children might be encouraged to shout it out. This fingerplay can be used when tracing the shape or drawing it and can be used to help differentiate between the square and the rectangle.

Fingerplays and chants can be invented by adapting favorite short poems and can include motion or action. The teacher can invent fingerplays or have children help to invent some. For example, after sighting a helicopter, this easy, concrete fingerplay was invented:

WORDS	ACTIONS
Up and down,	Children move up and down
Up and down.	with the words, arms out to the
Round and round,	sides, then spin
Round and round.	in a circle.
The helicopter . . .	Children run off
Goes off to town.	to a corner of the room.

Every caregiver of young children has a varied repertoire of fingerplays and chants. They may be recorded on file cards that are easy to use and store. Fingerplays for transitions, basic concepts, holidays, and even commonplace concepts such as naptime can simplify the daily routine and enhance a program. One source of fingerplays is the book *Finger Frolics 2* by Liz Cromwell[1]. It provides a wide range of easy-to-learn fingerplays.

[1] Cromwell, L. (1997). *Finger Frolics 2*. Kenmore, NY: Partners Press.

Rhymes

Rhymes can be simple poems and chants. They can be used as one would use the fingerplay or chant. Silly rhymes are particularly enjoyable even for young toddlers and are easily created. Children love rhymes that use their names or the names of friends and family members.

Rhymes have been passed down from generation to generation. There are rhymes for jumping rope, learning colors, and just about anything else children find important, frightening, or silly.

"One, two, buckle my shoe"; "Blue, blue, God loves you"; "One potato, two potato, three potato, four"; "Lizzy Borden took an axe . . . " are all rhymes that most remember from childhood. Horrendous rhymes were often created as a way of helping children express and cope with fear. "Ring around the Rosie" was originally an expression of children's fears about death and the terrible processing of bodies during the plague in England. "Ashes to ashes, we all fall down" was play-acting the deaths that the children feared. Ridicule is one way that children diminish and process fears. New rhymes are forever adding to the heritage that one group of children passes to the next as a ritual part of childhood.

MOTHER GOOSE TALES/NURSERY RHYMES

Who was Mother Goose? There are various versions of the origin of Mother Goose. Some credit the term to the French author Charles Perrault, who in 1697 referred to the rhymes as those told by an old woman tending geese. Others attribute Mother Goose to the English author, John Newbury, who first used the term in a book he published in 1765. Still others claim that Mother Goose was a Boston woman by the name of Elizabeth Goose. She was the mother-in-law of a publisher of a slim volume titled *Mother Goose Melodies for Children* published in Boston in 1719. Though the proof is lost in the archives of the Antiquarian Society Collection in Worcester, Massachusetts, it is unimportant who first used the term. Mother Goose is known by children all over the world as a symbol of rhymes and the enjoyment gained from their use.

Mother Goose Activities

Mother Goose stories are easily used to stimulate language acquisition and teach social behavior rules. They can be used for their humor as simple flannelboard stories or as dramatic productions with props and costumes. They can be adapted for art activities as well.

Many of the Mother Goose tales are found in collections. A large collection will offer many rhymes that the teacher may never have seen or heard. They can be used at storytime, circle time, or even for transitions. "Jack be nimble, Jack be quick . . ." can be a transition rhyme for leaving the room. Children can say the rhyme as they jump over a paper candlestick while leaving the room one by one.

Several Mother Goose tales have been made into picture books with beautiful illustrations. Two good choices of Mother Goose stories are *Sing a Song of Mother Goose* by Barbara Reid and *The Orchard Book of Nursery Rhymes* by Zena Sutherland. Stories such as Jim Aylesworth's *The Completed Hickory Dickory Dock* pick up where the original tales leave off.

In addition to Mother Goose, rhymes from other countries or collections such as *Gregory Griggs and Other Nursery Rhyme People* by Arnold Lobel are also useful. For example, "The Farmer of Leeds" is a wonderful spring rhyme about the grass growing. It can lead into a grass-growing activity using sponges. The sponges can be cut into the shape of a person, then grass seeds added where a person's hair would grow. When they are placed upright in a dish of water, grass hair will sprout. Such an activity adds much to the enjoyment of the rhymes.

Nursery Rhymes

Collections of Mother Goose and other nursery rhymes have always been passed around, added to, changed, and revised. Some were originally written as political satires poking fun at the king or government from the safety of street songs and children's rhymes. These changes explain why rhymes vary from country to country and from region to region within a country.

"Mary Had a Little Lamb" is an example of a Mother Goose rhyme that was added to the collection well after many of the original rhymes were written. The tale was originally written by Sarah Josepha Hale and was first published in 1830. Contemporary writers such as Ruth I. Dowell are continuing to add to the Mother Goose collection with such tantalizing titles as "I'm Rather Short, Larry Bird," "Pennsylvania Pete," "Mama's Poppin' Popcorn," and "Myrtle Was a Turtle."

The traditions and wording of rhymes are important to children. The tongue twisters and secret words found in so many rhymes are like echoes of ancient fireside rituals. They provide children with reassurance and control over the mysteries of the adult world. Such carefully followed advice as "Step on a crack, break your mother's back" or "See a pin and pick it up, all the day you'll have good luck" are part of our treasured childhood memories.

FABLES/FOLK TALES/FAIRY TALES

For young children, fables, folk tales, and fairy tales constitute a treat that teaches and inspires. Many convey a society's value system; others are simply entertainment. Handed down through oral tradition, they were told to each new generation by storytellers, people revered by earlier cultures, until they were eventually preserved in written form.

Fables

A fable is a story used to teach a moral to people. Most use animals as the characters, but this is not always the case. Other fables may use people or inanimate objects as characters. Fables with animal characters are called *beast fables.* Fables are found in every culture throughout the world. In the West, people are most familiar with the fables credited to Aesop. Many other fables have also become part of the English speaking tradition. These include Uncle Remus stories by Joel Chandler Harris, as well as Rudyard Kipling's *Jungle Book.* Phrases from the fables often find their way into common language: "That's just sour grapes," and "No use crying over spilt milk."

Fables can be used for both enjoyment and discussion of the morals they contain. An attractive source of fables is *Anno's Aesop* by Mitsumasa Anno. Classroom activities related to fables include creating fables about school rules or table manners, illustrating the fables, and acting out the fables.

Folk Tales

Folk tales are the common man's fairy tale. They are unadorned stories. As with fairy tales and legends, folk tales share common plots in which good overcomes evil and justice is served. Every culture possesses these tales. They serve to explain society, history, and natural phenomena and offer a sense of security while sometimes poking fun at things people wish to change.

Folk tales have existed since well before recorded history. They developed through an oral tradition, because few people could read at the time most folk tales were authored. Folk tales have served to teach, to entertain, and to explain the world to each new generation of listeners. Children's literature today encompasses a marvelous variety of such tales from throughout the world. Rosemary Wells presents children with a classical tale in *Max and Ruby's First Greek Myth: Pandora's Box*, using a story-within-a-story device to introduce young children to the genre of myth. The quickly paced text is combined with humorous illustrations that gives the tale a clever twist. In contrast, Joanne Compton presents a more modern version of "Cinderella" to create a distinctly American story in *Ashpet: An Appalachian Tale*.

Author Joanne Compton. Used by permission of Holiday House, New York.

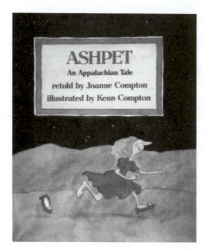

Ashpet: An Appalachian Tale *retold by Joanne Compton.* Reprinted by permission of Holiday House, New York.

Recently published versions of traditional folk tales keep the genre very much alive with contemporary language and appealing illustrations. Michael Emberly, in his book *Ruby*, recounts a variation of "Little Red Riding Hood." Using a contemporary city as the setting, a clever mouse named Ruby attempts to bring goodies to her grandma on the other side of town. A conniving cat plays the part of the wolf, but Ruby proves much too clever for the cat. Jon Scieska presents a folk tale from a different perspective in *The True Story of the Three Little Pigs*. This version, told from the wolf's point of view, has the beast pleading that he was framed. The tale would be a great accompaniment to a telling of the traditional story.

Most cultures cherish their folk tales. Such stories make for good reading while helping children to broaden their understanding of the cultures of the world. Many of the tales use animal characters, a familiar device to most young readers. Native American cultures have plenty of tales to share. Janet Stevens retells a Ute tale in *Coyote Steals the Blanket: A Ute Tale*. In this story, Coyote ignores Hummingbird's warning and steals a beautiful blanket. The miscreant finds himself pursued by a magic boulder from which only Hummingbird can save him.

TIPS FOR TEACHERS

Commit some folk tales to memory and share them through oral storytelling around a flashlight-powered campfire.
- *"The Three Little Pigs."*
- *"The Hare and the Tortoise."*
- *African "pourqoui" tales.*
- *Caribbean trickster stories.*

Coyote appears as a rascally character in many American cultures. In *The Tale of Rabbit and Coyote*, Tony Johnston draws a story from the culture of Oaxaca, Mexico, where the two antagonists crash from adventure to adventure in an extended saga. In a surprising but pleasant departure from his typical style, Tomie dePaola's illustrations of the blue coyote and purple rabbit will evoke howls of laughter from young listeners. Tales from a number of native American cultures are included in *Thirteen Moons on Turtle's Back* by Joseph Bruchac and Jonathan London. The collection is symbolic of the thirteen cycles of the moon during the calendar year and the thirteen scales on the back of a turtle. The stories reflect a culture that is close to the rhythms of nature. Rich illustrations by Thomas Locker set wonderful moods for the tales.

The continent of Africa is another rich source of folk tales at their best. Ashley Bryan uses playful rhythmic prose to share *The Story of Thunder and Lightning*, based on a Nigerian tale. Mother Thunder and active son Lightning are banished to the sky after the latter character has caused one too many problems for the villagers. The author's vibrant watercolor illustrations create a genuine African feel to the story. In another Nigerian tale explaining why things are as they are, Mary-Joan Gerson presents the story *Why the Sky Is Far Away*. This tale includes important global themes such as wastefulness, greed, garbage, and the problems of feeding the world's people. Tololwa Mollel continues the use of the African "pourquoi" tale in *A Promise to the Sun*. This tale tells why bats live in caves and why the sun pauses on the horizon before setting. The narrative includes the themes of loyalty, trust, and the importance of keeping promises. Using a trickster tale format, Gerald McDermott tells the story of *Zomo the Rabbit*. This tale is a forerunner of rabbit trickster tales from the Caribbean and the American South, where the main character becomes Br'er Rabbit.

Fairy Tales

Fairy tales are folk stories or legends in which an author incorporates additional aspects of literature. They tend to be more involved and more polished than folk tales and legends.

Concern has been expressed by some about the impact of these tales on young children. They can be frightening and sometimes include violence. The justice served in the tales can be swift and bloody, and some of the tales are grim and graphic. The best judge of whether these stories should be used is someone who knows the children. However, one should consider the fact that childhood is full of frightening monsters and unknown fears. Adults sometimes fail to realize that children will invent these fearsome characters as part of their way of developing coping skills. Using the tales may help children by providing positive role models. Listening to stories about the devotion of the good characters and the destruction of evil forces can reassure children that their own inner conflicts and fears will likewise be settled and resolved positively.

Varying types of fairy tales are found in literature. Some are humorous, while some use beasts to represent ideas or traits. Some answer "why" questions, while others are filled with magic and wonder. Frequently recurring themes and ideas in fairy tales include the number 3, characters who are all good or all bad, long journeys, and distant times and places. Fairy tales provide heroes who at times use their might. Unlike television characters, however, the hero of a fairy tale will more often use wit, cleverness, and intelligence to defeat a foe. These are admirable traits for a child to aspire to.

There are some tales that contain excessive violence. Look for versions that include less violence and might be more suitable for young listeners. Children do find the tales both enjoyable and reassuring. The endings always seem to reaffirm that the world is right again and that order has been restored.

The traditional fairy tale continues to be published in new versions. Eric Kimmel presents a fitting example in *The Three Princes*, a story in which a princess determines which of her suitors she will marry. Sending the three princes out in search of the greatest wonder they can find, she proves herself wise indeed

Author Eric Kimmel. Courtesy/photo credit: Doris A. Kimmel.

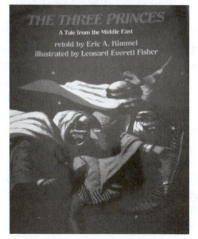

The Three Princes retold by Eric Kimmel. Reprinted by permission of Holiday House, New York.

Fairy Tales are a traditional part of childhood. Illustrations by Karen Milone, reprinted by permission of Troll Associates, from *The Wild Swans* by Hans Christian Anderson, © 1981 by Troll Associates.

in selecting her husband. A hilarious variation on a traditional fairy tale is Jon Scieska's *The Frog Prince Continued*. The story picks up just after the happily-ever-after ending of the original tale. Unhappy with his new life, the frog seeks a witch who will turn him back into a frog. To his dismay and to the delight of the reader, the frog prince keeps running into witches from other fairy tales. A new fairy tale can be created, as has been done by William Stieg in *Shrek*. The story is given a unique twist by turning the traditional elements upside down. Everything turns out fine in the end, though, because Shrek and his princess are pleased to live horribly ever after. A variation of the Cinderella story is found in the Algonquin tale, *The Rough-Face Girl*, retold by Rafe Martin. The tale deals with the theme of what is real beauty.

Different Versions

Contrasting versions of the same story is a way to explore the content and to help children respond to the stories. Children can be encouraged to discuss how they feel about the stories and the varied resolutions of the plot. Take, for example, the story of Hansel and Gretel. It is a scary story that can reaffirm the importance of parental care, the danger of going off alone, and the resolution of a child's fear of being alone. The story addresses the themes of stepmother and stranger. In one version, retold by Linda Hayward, the wicked stepmother leaves, and the children find their way home by their own devices. In another version, retold by Barbara Shook Hazen, the children cleverly escape from the witch, leave with a bag of jewels, and return home to find a reformed and repentant step-mother with whom they live happily ever after. After reading the two versions, one might discuss with the children which version they liked best and their reasons for choosing that version.

Encouraging responses to the literature allows children to bring up hidden fears and issues. Verbalizing can help children understand that others share and understand their feelings. It is important to validate children's rights to their feelings. One should not allow ridicule or negative attitudes to impede these discussions.

Legends

Ethnic tales, myths, and legends lend themselves to the preschool program. For example, when teaching about the earth traveling around the sun, the Greek myth about Apollo and his chariot can be included. When teaching about safety and the need to avoid yelling in the pool or yard, the story of "The Boy Who Cried Wolf" can be used to illustrate the dangers in pretending to need help. When teaching about sharing, "The Fisherman and His Wife" can be used to illustrate what happens when greed gets out of control.

Folk tales and legends can encourage language acquisition with their effective use of repetition of words and word sounds such as "Fee, fie, foe, fum"; "All the better to see you with my dear"; and "Who is the fairest of them all?" Children naturally join in with the words of the story. Local tales, ethnic legends, and ethnic tales can also be helpful in integrating minority children into the mainstream within the classroom. Sharing one's cultural heritage is a strengthening and unifying way to build understanding among children while helping each child's ego development. Parents, churches, and libraries can often supply tapes or stories that would meet the needs of the class. Cultural storytellers can also be invited to come to tell tales to the children.

PICTURE BOOKS/WORDLESS PICTURE BOOKS

A picture book is a special kind of book for a special audience. Unlike the child who can read many words, younger children gain much of their understanding of a story from the illustrations and through listening to the story. A picture book must possess a well-developed plot, theme, setting, and characterization. It should also use an appropriate style, print dimension, and page size. In addition, a picture book must have a special unity between text and illustration. The two must provide an understandable telling of the story for those who are not yet fluent readers. In most picture books the words printed on the page are not always necessary to comprehend the action, flow, and intent of the story. The author, illustrator, and reader of a good picture book enjoy a communal experience that transcends the written language.

In some picture books, words have been completely eliminated. *Window* by Jeannie Baker is an illustrated wordless picture book with an environmental message. The story begins with a mother and baby boy looking out their window at the wilderness. As the boy grows older, the signs of civilization creep in. By the time the boy grows to adulthood, the wilderness has disappeared and a city has taken shape.

CONCEPT BOOKS

Concept books, which include counting and ABC books, are an area of children's literature that has seen tremendous growth and some interesting developments over the past few years. They may be pop-up books, pop-out books, poke-through-the-hole books, puppet books, books cut into shapes, books cut into puzzles, big books, mini books, and textured books. With such talented artists as Peter Seymour, Bruce McMillan, Tana Hoban, Eric Carle, Richard Scarry, and Dr. Seuss involved, it is not a problem finding a good concept book. Rather, the problem is making a decision as to which is most appropriate for a particular purpose. Concept books are fun to use, and they help motivate children to learn about spatial concepts, numbers, and colors.

In selecting concept books, some general guidelines might be kept in mind. First, the concept should be clearly described and illustrated in the book. The facts included should have validity. If the book is about magnetism, the illustrations shouldn't show a magnet picking up pennies because magnets are not attracted to copper. The illustrations should possess numerical accuracy as well. If a counting book indicates that there are five objects on a page, there should be five objects on the page. The presentation of the concept should be interesting. If the teacher has to struggle to keep the children focused on the book, the book is probably boring. A good concept book motivates children to use it. They will want to listen to the story and look at the pictures. All these books should be constructed sturdily so that children can use them after the teacher has presented them. Finally, the book should have a sustaining factor. The children should be drawn back to the book after the initial reading by an adult. If this does not occur, perhaps the book wasn't an appropriate choice in the first place. These guidelines, of course, assume that other criteria, including age-appropriateness were followed as well.

Counting Books

Many teachers will use several different books for each concept they teach. If the concept is counting, for example, it could be introduced with Eric Carle's *1, 2, 3 to the Zoo*. At storytime, the teacher could share Michael Bond's *Paddington's 123*. John Lobban's endearing illustrations are always welcome. The day could end with a reading of Ezra Jack Keats's *Over in the Meadow* and a homework mission for children to check their own yards for things read about in the story.

Several additional books might be useful to enrich and expand the concept of counting and numbers. *One, Two, Three, Count With Me* by Catherine and Laurence Anholt invites children to count groups of objects by color, size, letters, and days of the week as they visit areas such as a playground, farm, and backyard. A similar book, featuring many multiethnic characters, is *One, Two, Three, Play With Me* by Laura Kvanosky. *Willy Can Count* by Anne Rockwell is based on a little boy's walk down a country lane accompanied by his mother. It is sure to be read over and over. Charles Sullivan uses humorous poetry and a wide range of art in his counting book, *Numbers at Play*. Counting books featuring farm animals include *Ten Pink Piglets: Garth Pig's Wall Song* by Mary Rayner and *Over on the Farm* by Gwenda Turner. *Counting Cranes* by Mary Beth Owens is an environmentally conscious counting book that presents the life cycle and migration patterns of whooping cranes.

The books can always be left out for the children to use independently in the classroom. They will often discover that it is more fun to share counting with a friend using books and blocks than to use a workbook page or a ditto to learn the same concept. The social skills used are also developmentally beneficial for children. Additional activities that can be coordinated with concept books include creating concept books with real objects and magazine pictures, creating concept posters centered around a book, and acting out a concept with blocks, pillows, or other props.

Alphabet (ABC) Books

The alphabet comprises most of the symbols used in our written language. The more comfortable children become with the letters and their sounds, the less confusing written language will be for them. Since it should not be expected that children will learn the letters and sounds until the elementary school grades, there should be no pressure on them to repeat, write, or memorize the letters. If children learn the letters on their own, that is fine, but it should not be an expectation. The goal is familiarity and confidence with language and meaning.

Alphabet books have a long history. Many illustrators of both children's and
adult books have designed ABC books in their careers. In fact, there are literally
hundreds of alphabet books from which to choose. They are found in every imag-
inable illustration technique from wood carving to etching to photography.

Selecting Alphabet Books

In selecting ABC books, certain general criteria may be helpful. The objects
depicting the letters should be an appropriate size and readily identifiable. A limited number of objects should be used, perhaps one or two per letter. The lettering
choice should be particularly legible. Ordinarily, the letter is best placed on the
page with the illustrations. The objects should be clearly representative of the
sound of the letter. The design of the book should be colorful and attractive.

It is important that these criteria be considered. It is especially important that
the page be designed so that most children will be able to successfully find the letter and objects. The letter sounds should be heard clearly in the name of the

Willy Can Count *by Anne Rockwell.*
Reprinted by permission of Little,
Brown Publishers, Boston.

objects used. For example, the letter "T" should use objects such as a tiger, top, or teacup for its illustration, rather than objects in which the "T" sound is blended, such as three, tree, or throat. Other letters to examine in ABC books include "S," "W," and "D." The letters "C" and "G" should be illustrated with objects representing the hard sound of the letter (e.g., cat for "C"; girl for "G"). The concept of hard and soft sounds for the same letter is often confusing to young children.

Humor is often found in many successful ABC books. *Alphabet Animals* by Charles Sullivan combines light humorous poetry with folk art, sculpture, line art, painting, and photographs.

A creative approach to the alphabet book is found in Steven Schnur's *Autumn, An Alphabetic Acrostic*, illustrated in radiant linoleum cuts by Leslie Evans. When the lines are read vertically, a message is discovered. This book is a treat for the eyes and the ears.

A striking alphabet book with a twist is *Aardvarks Disembark!* by Ann Jonas. After the flood, Noah calls roll, and the animals leave the art. After the letter "Z," however, many more animals get off, including some extinct and endangered species, rarely seen in picture books. A somewhat related title is *Aster Aardvark's Alphabet Adventures* by author/illustrator Steven Kellogg. His zany illustrations and witty language will delight readers of all ages.

A game motif is combined with paintings by Picasso, Botticelli, and others to locate objects from A to Z in Lucy Micklethwait's *I Spy: An Alphabet in Art*. Jenny Williams uses objects from daily routines to introduce very young children to the alphabet in her book, *Everyday ABC.* Finally, author/photographer Tana Hoban's book, *26 Letters and 99 Cents*, invites children to participate by matching objects with initial letters in a combination alphabet-and-counting book.

Alphabet Activities

As with numbers, a set of coordinated activities to go along with alphabet books may be developed. After reading an animal alphabet book, children can draw or paint an animal for a particular letter. After reading an object ABC book, a letter hunt can be organized to search the room for objects beginning with the same letter. Cooking something beginning with a certain letter can be combined with other concepts. If the letter is "S," one could make strawberry sundaes. The letter "N" could be reinforced by having each child draw nine objects of their choice. The group could construct its own tactile alphabet book, alphabet sock puppets, or language-experience story. A *language-experience story* is a story dictated by the children and recorded by the teacher on the chalkboard or a poster book. The story is ordinarily about an experience all the children understand or have shared. If a language-experience story is used, perhaps based on words beginning with a particular letter, the focus should be on meaning rather than on recognizing a letter. The main function of learning about letters is to arrive at the meaning of the printed words.

Many activities can spring from ABC books. Courtesy Diana Comer.

FICTION: REALISTIC FICTION/FANTASY FICTION

The main purpose of fiction is to entertain the reader. However, its purpose is often to inform and persuade as well. Fiction is a narrative that comes from the imagination of the author rather than from history or factual information. Fiction gives the reader the author's vision of reality in concrete terms.

Realistic Fiction

Realistic fiction is a story that could have happened, and some parts of it may be from the author's own experiences. The author of realistic fiction is often trying to help children deal with a situation or problem. The world is presented as the author perceives it. The reader is not asked to believe in purple cows or singing dogs. Yet this is fiction, because the scenes, characters, and dialogues spring from the author's imagination. Nevertheless, the imaginary content is based on truth as the author sees it. Robert Cormier, in explaining his purpose in writing realistic fiction, stated, "I was trying to write realistically even though I knew it would upset some people. The fact is the good guys don't always win in real life. . . I also wanted to indict those who don't try to help, who remain indifferent in the face of evil or wrongdoing. They are as bad or probably worse than the villains themselves."[2]

Realistic fiction helps children confront the good and bad human feelings within all of us. It allows readers to recognize that all people share these same human emotions and thoughts. Readers are able to explore their own feelings

[2] Hearne, B, & Kaye, M. (Eds.). (1987). *Celebrating children's books.* (p. 48). New York: Lothrop, Lee & Shepard.

Author Angela Johnson. Used by permission or Orchard Books, New York.

Author Eve Bunting. Courtesy Eve Bunting.

from a safe distance through the characters. Jane Yolen tells a tale of birth, growth, love, loss, and intergenerational kinship in *Honkers*. Leslie Baker's realistic watercolors have a hazy, comfortable feeling. The reality of separation and divorce is presented in *Friday's Journey* by Ken Rush. *What about My Goldfish?* by Pamela Greenwood focuses on moving. A similar book featuring an African-American family is *The Leaving Morning* by Angela Johnson. Eve Bunting explores the concepts of law, human dignity, and the ability to get along with others in *Smoky Night. The Tenth Good Thing about Barney* by Judith Viorst helps children learn to cope with death, in this case the death of a pet cat. Other topics that realistic fiction may help young children understand include school social situation, old age, illness, and sibling rivalry.

Historical Fiction

Realistic fiction also includes historical fiction, which provides an imaginary story based on a historical event or person. The author goes beyond the facts to create a fictional piece. An increasing number of books are becoming available in this area. Brinton Turkle's books about Obadiah are a series of historical but fictional accounts of Nantucket Island in colonial times. *A Picture Book of Harriet Tubman* by David Adler chronicles the life and accomplishments of the woman who led slaves to freedom on the underground railroad. It is a very readable book that conveys the quiet dignity of an extraordinary woman. *Klara's New World* by Jeanette Winter introduces children to the fact that immigration has been a major factor throughout history. Westward expansion is the topic of *Going West* by Jean Van Leeuwen, *Snowed In* by Barbara Lucas, and *Across the Blue Mountains* by Emma Clark. Using settings in the early twentieth century, *Harvest Song* by Ron Hirschi points to the agricultural background of the United States, while *Moving to Town* by Mattie Lou O'Kelley presents the theme of industrialization. Eleanor Coerr details the life of Carlotta Myers, the nineteenth-century balloonist, in *The Big Balloon Race*. Many of these books provide an added bonus of including women and minorities in nontraditional roles. Historical fiction written at a higher reading level can also be read aloud.

Fantasy Fiction

Many of the stories written for children are fantasy stories. An author of a fantasy asks the reader to suspend the rules of reality. A fantasy takes place in a nonexistent world and may include unreal characters. The use of physical or scientific principles unknown to the reader's experience is also found in fantasies. David Wiesner presents a "what if" concept in his Caldecott Medal book *Tuesday*. What if pigs could fly is answered in this light-hearted flight of fantasy.

TIPS FOR TEACHERS

Have children respond to fantasy by creating a picture related to the tale.
- *Provide children with a variety of materials (e.g. buttons, wallpaper samples, paint, glue, fun fur, feathers, fabric) to create a scene from the fantasy world.*
- *Read a folk tale from another country, and ask children to draw a scene showing what they think the foreign scene might look like.*
- *Give children clay and pipe cleaners to create sculptures of a fantasy character from a tale.*

In fantasy, imagination is stretched and brought into an art form. The author, illustrator, and reader all share the new experience. Fantasy is accepted readily by children because their imaginations allow the belief that anything is possible.

Magic, imaginary worlds, and marvelous creatures are all real to children. What they can imagine, can exist. Paula Fox explains, "Imagination is random and elusive. We deduce its presence by its effects, just as we deduce that a breeze has sprung up, a breeze we can't see, because we hear and see the rustling of the leaves in a tree. It is the guardian spirit that we sense in all great stories; we feel its rustling."[3]

A sense of humor is a powerful and positive coping mechanism not only for children, but for adults as well. It helps one to deal with the stress of modern life. The humor often found in fantasy fiction is contagious and healing. Few children can resist the silliness in Judith Barrett's *Animals Should Definitely Wear Clothes*. It hits preschoolers right in the funnybone. *Cloudy with a Chance of Meatballs*, also by Judith Barrett, creates a crazy world with pancakes and maple syrup covering the streets. A world is constructed that is quite different from the child's reality. The antics of the city-dwelling Lyle the crocodile, a character in several of Bernard Waber's books, amuse and delight young readers. Much loved author/illustrator Dav Pilkey shares a humorous fantasy journey in *When Cats Dream*. Surreal images of the dreams echo the world of modern art.

Fantasy fiction may have absurd characters, imaginary characters, or animals who behave as people. Fantasy fiction can be based on real world settings, or call for reality to be totally suspended and substitute almost anything in its place. Yet all fiction must still provide the basic components of a clearly defined plot, believable characters, an appropriate setting, and relevant themes. Without these skillfully woven into the story, the book fails to move the reader. *Sarah's Unicorn* by Bruce Coville is a superb example of fantasy fiction with each of these elements combined in a way that makes the reader truly care about the outcome.

NONFICTION/INFORMATIONAL BOOKS

Nonfiction books are written for the purpose of providing factual information. Such books for young readers use either a text or a narrative format. The latter is often used because of its familiarity to children. The author of such books has an obligation to impart only accurate information to children. Misinformation, misleading information, and outdated information may occur because a book is old or because new information has been discovered, in which case the reason for the inaccuracies should be explained to the children if the book is used, and, of course, accurate information should be supplied.

Presenting Information

Antiquated books can be useful for showing children how people used to think about a topic, but the teacher should ensure that children understand the correct information. It is good for children to become aware of the fact that information is not absolute, especially in the area of science. The teacher should always pref-

---

[3] Hearne, B, & Kaye, M. (1987). *Celebrating children's books*. (p. 24). New York: Harper & Row.

ace science information presentations with such phrases as, "At this time, this is the information that we believe to be true about . . . ." Children will gain from the understanding that information changes with more research. For example, a book about animals that states that giraffes make no sound need not be discarded. The photographs of the giraffe and perhaps much of the text can still be used. The teacher can simply add the correct information. Although it was once thought that giraffes made no sound, it is now known that they do make throaty sounds of communication.

Learning that information changes fosters the beginnings of critical thinking. A child with a specific interest may even have more current information than either the book or the teacher. Children should be encouraged to question information they feel is wrong. Also, resource books and telephone calls to verify information teach children, through example, an important lesson: a primary reason for learning to read is to find answers to questions.

Subtle misconceptions can trickle into a curriculum through a lack of knowledge. The same teacher who would never knowingly bring prejudice into the classroom by reading offensive material might perpetuate misconceptions about native Americans and pilgrims at Thanksgiving. Will the children learn that native Americans no longer live the way they did during colonial times? Will the teacher update the class on current native American lifestyles? If not, then an inaccurate portrayal of an entire cultural group is being given to every child in the class. The sensitive teacher will provide the whole truth.

In choosing factual books, certain guidelines may be helpful to consider:
1. The book should be checked for accuracy or information;
2. Note the copyright date to ensure that the material is as up-to-date as possible;
3. When charts or pictures are used, they should be simple, clear, and easy to read;
4. The readability of the material should be appropriate for the children's age group.

Selecting Books

When selecting informational books for young children, it is important to realize that many fiction titles should be included along with nonfiction ones, because a great amount of carefully researched and accurate information is provided by some fiction authors. Young children are particularly open to learning things through narrative stories. A good example of an informative narrative story is Karla Kuskin's *The Philharmonic Gets Dressed*. Through the story, children learn about the different sections of an orchestra. Songs are used to teach about the characteristics of insects in *A Creepy Crawly Song Book* by Hiawyn Oram. Songs such as "The March of the Worker Ants," "The Ladybug's Lullaby," and "Slow, Slow Snail" present information with humor and style.

Opportunities exist for correlating different content areas. The ladybug lullaby can be used to introduce the familiar line "Ladybug, ladybug, where are you going?" that is used in Julia Finzel's math-concepts book, *Large as Life*. Additional math concepts such as looking, thinking, and counting can then be introduced through Paul Giganti's *Each Orange Had Eight Slices*, which can lead into discussions of fruit, color, or nutrition. Over the past decade, a rapidly growing number of books has been published dealing with social studies and science for young children. In each of these areas, nonfiction books can be combined with fiction books to present an abundance of factual information.

Social Studies

The study of community and the development of one's place in the world is addressed in most early childhood programs. A good beginning place is Cynthia Rylant's *Everyday Town*, a board book that identifies the vehicles, parades, lights, pigeons, and buildings that comprise a town. Turn-of-the-century town life in rural Maine is depicted in Jacqueline Briggs Martin's *The Finest Horse in Town*. A sense of the westward movement is conjured up in *Train Song* by Diane Siebert. Young children will enjoy rolling place names like Abilene and North Platte off their tongues. Contemporary midwestern small-town life is lovingly portrayed in *Climbing Kansas Mountains* by George Shannon. A multicultural intergenerational look at life in a big city from a Hispanic viewpoint is presented in *Abuela* by Arthur Dorros. An African-American family is featured in another book on city life, *Morning Sounds, Evening Sounds* by Cecile Schoberle. A book featuring city life comprising many cultures is Eileen Spinelli's *If You Want to Find Golden*.

Books abound that present the multiculturalism found in society. Many are wonderful stories that happen to provide accurate information on the cultures that make up our international society. Native American culture is depicted in *The Shepherd Boy* by Kristine Franklin, the story of a boy who has an important role to play in his family's livelihood. The concept of passing cultural values to the next generation is presented in *Pueblo Storyteller* by Diane Hoyt-Goldsmith. April, a ten-year-old living in the Cochiti Pueblo near Santa Fe, learns about the bread, pottery, drums, storytelling, and ceremonies of her people.

Hispanic and Asian cultures are increasingly featured in books for young people. In *Treasure Nap* by Juanita Havil, Alicia learns of her great-grandmother's emigration from Mexico to America. The treasures that her great-grandmother brought with her were not valuable in themselves; the serape, the wooden birdcage, and the musical pipe called a *pito* gathered their value from the fact that they represented cherished aspects of her native culture. In *Amelia's Road* by Linda Jacobs-Altman, the life of the migrant farm worker is given dignity and realism. Amelia hates roads because they always symbolize the travel that deprives her of the permanence she longs for. Illustrator Enrique Sanchez's lush greens and browns provide a moving contrast between the bountiful land and the austerity of Amelia's life. In *Who Belongs Here? An American Story* by Margy Burns Knight, readers are confronted with the contradictions of America. Nary, a young Cambodian, escapes a bloody civil war in his homeland by emigrating to America, only to encounter prejudice. The book calls out for discussion about tolerance, stereotyping, social change, and cultural heritage. Finally, Minho and his mother provide a universal look at the obvious similarities of all people as they experience the sights and sounds of the city during an afternoon of errands in *One Afternoon* by Yumi Heo.

Two beautiful books by Angela Johnson, one of a number of fine African-American writers of children's books, are a good place to begin exploring African-American culture. Like others mentioned here, they present genuine pictures of a culture rather than a stereotyped view of a people. In *One of Three*, the young narrator tells a story that presents a vivid picture of African-American life. *Joshua by the Sea* is a poetic story of a family's love that all children will easily respond to. Rhonda Mitchell's glowing watercolor illustrations are an added bonus. In *A Million Fish . . . More or Less* by Patricia McKissack, the reader is transported to the African-American culture of the Bayou Clapateaux in Louisiana. While fishing one day, Hugh Thomas catches both fish and a penchant for creating and sharing hilarious tall tales. This story really answers the question of why the oral tradition is so important.

The family is a long-cherished facet of African-American culture. Elizabeth Fitzgerald Howard creates a story of generations in *Aunt Flossie's Hats (and Crab Cakes Later)*. It is a warm story of two girls who visit their aunt for stories, an opportunity to play with a hat collection, and an outing for crab cakes. Another story by Angela Johnson is *When I Am Old With You*, in which readers share the warm bond between a child and grandfather. The two are both individuals and universal characters. The universality of all people is brought out in *Brothers and Sisters* by Maxine Rosenberg. In this story three sets of siblings, depicting different ethnic backgrounds, share stories about their lives that show the common bonds among all.

World cultures are represented in many books for young readers. A good first choice is *Houses and Homes* by Ann Morris. Using photographs by Ken Heyman, the book presents the similarities and differences of a wide variety of

One Afternoon *by Yumi Heo.* Used by permission of Orchard Books, New York.

Author/illustrator Yumi Heo. Used by permission of Orchard Books, New York.

houses and cultures from around the world. In *Little Elephant's Walk* by Adrienne Kennaway, Little Elephant and his mother roam the African plains and rain forest. It is a good book to begin discussions about natural harmony, food chains, and ecosystems. Another excellent choice for learning about Africa is Catherine Stock's *Where Are You Going, Manyoni?*, which follows a young African girl as she makes the long trek from her home to school near the Limpopo River in Zimbabwe. Using spectacular watercolor illustrations and rich language, Stock depicts the East African vegetation, wildlife, and culture. Moving to another culture, one might select Ryerson Johnson's *Kenji and the Magic Geese*. In this story, a poor Japanese family is forced to sell its prized painting of five geese in flight. Kenji takes dramatic action to save the painting. The tale provides a subtle picture of Japanese life, values, and cultural heritage.

Joshua by the Sea *by Angela Johnson.* Used by permission of Orchard Books, New York.

Science

Young children are fascinated with nature, the world around them, and the way things work. Chris Babcock's *No Moon* provides a hilarious introduction to the world of science. It involves Martha, a histrionic cow who, deciding that life is too dull, refuses to give milk until she becomes a "cowsmonaut." After a stampede through New York City, Martha arrives at the Museum of Natural History, where a creative solution is achieved. Mark Teague's illustrations make the most out of each situation. Robert Yagelski's *The Day the Lifting Bridge Stuck* presents another amusing science-related story. It is a good book to begin a discussion on technology in our lives and our dependence on it. Purely nonfiction titles include Angela Royston's *Big Machines*, David Macaulay's *The Way Things Work*, and Michelle Koch's *World Water Watch*. A resource book for creating recycled-material craft projects for five- to seven-year-olds is *Cups & Cans & Paper Plate Fans: Craft Projects from Recycled Materials* by Phyllis and Noel Fiarotta.

TIPS FOR TEACHERS

Create a picture book telling about the science project in which the children took part.
- *Have a parent volunteer take photographs of the project or field trip to illustrate the story of the event.*
- *Tape record the event as an aid to creating the book.*
- *Make multiple copies of the book for children to read and thus relive the experience.*

Physical science topics are presented in books about the sun, stars, space, seasons, and the elements. In *I'll See You When the Moon Is Full* by Susi Fowler, a father leaving on a business trip explains the phases of the moon to his little boy. Using color photographs, Ian Graham's *Looking at Space* presents the sun, moon, constellations, and galaxies, and the tools of space exploration. Reeve Lindbergh's *What Is the Sun?* presents similar information in a question-and-answer rhyming format. A family learns about the mythical shapes in the night sky in Natalie Kinsey-Warnock's *On a Starry Night*. David McPhail's illustrations provide a deep, rich, velvety black background for the text. The topic of the sun is approached through a gentle narrative in Susan Winter's *My Shadow*.

The element of water is explored in books dealing with winter, rain, and the seashore. *North Country Night* by Daniel San Souci presents the activity of a north country forest covered with a fresh blanket of new snow. A woman explains the solstice to her granddaughter in Jean Craighead George's *Dear Rebecca, Winter Is Here*. The change from autumn to winter is also presented in Ben Schecter's *When Will the Snow Trees Grow?* Water is explored as both a freshwater and saltwater phenomenon in Mike Thaler's *In the Middle of the Puddle* and Charlotte Zolotow's *The Seashore Book*. The latter book is also a good transition

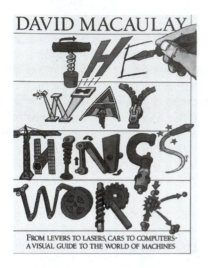

The Way Things Work *by David Macauley.*
Reprinted by permission of Houghton Mifflin Co.

from physical science to life science. Wendell Manor's breathtaking paintings let the reader almost feel and smell the salt air and smooth shells.

Life science exploration can emerge from the ocean theme through *The Magic School Bus on the Ocean Floor* by Joanna Cole and Bruce Degen. Children will enjoy thoroughly the character of Miss Frizzle and her wacky ever-changing outfits in the "magic school bus" series of books. Continuing with ocean life, young readers will respond positively to Bruce McMillan's *Going on a Whale Watch* and feel right at home with the multicultural tour group in Aliki's *My Visit to the Aquarium.*

A wide assortment of animals are presented to young children in Hana Machotka's *Terrific Tails*, Ron Hirschi's *A Time for Babies*, and Denise Fleming's *In a Small, Small Pond*. The four basic aspects of growth are developed in an

Author/illustrator Mike Thaler. Courtesy Mike Thaler, "America's Riddle King."

interactive and uncluttered manner in Linda Martin's *Watch Them Grow: The Amazing Ways That Animals and Plants Change as They Grow*. Opportunities for investigating specific animals in more depth are readily available in books such as Joanne Ryder's *Dancers in the Garden* (about hummingbirds) and Sandra Lee's lively text titled *Koalas*. An investigation of the human body is presented in *The Magic School Bus Inside the Human* Body by Joanna Cole and Bruce Degen. The process by which animals and plants reclaim the land is vividly presented in *McCrephy's Field* by Christopher Lynne Myers. Finally, a good naptime science choice is Wendy Lewison's *Going to Sleep on the Farm.*

POETRY

Poetry is not stuffy! It is not boring! It is not just for greeting cards! A poem is a song without notes. It is the form used for the most intense and imaginative writing about our world and ourselves. Poetry is lyrical, succinct, heart-touching, and also great fun. The poet selects each word carefully so the impact of what is said and meant is startling to the reader or listener. No matter what the rhyme patterns, the rhythm and the cadence of a good poem attract children in much the same way as a song or a jingle. The descriptive use of language conjures up visions in the head of the listeners so that they almost feel they have witnessed the action of the poem. Winnie-the-Pooh is a favorite poetic character, yet few children are consciously aware that the story of Christopher Robin is written in poetry. They just know that the story is a favorite.

Poetic Devices

Formal poetry has metered verse. It uses syllables, line length, and special structures to create the differences in haiku, tanka, cinquain, sonnet, limerick, and two-word poetry. Frequently used devices in poetry written for children are onomatopoeia, personification, simile, metaphor, and alliteration. *Onomatopoeia* is the use of specific words because their sound suggests what is happening in the poem (e.g., pop, sizzle, hiss, bang). *Personification* occurs when human characteristics or emotions are given to animals or inanimate objects (e.g., Pop, pop, pop! I'm inside out and warm and hot! Do not fail to put butter and salt on my top!). A *simile* is used to compare two things that are different, using words such as "like" and "as" (e.g., the puddle was as wet as a puppy's nose, or her hair was as soft as a fire's glow). A *metaphor* is an analogy that gives some of the characteristics of one object to a second object (e.g., my crumb of bread is the giant feasty for all the little ants and buglike beasties). *Alliteration* is the repetition of the initial consonant of a word several times in a line (e.g., Little Lyle laughed loudly).

Using Poetry

With young children, poetry written beyond their reading level can be used. It should be read with expression and tied to the children's level of understanding. Although poetry can be shared simply as a type of literature, another fine use is to integrate it with other thematically related forms of literature. For example, if the unit theme is animals, poems to be read might include "The Hippopotamus" by Jack Prelutsky, "Roger the Dog" by Ted Hughes, and "The Crocodile: by Lewis Carroll.

Poetry weaves itself into children's thinking in a number of different ways. Lee Bennett Hopkins collects and presents theme-related poetry. In his book *April Bubbles Chocolate*, twenty-six poets present diverse moods and subjects as they wander through the alphabet with the reader. It's great fun trying to guess what the subject of each letter will be. *Balloons and Other Poems* by Deborah Chandra presents a collection of imaginative poems that suggest new ways of looking at common objects and events. In *Paddy Pig's Poems*, Donald Charles introduces us to a storybook character who is himself a Victorian poet. None of his friends appreciates his unusual endings, but Paddy turns the tables on them in the end. In some books, the entire narrative is told in poetic form. Good choices for sharing this type of poetry include *Rachel Fister's Blister* by Amy MacDonald, *When Crocodiles Clean Up* by Roni Schotter, illustrated by Thor Wickstrom, and *Silly Sally* by Audrey Wood. Poetry is especially powerful when dealing with emotions, as in *Night on Neighborhood Street* by Eloise Greenfield. Set in an African-American urban neighborhood, this story contrasts the harsh realities of urban life with the people's feelings of friendship and closeness.

Dorothy Aldis and Leland B. Jacobs also write simple, self-explanatory poems. They write about everyday things like curbstones and the circus. "Hush-a-bye Baby" is a simple poem inspired by the native American custom of hanging cradles from birch trees. It was written by a pilgrim who was impressed by the custom.[4] It has been called the first poem of rhyme written in the new world, a lullaby rhyme:

> Hush-a-bye baby, on the treetop,
> When the wind blows, the cradle will rock.
> When the bough breaks, the cradle will fall,
> And down will come baby, cradle and all.

This Boston area version of the lullabye first appeared in print in 1765 in *Mother Goose's Melody*. Children have no problem understanding the meaning of the piece, but adding this other information makes it more interesting.

Shel Silverstein is one of the best known children's poets. He captures children's imaginations with topics from spaghetti to trees. His black and white line illustrations add much to his fine words.

Robert Louis Stevenson and Henry Wadsworth Longfellow are two traditional favorites. Many little girls, especially on off days, feel a kindred spirit with Longfellow's daughter who inspired the poem that begins, "There was a little girl, who had a little curl right in the middle of her forehead . . . ." If a child is sick in

---

[4] Panati, C. (1987). *Extraordinary origins of everyday things*. New York: Harper & Row.

bed, Stevenson's "The Land of Counterpane" is *must* reading. It is especially comforting when the child can use toy soldiers to act out the sheet battles. Stevenson's language is always vivid. From the poem "My Shadow," note the expressive lines:

> For he sometimes shoots up taller
> like an India rubber ball,
> And he sometimes gets so little
> that there's none of him at all.

Stevenson's lines show how timeless and universal good poetry can be for children. Many fine poets have written verses for children: Walter de la Mare, Langston Hughes, Edward Lear, Lewis Carroll, John Ciardi, Odgen Nash, Carl Sandburg, William Blake, and Eve Merriam.

Fostering Creativity with Poetry

Because of its powerful images, poetry naturally lends itself to visual creativity in such books as *Riddle-icious* by Patrick Lewis. Each page of this book contains a rhyming riddle with plenty of clues to the solution right on the page. Debbie Tilley's playful artwork provides the hints. Powerful feelings are played out in the rhymed narrative of *The Upstairs Cat* by award-winning poet Karla Kuskin. Her tale about two antagonistic cats who must share the same house is heightened by Howard Fine's dramatic oil painting illustrations.

Two-word poetry is an easy way to involve young children in creating nonsense verse. The two words, one a noun and one an adjective, can rhyme or not. They can be silly or not. They can be added to other two-word verses to create larger nonsense poems. Illustrations are always a pleasant follow-up to a poem such as

> Sleeping farmer rubbed his purple eyes.
> A polka-dot pig with a talking dog.
> Wow cow and golly gee, what a sight to see.

It may not be memorable poetry, but it is fun and demonstrates the sense of creativity and excitement that surrounds poetry.

Finally, no discussion of poetry for children would be complete without considering the work of Jack Prelutsky. A prolific writer, his books address most of the major holidays with such titles as *It's Valentine's Day*, *It's Thanksgiving*, and *It's Christmas*. Other titles such as *Rainy, Rainy Saturday*, *Rolling Harvey down the Hill* and *The Kid on the Block* address themes of loneliness, friendship, and family relationships.

Poet Jack Prelutsky. Courtesy Jack
Prelutsky.

Selecting Poetry

Criteria for selecting poetry to use with children should focus on content rather than the technical aspects of meter and rhyme scheme. The poetry should be melodic, with the rhythm and beat alive and clear. It should have vivid language. While poetry can be about any thought-provoking topic, it should be interesting and relevant to the audience. A variety of classic, contemporary, nonsense, and one's own poetry should be included to give children a broad exposure. This will allow children to appreciate all types of poetry and to develop individual preferences. One should always remember that poetry is meant to be read aloud. Decide how the poem ought to be read before reading it to an audience. Then, read it with feeling.

TIPS FOR TEACHERS
Create a file-card library of poems to use throughout the year on topics to be explored.
- *Holiday poem cards.*
- *Seasonal poem cards.*
- *Activity-related poem cards.*

When introducing a poem, it is important to set the mood for what is to come. Care should be taken not to over-explain the poem prior to the reading. Since poetry touches us in different ways, children should be allowed to experience the poem with their own imaginations. Never make children memorize a poem.

Reread it often if the children enjoy it, but don't require memorization. Use an abundance of humorous poetry. Start writing poetry for the children as soon as the reading of poetry is introduced. The two are partners in developing a full appreciation and enjoyment of poetry.

AWARDS AND PRIZES IN CHILDREN'S LITERATURE

Outstanding works by children's authors and illustrators are recognized through a variety of awards and honors. These include formal awards and medals, magazine awards, and library awards. The most famous award for picture books is the Caldecott Medal. This American award is given each year to an illustrator by the Association for Library Services to Children. The Caldecott Medal is named for the British illustrator of children's books, Randolph Caldecott (1846–1886). It was first given in 1937 when Frederic G. Melcher established it, as he had the Newbury Award in 1922. The Caldecott Medal is limited to a resident or citizen of the United States. It is ironic that this "Americans only" award is named after a British subject. Although not every well-known children's book illustrator has received this award, many have, and many others have been honored as runners-up. A Caldecott Medal–winning book has a gold seal with the award on the cover. Caldecott Honor Award–winning books (the runners-up) have a silver seal on their covers.

A list of winning books provides a good starting point for a search for quality books. (Winners of the Caldecott Medal are listed in Appendix B.) However, it is important to remember that an award does not necessarily mean that a book is appropriate for a given class or for a teacher's purpose. One should keep in mind that it is adults who give the award, based on criteria developed by adults. The genuine award for a quality book is the enthusiastic response of generations of children to a particular work. Today's award winners await the test of time.

Other awards for excellence in children's poetry, illustrations, and writing are given in the United States and in other countries. The Kate Greenaway Medal is given by the British Library Association for distinguished work in the illustration of children's books. The Amelia Frances Howard-Gibbon Medal is a similar award given to a Canadian citizen by the Canada Library Association. The Laura Ingalls Wilder Award is given every three years by the Association for Library Services to Children to an author or illustrator whose books, published in the United States, have made a substantial contribution to children's literature. The Newbury Medal is given annually by the same organization to a United States author for the most distinguished contribution to children's literature during the past year. Other awards for children's literature are listed in *Children's Books: Awards and Prizes*.[5] Any time authors, poets, or illustrators win one of these prestigious awards, their work has been chosen from over 4,500 books printed annually.

To learn about new works by favorite illustrators or authors, refer to *Books in Print*, published annually by R. R. Bowker. There are three volumes in the set: an index by author's name, an index by title, and a volume with publishers' updated

---

[5] *Children's books: Awards and prizes.* (1993). New York: Children's Books Council.

information. If interested in specific subject matter, the four-volume annual *Subject Guide to Books in Print* may be useful. It too is published by R.R. Bowker. *Something About the Author*, published by Gale Research in Detroit, Michigan, is an invaluable source of information about writers and illustrators of children's books. It has been published for over twenty years, with new volumes added annually. All of these resources are found in the library.

SUMMARY

Expose children to a wide variety of quality literature. The purpose of exposing children to literature is, first and foremost, to help them gain meaning. This is an important step on the road to literacy. There is a tremendous range of literature available to young children. Even if children are not yet reading, they can benefit from listening to stories written several years above their reading level. The literature can be used to reinforce other activities, or it can serve as a starting point for an activity. Basic to all of this is the fact that, again, literature should help create meaning. It should serve as a means of deepening our enjoyment of life and helping us to make sense of our world.

QUESTIONS FOR THOUGHT AND DISCUSSION

1. What is a fingerplay?
2. What is a chant?
3. What is a rhyme?
4. What is the difference between fantasy and realistic fiction? Why should a teacher use each type?
5. Why should a teacher use Mother Goose tales?
6. How can fingerplays be used in the classroom?
7. What are the differences between fable, folk tale, and fairy tale?
8. What are the dangers of using fairy tales with young children? How can these dangers be avoided?
9. How should one select nonfiction books?
10. Why are picture books important in an early childhood classroom?
11. Why is it permissible to use poems that are written above a child's reading level?
12. How should one select poetry?
13. How should one use poetry with children?

CHILDREN'S BOOKS CITED

Adler, D. (1992). *A picture book of Harriet Tubman*. New York: Scholastic.

Aliki (1993). *My visit to the aquarium*. New York: HarperCollins.

Altman, L.J. (1993). *Amelia's Road*. New York: Lee & Low.

Anholt, C., & L. (1994). *One, two, three, count with me*. New York: Viking.

Anno, M. (1989). *Anno's Aesop*. New York: Orchard.

Aylesworth, J. (1990). *The completed Hickory Dickory Dock*. New York: Atheneum.

Babcock, C. (1993). *No moon*. New York: Crown.

Baker, J. (1993). *Window*. New York: Puffin.

Barrett, J. (1980). *Animals should definitely wear clothes*. New York: Atheneum.

Barrett, J. (1978). *Cloudy with a chance of meatballs*. New York: Atheneum.

Bond, M. (1996). *Paddington's 123*. New York: Puffin.

Bruchac, J., & Locker, J. (1992). *Thirteen moons on turtle's back*. New York: Philomel.

Bryan, A. (1993). *The story of thunder and lightning*. New York: Atheneum.

Bunting, E. (1994). *Smoky night*. San Diego, CA: Harcourt Brace Jovanovich.

Carle, E. (1969). *1, 2, 3 to the zoo*. New York: Collins World.

Chandra, D. (1990). *Balloons and other poems*. New York: Farrar, Straus, Giroux.

Charles, D. (1989). *Paddy Pig's poems*. New York: Simon and Schuster.

Clark, E. (1993). *Across the blue mountains*. San Diego, CA: Harcourt Brace Jovanovich.

Coerr, E. (1981). *The big balloon race*. New York: Harper & Row.

Cole, J., & Degen, B. (1990). *The magic school bus inside the human body*. New York: Scholastic.

Cole, J., & Degen, B. (1992). *The magic school bus on the ocean floor*. New York: Scholastic.

Compton, J. (1994). *Ashpet: An Appalachian tale*. New York: Holiday House.

Coville, B. (1979). *Sarah's unicorn*. New York: Harper & Row.

Dorros, A. (1991). *Abuela*. New York: Scholastic.

Emberly, M. (1990). *Ruby*. Boston: Little, Brown.

Fiarotta, P., & Fiarotta, N. (1993). *Cups & cans & paper plate fans: Craft projects from recycled materials*. New York: Sterling.

Finzel, J. (1991). *Large as life*. New York: Lothrop, Lee & Shepard.

Fleming, D. (1993). *In a small, small pond*. New York: Holt.

Fowler, S. (1994). *I'll see you when the moon is full*. New York: Greenwillow.

Franklin, K. (1994). *The shepherd boy*. New York: Atheneum.

George, J.C. (1993). *Dear Rebecca, winter is here*. New York: HarperCollins.

Gerson, M. (1992). *Why the sky is far away*. Boston: Little, Brown.

Giganti, P. (1992). *Each orange had eight slices*. New York: Greenwillow.

Graham, I. (1991). *Looking at space*. New York: Scholastic.

Greenfield, E. (1991). *Night on Neighborhood Street*. New York: Dial.

Greenwood, P. (1993). *What about my goldfish?* New York: Clarion.

Havil, J. (1992). *Treasure nap*. Boston: Houghton Mifflin.

Heo, Y. (1994). *One afternoon*. New York: Orchard.

Hirschi, R. (1991). *Harvest song*. New York: Cobblehill/Dutton.

Hirschi, R. (1993). *A time for babies*. New York: Cobblehill/Dutton.

Hoban, T. (1992). *26 letters and 99 cents*. New York: William Morrow.

Hopkins, L.B. (1994). *April bubbles chocolate*. New York: Simon and Schuster.

Howard, E. (1991). *Aunt Flossie's hats (and crab cakes later)*. New York: Clarion.

Hoyt-Goldsmith, D. (1992). *Pueblo storyteller*. New York: Holiday House.

Johnson, A. (1994). *Joshua by the sea*. New York: Orchard.

Johnson, A. (1992). *The leaving morning*. New York: Orchard.

Johnson, A. (1991). *One of three*. New York: Orchard.

Johnson, A. (1990). *When I am old with you*. New York: Orchard.

Johnson, R. (1992). *Kenji and the magic geese*. New York: Simon and Schuster.

Johnston, T. (1994). *The tale of Rabbit and Coyote*. New York: Putnam.

Jonas, A. (1994). *Aardvarks disembark!* New York: Puffin.

Keats, E.J. (1972). *Over in the meadow*. New York: Four Winds.

Kellogg, S. (1992). *Aster Aardvark's alphabet*. New York: William Morrow.

Kennaway, A. (1992). *Little Elephant's walk*. New York: HarperCollins.

Kimmel, E. (1994). *The three princes*. New York: Holiday House.

Kinsey-Warnock, N. (1994). *On a starry night*. New York: Orchard.

Kipling, R. (1996). *Jungle Book*. New York: Viking.

Knight, M. (1993). *Who belongs here?* Gardiner, ME: Tilbury.

Koch, M. (1993). *World water watch*. New York: Greenwillow.

Kuskin, K. (1982). *The philharmonic gets dressed*. New York: Harper.

Kuskin, K. (1997). *The upstairs cat*. New York: Clarion.

Kvanosky, L. (1994). *One, two, three, play with me*. New York: Dutton.

Lee, S. (1994). *Koalas*. Chicago: Child's World.

Lewis, P. (1997). *Riddle-icious*. New York: Alfred A. Knopf.

Lewison, W. (1992). *Going to sleep on the farm*. New York: Dial.

Lindbergh, R. (1994). *What is the sun?* Cambridge, MA: Candlewick.

Lobel, A. (1978). *Gregory Griggs and other nursery rhyme people*. New York: Greenwillow.

Lucas, B. (1993). *Snowed in*. New York: Bradbury.

Macaulay, D. (1988). *The way things work*. Boston: Houghton Mifflin.

MacDonald, A. (1990). *Rachel Fister's blister*. Boston: Houghton Mifflin.

Machotka, H. (1994). *Terrific tails*. New York: Morrow.

Martin, J.B. (1992). *The finest horse in town*. New York: HarperCollins.

Martin, L. (1994). *Watch them grow: The amazing ways that animals and plants change as they grow*. New York: Dorling Kindersley.

Martin, R. (1992). *The rough-face girl*. New York: G.P. Putnam's Sons.

McDermott, G. (1992). *Zomo the Rabbit*. San Diego, CA: Harcourt Brace Jovanovich.

McKissack, P. (1992). *A million fish . . . more or less*. New York: Knopf.

McMillan, B. (1992). *Going on a whale watch*. New York: Scholastic.

Micklethwait, L. (1992). *I spy: An alphabet in art*. New York: Greenwillow.

Morris, A. (1992). *Houses and homes*. New York: Lothrop, Lee & Shepard.

Myers, C., & Myers, L. (1991). *McCrephy's field*. Boston: Houghton Mifflin.

O'Kelley, M.L. (1991). *Moving to town*. Boston: Houghton Mifflin.

Oram, H. (1993). *A creepy crawly song book*. New York: Farrar, Straus, Giroux.

Owens, M.B. (1993). *Counting cranes*. Boston: Little, Brown.

Pilkey, D. (1992). *When cats dream*. New York: Orchard.

Prelutsky, J. (1980). *It's Christmas*. New York: Greenwillow.

Prelutsky, J. (1982). *It's Thanksgiving*. New York: Greenwillow.

Prelutsky, J. (1983). *It's Valentine's Day*. New York: Greenwillow.

Prelutsky, J. (1984). *The new kid on the block*. New York: Greenwillow.

Prelutsky, J. (1980). *Rainy, rainy Saturday*. New York: Greenwillow.

Prelutsky, J. (1980). *Rolling Harvey down the hill*. New York: Greenwillow.

Rayner, M. (1994). *Ten pink piglets: Garth Pig's wall song*. New York: Dutton.

Reid, B. (1994). *Sing a song of Mother Goose*. New York, Scholastic.

Rockwell, A. (1989). *Willy can count*. Boston: Little, Brown.

Rosenberg, M. (1991). *Brothers and sisters*. New York: Clarion.

Royston, A. (1994). *Big machines*. Boston: Little, Brown.

Rush, K. (1994). *Friday's journey*. New York: Orchard.

Ryder, J. (1992). *Dancers in the garden*. San Francisco: Sierra Club.

Rylant, C. (1993). *Everyday town*. New York: Bradbury.

San Souci, D. (1990). *North country night*. New York: Bantam Doubleday Dell.

Schecter, B. (1993). *When will the snow trees grow?* New York: HarperCollins.

Schoberle, C. (1994). *Morning sounds, evening sounds*. New York: Simon and Schuster.

Schotter, R. (1993). *When crocodiles clean up*. New York: Macmillan.

Schieszka, J. (1991). *The frog prince continued*. New York: Viking.

Schieszka, J. (1989). *The true story of the three little pigs*. New York: Puffin.

Schnur, S. (1997). *Autumn, an alphabetic acrostic*. New York: Clarion.

Shannon, G. (1993). *Climbing Kansas mountains*. New York: Bradbury.

Siebert, D. (1990). *Train song*. New York: Crowell.

Spinelli, E. (1993). *If you want to find Golden*. Morton Grove, IL: Albert Whitman.

Stevens, J. (1993). *Coyote steals the blanket: A Ute tale*. New York: Holiday House.

Stieg, W. (1990). *Shrek*. New York: Farrar, Straus, Giroux.

Stock, C. (1993). *Where are you going Manyoni?* New York: Morrow.

Sullivan, C. (1991). *Alphabet animals*. New York: Abrams.

Sullivan, C. (1991). *Numbers at play*. New York: Rizzoli.

Sutherland, Z. (1990). *The Orchard book of nursery rhymes*. New York: Orchard.

Thaler, M. (1988). *In the middle of the puddle*. New York: Harper.

Tololwa, M. (1992). *A promise to the sun*. Boston: Little, Brown.

Turner, G. (1994). *Over on the farm*. New York: Viking.

Van Leeuwen, J. (1992). *Going west*. New York: Dial.

Viorst, J. (1972). *Alexander and the terrible, horrible, no good, very bad day*. New York: Atheneum.

Viorst, J. (1971). T*he tenth good thing about Barney*. New York: Atheneum.

Wells, R. (1993). *Max and Ruby's first Greek myth: Pandora's box*. New York: Dial.

Wiesner, D. (1997). *Tuesday*. New York: Clarion.

Williams, J. (1992). *Everyday ABC*. New York: Dial.

Winter, J. (1992). *Klara's new world*. New York: Knopf.

Winter, S. (1994). *My shadow*. New York: Doubleday.

Wood, A. (1992). *Silly Sally*. San Diego, CA: Harcourt Brace Jovanovich.

Yagelski, R. (1992). *The day the lifting bridge stuck*. New York: Bradbury.

Yolen, J. (1993). *Honkers*. Boston: Little, Brown.

Zolotow, C. (1992). *The seashore book*. New York: HarperCollins.

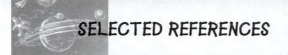

SELECTED REFERENCES

Children's Books: Awards and Prizes. New York: Children's Book Council, 1993.

Cummings, P. (1992). *Talking with artists*. New York: Macmillan.

Davis, R. (1990). *Art and children: Using literature to expand creativity*. Metuchen, NJ: Scarecrow.

Freeman, J. (1990). *Books kids will sit still for*. New Providence, NJ: Bowker.

Jett-Simpson, M. (Ed.). (1989). *Adventuring with books*. Urbana, IL: National Council of Teachers of English.

Kobrin, B. (1988). *Eyeopeners!* New York: Penguin.

Pigdon, K., & Woolley, M. (1993). *The big picture: Integrating children's learning*. Portsmouth, NH: Heinemann.

Redleaf, R. (1993). *Busy fingers, growing minds*. St. Paul, MN: Redleaf.

Rosen., M., & Nicolls, J. (1994). *Count to five and say "I'm alive."* York, ME: Stenhouse.

Rudman, M.K. (Ed.). (1993). *Children's literature: Resources for the classroom*. Norwood, MA: Christopher-Gordon.

Sutherland, Z., & Arbuthnot, M.H. (1991). *Children and books*. New York: HarperCollins.

Trelease, J. (1995). *The new read-aloud handbook*. New York: Viking Penguin.

Warren, J. (1984). *More piggyback songs*. Everett, WA: Warren.

Adventure is worthwhile in itself.

– Amelia Earhart

5 Magic Motivations

Y ou gotta shake, shake, shake your sillies out" is the start of a wonderful song by Raffi, the popular singer of children's music. Raffi knows, as does every teacher, that young children need to wriggle. Even when they try to be still, they seem to shake, shimmy, and move about. The individual movements of each child combine with those of others in a subtle wrestling ballet. This interaction can progress, if left unattended, into a brawl.

Every storyteller has experienced the following situation: Child one taps child two . . . child two reacts with a subtle kick to child one . . . child one counters with a leg pinch . . . child two holds in a yell while stretching a leg into child one's back . . . child one escalates the action with a solid shove . . . and so on. It is always better to avoid this situation in the first place rather than trying to correct it after the dynamics have begun. Such restlessness can usually be avoided by presenting a story of real interest to the children and engaging them in an enthusiastic sharing of the storytelling experience.

CAPTURING THE ATTENTION OF CHILDREN

Totally eliminating unacceptable peer behaviors may not be possible. However, much can be done to decrease them. Children often engage in inappropriate behaviors when they do not perceive any acceptable behaviors that are of interest to them. Many poor behaviors can be avoided or minimized by using a combination of planning, common sense, and creativity in the presentation of stories. Nevertheless, the teacher who attempts to have perfectly still and quiet children during any activity, including a story reading, is destined to fail. This does not mean that children cannot sit reasonably still or that they should not be expected to listen. But success will depend on realistic expectations of children's behavior as well as the ability to engage, motivate, and plan for the children. Planning to work with the normal wriggles and giggles makes more sense than trying to totally eliminate them.

Transitions are important for all young children. Don't expect children to leave free play or an outdoor activity, and immediately sit still for a story. Without some type of transition activity, a smooth change from active play to passive sitting is nearly impossible for many children. Once settled with a transition song or fingerplay, children want to listen to the story. And children will listen if the teacher has set the stage for the story in a way that motivates them to listen.

Listening is a crucial language skill as well as an important socialization life skill. Telling and reading stories to children can help them increase their listening attention span in a natural and enjoyable manner. Assuming that the book choice is appropriate and that the setting for telling the story is comfortable, one can consider other factors that affect the story reading.

Planning the Sharing of a Story

Planning a story is an interesting and challenging activity for anyone who understands how the teacher, child, and story must interact. Keep in mind that sharing is a two-way street between teacher and child. Too often, reading a story appears to be so simple a process that a plan is forgotten or not developed. A good lesson plan stretches the teacher's thinking to include planning for disaster. Planning for potential problems within a story-sharing session can help eliminate them. The teacher must plan for wriggles, giggles, and other possible disruptions. This can be done by analyzing not only the choice of books, but the method of presentation as well. A lesson plan is an organized way to look at the components of a lesson. It allows one to see how the various pieces fit together, what is missing, and what can be changed. It can also provide a record of the title, author, and publisher of the book, and most important, the children's response to the story. This record will assist the teacher in revising the plan for the next time the book is shared with children. A lesson plan form makes the recording and planning easier. Figure 5–1 contains a sample lesson plan form. For each book, objectives, motivation, sharing procedures, and evaluation are recorded.

TIPS FOR TEACHERS
Maintain an awareness of the interests of the children.
- *Follow the children's lead by listening to the topics they are discussing.*
- *Have alternate books and activities ready in case a different direction in the activity is appropriate.*
- *Know what is important to individual children by communicating regularly with families.*

Objectives. Objectives refer to the changes seen in a child as a result of interacting with a story. Many of these changes are related to feelings, attitudes, discovery of self, and new understandings of the world. Objectives focused primarily on remembering factual information from a story are misguided when using literature with young children. Literature should help the child grow spiritually, emotionally, and mentally. Take, for example, the reading of a story in which one of the characters is blind. It is far better for a child to learn about the common humanity

```
┌─────────────────────────────────────────────────────────────┐
│                    Literature Lesson Plan                     │
│                                                               │
│   Subject _____   Date _____                 │
│                                                               │
│   Title _____    Author _____        │
│                                                               │
│   Publisher _____     Year of Publ. _____       │
│                                                               │
│   Source (if applicable) _____    │
│                                                               │
│   Materials Needed _____    │
│                                                               │
│   Concepts included: _____    │
│                                                               │
│   Objectives: At the end of the lesson, the students will . . . │
│                                                               │
│   1. _____    │
│                                                               │
│   2. _____    │
│                                                               │
│   Motivation: To involve the children, I will . . .           │
│                                                               │
│   _____    │
│                                                               │
│   _____    │
│                                                               │
│   _____    │
│                                                               │
│   Sharing: To achieve the lesson objectives, I will . . .     │
│                                                               │
│   _____    │
│                                                               │
│   _____    │
│                                                               │
│   _____    │
│                                                               │
│   _____    │
│                                                               │
│   Evaluation: At the conclusion, the children will be able to . . . │
│                                                               │
│   _____    │
│                                                               │
│   _____    │
│                                                               │
│   _____    │
│                                                               │
│   Attach file card with any poem or fingerplay used by teacher. │
└─────────────────────────────────────────────────────────────┘
```

Figure 5–1. Literature lesson plan. Courtesy Walter Sawyer.

of all people regardless of their disability than for the child to learn a definition for the word "blind." In most cases, recalling something such as the specific disability isn't nearly as important as the message of understanding and accepting human differences. Therefore, it is important to think carefully about what a book should accomplish. The teacher must consider the curriculum, the book's purpose, and the development of the children in deciding upon the objectives of the lesson.

Involving children in the telling of the story is a motivational tool.

Motivation. Motivation is a critical key to successful storytimes. Simply stated, motivation is the process of leading children into a desire to listen to and interact with the story. It is the way children come to see the story as having interest and meaning for themselves. Story motivations can include the use of objects, sounds, fingerplays, games, and personal recollections. Objects such as mystery boxes, silk scarves, and large feathers can bring fun to the activity. Motivations are usually brief but can be more lengthy if necessary. A good motivation is one that works!

Consider the possibilities for sharing *The Berenstain Bears* and the *Spooky Old Tree* by Stan and Jan Berenstain. Before the story, one might place a stick, a piece of rope, and a flashlight into a box or bag. Ask the children to feel the objects and guess what they are. By suggesting how these relate to the story, you can give the children a reason to be interested and involved in the story. Approaching the same story from a different direction, one might display a large picture of a bear and ask the children how they might feel if they met such a bear. With just a bit of acting, the teacher might portray a fearful shaking and with a frightened voice ask the children what kinds of things scare them. This particular story is just a bit scary, but great fun for even older infants and toddlers. The excitement mounts as readers follow the bear children through the spooky old tree. All ends well. The adult should remember to wink at the children from time to time while pretending to be scared. This subtle clue will assure children that it is all in fun while still maintaining the feeling of being scared.

Consider the book *Amazing Grace* by Mary Hoffman. In the story, Grace wants to play the role of Peter Pan in her class play. Through family support, Grace learns that she can be anything she wants to be. Children can be motivated with lead-in questions such as, "Has anyone ever told you that you can't do something that you really wanted to do? How did that make you feel? What did you do about it? What do you think Grace likes to do (show the cover to the children)?" An appropriate version of the actual story of Peter Pan can be shared as well. Tinkerbell, fairy dust, Captain Hook, pirates, and buried treasure can be made a real part of the storytelling, with simple props such as foil-covered cardboard swords, glitter, play money, and handkerchiefs. Continuing with the pirate theme, a reading of *Tough Boris* by Mem Fox can be followed with a treasure hunt activity using hand-drawn treasure maps with picture clues.

If the book used is *A Snowman on Sycamore Street* by C.B. Christiansen, the teacher could motivate the children by hiding a real snowman behind one's back. After guessing what is being hidden, the children could be shown the snowman. This activity might be followed by asking them if they would like to have a real live snowman to play with. An alternative activity might include a pantomime of the making of a snowman. Still another idea might be to place a scarf, hat, and pieces of coal in a box or bag and ask the children to think of something that could be made using these items.

The ideas and objects used to engage children are limited only by the teacher's imagination. Some motivational objects can be held by the children during the story. If a particular child has difficulty attending to a story, that child might be asked to hold the stuffed animal or to wear the fireman's hat. Some use a rotating list of students for sharing the story motivation objects. A clever teacher keeps an eye open at yard sales and flea markets for stuffed toys and props to be used as future motivation tools. Post-holiday sales are good sources for materials related to holiday stories.

Sharing. The plan for sharing a story includes ideas for making the story interesting and meaningful to children. Jim Trelease's *The Read-Aloud Handbook* contains an excellent chapter on reading a book to children.[1] Jim Trelease's summary suggests some questions to consider when developing the plan for the actual reading of picture books: How will I make sure that everyone can see the pictures? Will I read every word, or will I summarize some parts? What pace or speed of reading will I use? What can I tell the children about the author? Will I have the children draw a picture of the story during or after the reading? Where are the suspenseful parts where I can pause for questions and discussion?

In addition to these questions, keep in mind some additional factors. First, make sure there is enough time to finish the book. Second, try to use a variety of unfamiliar books. It is more difficult to create interest in a book when children

[1] Trelease, J. (1995). *The New Read-Aloud Handbook.* New York: Penguin.

Teacher with cotton "snow" prepares the children to focus on an upcoming story about winter. Courtesy Diana Comer.

already know what is going to happen. If some children know the story, let them help tell it. Finally, be prepared to involve the children. Prompt them to ask questions at appropriate times. Discuss the story with them. Accept interpretations of the story that differ from one's own.

The end of the sharing should include a closure. Closure may include recalling all of the important points of the story. At this level, however, enjoyment and language growth will be the most common objectives. These are best assessed by observing the children's attention to the story and by listening to their discussion about the story. Children will enjoy retelling the story at this point, a most worthwhile activity.

Evaluation. The evaluation is the final part of the plan. At this point one needs to see if the objectives were met. This is when the teacher attempts to honestly determine what worked, what did not, and what could be changed to improve the story presentation the next time it is used. The sharing of the story can lead into a retelling or discussion of the story. The accuracy of the retelling can reveal the child's understanding of the original story. It might be an activity that relates to the story. For example, in *Listen Buddy* by Helen Lester, the theme of following directions play an important role. Children can show an understanding of the concept by creating and playing a game that requires following directions.

More Motivation Ideas

The best motivation for listening to a story is a great story. Consider *The Tale of Peter Rabbit* by Beatrix Potter, a great story that will engage most children's interest without much help. However, one might use stuffed toys or puppets to introduce the book. The teacher might also hold up a small jacket with a rip in it and ask the children how they thought it could have been torn. Still another approach might be to show the children a small watering can. After explaining how it might be a good hiding place for a small animal, the teacher could pull a small stuffed rabbit out of the can.

Mr. Bear Says Peek-A-Boo by Debi Gliori is a fun book for toddlers. The story motivation might begin by placing a blanket over the teacher's head. The teacher would say nothing until one of the curious toddlers pulled the blanket off. This action would lead right into the story. A similar procedure can be used for *The Most Beautiful Kid in the World* by Jennifer Ericsson, in which Annie changes outfits to look just right for grandmother's visit. The storyteller might begin by bundling up in a wild array of outlandish clothes, topped off with a huge coat or cape. Inviting children to pull off some of the pieces of clothing before the story begins will bring about both giggles and interest in the story.

There are a variety of ways to motivate children to listen to Nancy Tafuri's *Early Morning in the Barn*. One might stir interest for each animal story by making the sound of the animal or by pantomiming the animal's movements. A bag mask or stick puppet may be useful for a book such as this. Also, the storyteller could hide a stuffed or real animal in a box or cage. The children can be asked to find or guess what the animal is.

Emmy Payne's *Katy No-Pocket* can provide the storyteller with the opportunity for a comedy routine motivation activity. The teacher would come into the reading area with hands full of things, some of them dropping on the floor. While wearing clothes without pockets for the day, the teacher can use this humorous scene to begin talking to the children about the need for pockets. An alternative to this is to motivate using a picture of a sad, tearful, pocketless kangaroo named Katy. As the story progresses, the group can take off the tears, replace the frown with a smile, and add a sandwich baggie pocket to Katy.

TIPS FOR TEACHERS

Collect a box full of old clothes and props to be used during the transition to a story.
- *Get dressed up in a snowsuit to tell a winter or snow-related story.*
- *Wear a big straw beach hat for a summer story.*
- *Put on a football jersey and oversized sneakers to share a story about a sport.*

The teacher and child will use the scarf for music, movement, and story activities. Courtesy Diana Comer.

Another humorous motivational routine can be created by the teacher for Esphyr Slobodkina's *Caps for Sale.* Here, the teacher could walk slowly and carefully to the reading area while wearing a huge stack of hats. An alternative to this might include the use of a stuffed or puppet monkey. The toy monkey whispers only to the teacher, who then translates the message to the class. The monkey begins by whispering that it has a great story about other monkeys and hats. A hat or hats can be placed on the monkey as the story is told.

Hey, Al by Arthur Yorinks can be introduced by having the teacher rush into the reading area. Wearing a baseball cap and pushing a broom, the teacher rapidly pantomimes the activities of a janitor at work. Using the broom and a dust rag to clean under and around the children will create much fun and interest. A quieter approach to the same story would entail the teacher placing a janitor's cap, a fern, and a small broom into a box or bag. The children can be asked to identify what each one is and what they have in common.

Using *The Wretched Stone* by Chris Van Allsburg, the teacher can begin by having each of the children find a small rock outside. After washing and drying the stones, children can show, talk about, and feel their stones. The teacher could then explain that in many cultures stones are thought to have certain powers. Children could close their eyes and think of the special powers that their stones might have. This is just the right time to begin the reading of the story. Another story to create interest and excitement about an object such as a rock is William Stieg's *Sylvester and the Magic Pebble.* The teacher might begin by having the children guess what is concealed in a hand. After revealing a brightly colored

Author/illustrator Chris Van Allsburg. Courtesy Chris Van Allsburg.

pebble, the children could be told that the pebble contains magic just like the one in today's story. Another way of gaining each child's involvement is to give each child a magic pebble to hold for the story reading. The pebbles can help the children think of a picture of their own wishes. Children can paint them, weigh them, and create new stories about them They can then draw their wishes and take their special pebbles home.

Children are usually quite aware of their own health and familiar with doctors and nurses. *My Dentist* by Harlow Rockwell and *Bobby Visits the Doctor* by Martine Davison are two books on this topic to which children will be able to relate. The teacher might begin by entering the reading area wearing medical garb, either real or homemade. Using medical tools from a box, the teacher would pantomime a medical exam with a doll or puppet. An alternative to this might be to use a doll, animal, or puppet in place of the teacher. Having an alligator doctor do a medical exam on an elephant would surely create interest.

IDENTIFYING POSSIBLE PROBLEMS

It is important for the storyteller to be familiar with the story being presented so that problems can be anticipated. Even if a book is age-appropriate, it may be uninteresting or confusing for the children. One should be ready to add some excitement to the reading by involving the children in the story. There are a variety of ways to do this. One may pause to ask the children what they think will happen next. Other aspects of the presentation may be changed as well.

The effective use of voice will often help children focus on what is being said. One can keep younger children involved in the rather lengthy book *Green Eggs and Ham* by Dr. Seuss by periodically asking them, "Will he eat the green eggs and ham this time?" When the children respond with a "No," the teacher should quickly read the ever growing list of negative responses from the character in the book. Older children thoroughly enjoy this story and have little trouble staying with it. Even though the book is written as an early reader, younger children can follow it if the storyteller provides the rhyming words for the repeating phrases. Follow up the reading by cooking scrambled eggs, using green food coloring in them. This will re-create the experience. In conjunction with this story, one might also read *Friday Night at Hodges' Cafe* by author/illustrator Tim Egan.

When conducting a lesson involving science or social studies, it is quite valid to use the pictures in books geared for older children when the subject cannot be found in age-appropriate books. If the pictures are clear and large, the book can be used by omitting the text that is too difficult. The information contained in those sections can be paraphrased for the children. It is recommended, however, that age-appropriate books be used whenever possible.

The Importance of Prereading

Prereading the story allows the teacher to know where emotional support may be needed, especially with young children. Tomie dePaola's *Nana Upstairs and Nana Downstairs* has a very sad part in the middle of the story. Knowing this ahead of time, the teacher can anticipate the need for support if or when the children seem upset. This depends on the class. During the story, one might ask such questions as, "How do you think Tommy feels? . . . Would you feel this way? . . . There are more pages in the book; would you like to see what happens?" It is a healthy sign when a book such as this can arouse empathy for a character.

TIPS FOR TEACHERS
Listen to tape recordings of yourself reading a story in order to evaluate your presentation.
- *Check to see if your voice is appropriately dramatic from beginning to end.*
- *Do you use appropriate volume, pitch, and pauses?*
- *Note spots in the reading where a pause for comments, questions, or predictions would be appropriate.*

Many books can arouse children's emotions, and one must be sensitive to this potential. The teacher needs to anticipate reactions when using books that deal with death, divorce, new babies, and so forth. A reading can be a wonderful support for children coping with a similar situation in real life. It can also cause a disruption as children deal with the surfacing of their feelings. When planning to use such books to help a child, have that child sit next to an adult in the room. Be ready to provide support to the child. Allow time at the end of such stories to discuss all the children's feelings. Let them know at the beginning of a book that there will be time to talk after the story. This minimizes disruptions. Allow all the children to respond to the story after it is finished.

◎ Children's Interests

The key to successful story sharing is to select books that are of true interest to children. The interests of adults may or may not be the interests of children. Although it is fine to expose children to new interests, it is important also to plan to satisfy their current interests. If the children are fascinated with dinosaurs, be sure to include books that relate to prehistoric times. If they are interested in superheroes, share storybooks which include such heroes. Be wary of books that seem particularly "cute." Such books are often designed to attract adults by their appearance rather than their interest to children. Flowery language and ornate illustrations will probably not attract most infants, toddlers, and preschoolers.

SMOOTH TRANSITIONS

Transitions are sometimes challenging for both teachers and children. Some children find it difficult to leave an activity in which they are truly involved. Although stories are usually viewed as enjoyable by most children, certain children react with acting-out behavior when storytime is mentioned. They equate storytime with negative thoughts of having to sit perfectly still. These children find it very difficult to sit still. A good transition makes it easier for them to shift gears and approach storytime with less anxiety.

Storytellers have found that songs, poems, and fingerplays are effective transitional activities. Children naturally respond to their rhythms. There are many short forms of rhymes that fit nicely into a transition time frame. Anyone who has ever heard a young child repeating a jingle knows that they are particularly responsive to rhyming words set to music. For this reason, they also pay attention to the songlike quality of fingerplays and other such transitional activities. An effective transition turns the child's attention to the next activity. Indeed, through being involved in the transition activity, the child already is involved in the shift to the next activity.

◎ Transition Ideas

Teachers may choose to either make up their own transition activities or borrow them from books such as *Piggyback Songs for School* by Jean Warren and Gayle Bittinger. Chanting messages or singing the message to a familiar tune are other ways to establish a pattern for change. For example, moving from art time to storytime may be done by singing the following rhyme to the melody of "O Tannenbaum":

"It's storytime! It's storytime!
Can we get ready for storytime?

Some other ways to facilitate transitions are to use unusual objects. Find a gaudy old rhinestone ring, the bigger and more colorful the better. Tell the children

Children's activities and interests can be used as a guide to selecting books for them. Courtesy Diana Comer.

that this is a magic ring given to you by a sorcerer. Hold up the ring for all to see. Make a special wish for the children. Adding a couple of phrases like "Abracadabra" will help put a feeling of magic into the children's desire to hear the story.

Magic wands can be great aids to transitions. One can use a water- and glitter-filled wand, a tinsel-filled wand, a glow-in-the-dark wand, or a light-up wand. Children love to see the wand waved in the air over their heads while the teacher chants magical words and phrases. The children realize that the wand is not really magic, but they love the fun of pretending. A wand draws their attention and that makes it work as a transitional tool.

It is comforting for children to know what will come next. For this reason, many storytellers use the same transitional song or poem at the beginning of each storytelling or reading session. A second song or poem may be added, but the storytime always begins with the familiar one.

Wriggle songs, poems, and fingerplays are also useful before a story begins. They allow movement prior to the story that helps to keep the children from needing to wriggle so much during the story. The best wriggle activities proceed from active wriggling to nose twitching or eye blinking that readies the children for a quieter time. Active participation of children is a key factor in any transition.

There are several good choices for de-wriggling children. In *Music: A Way of Life for the Young Child*[2] by Kathleen M. Bayless and Marjorie E. Ramsey, one can find a favorite song titled "Open, Shut Them." Written by Laura Pendleton MacCartney, this musical fingerplay has been around since the early part of the century. It is an excellent tool to guide children into an attentive listening attitude.

The use of a transition is a part of the planning. It eliminates many behavior problems by avoiding the conflicts caused by an abrupt change in routine. The child who tends to act out has more of an opportunity to choose acceptable behaviors when transition activities are provided.

A HEALTHY ENVIRONMENT

There are many strategies available to promote an enjoyable reading situation. Experience can be a valuable teacher, as it allows one to try different procedures over time. One can also learn from the experience that others have gained. No procedure, however, is effective every time with every child or group. Children and classes have distinct personalities. A procedure that works one time for one group may be ineffective at another time or with another group. The fact that there is no blueprint or plan that one can always follow is part of the challenge of working with children over time. Be willing to approach problems in new and creative ways.

Certain problems tend to occur more frequently than others. They include children sitting too close, causing disruptions during the reading, acting out, and demonstrating inappropriate peer relationships. One also has to be aware of which behaviors must be accepted as normal, how to regain the attention of the group after a disruption, and how to avoid using inappropriate procedures for dealing with problems.

Children Sitting Too Close

Youngsters need to have enough space to accommodate their normal movements. A most common solution to this is to place hearts, stars, stickers, or markers at the places where children are to sit. Encourage independence by asking children to find their own spaces. The seating arrangement may be in the form of a circle, semicircle, or a random pattern. Each child might be assigned a permanent spot, or children could choose an available spot. If permanent spots are assigned to children, names can be added to reinforce name recognition.

Another approach might be to have the children stand up and hold hands in a circle. After stretching out to a full arm's length between each child, they could let go of each other's hands and sit in the spot they are standing. This yields a

---

2 Bayless, K.M., & Ramsey, M.E. (1987). *Music: A Way of Life for the Young Child.* Columbus, Ohio: Merrill.

good space between each child. One might also tape a circle on the floor or carpet. A cross tape can be placed at each point where a child is expected to sit. Finally, using clear contact paper, tape each child's picture to the spot on the floor where that child is to sit. This works well for toddlers and younger children who cannot yet read their own names.

Disruptions During Reading

A disruption to the reading can occur for a variety of reasons that may or may not be related to the story. The most obvious solution to this problem is to establish eye contact with the child and send a brief nonverbal message, such as telling the story directly to that child for a moment. For example, the teacher might nod to the child and mouth the word "after." If this is not effective, one might verbally acknowledge the child but ask that he or she wait until the end to speak. If the interruption is pursuant to the story, the teacher might wish to allow the child to briefly share the information. The reading could then be continued.

Consider the possibility that the children need to stretch. Use a wriggle or giggle fingerplay, then continue the story. Make the story a serial story by continuing it later in the day or the next day. Engage the children in the story. Ask what might come next, what did the giant do, or how the bunny found her way home. Teachers must use their instinct, judgment, and knowledge of the group to decide which course of action to follow.

Acting-out Children

Every class seems to have one or two children who might be described as overly active or as mischievous. Their disruptive behavior is often termed "acting out." These children should be seated near the teacher before the reading begins. Children who are known to have difficulty sitting near each other should be seated apart.

Involving these children in the storytelling is effective. Give them the motivational items to hold during the reading. If they are made to feel that they have an important role during the storytime, they will have less need for attention. But in dealing with these children, remember that literature is its own reward. One doesn't grow to appreciate it by having one's silence "bought" for sitting through it.

A good approach for engaging the attention of especially active children is to have them create a special book to bring home, with something drawn on the page that represents the story read that day. The book title and author can be written on the page as well. In this way, children can talk about the story later, and parents can reinforce the story. By doing this, children learn that they are expected to attend to the reading so they can share it with their parents. Praise the whole group for doing a good job of listening and learning. All children should feel that they are part of a social group with certain responsibilities.

TIPS FOR TEACHERS

Plan in advance what you will do to help a child who acts out.
• Give all the children something to do during the reading, such as hand motions and oral responses to parts of the story, and make sure they know what they should do during the story.
• Have the active child become a helper in the telling of the story.
• Use great stories so acting out won't become a problem in the first place.

Peer Relations

Children do bump and nudge each other, often unintentionally but sometimes on purpose. When it appears that a safety problem exists or that a behavior is interfering with the reading, an adult must take some type of action. The goal is to have all engaged in the story. Therefore, the first course of action might be to simply motion for the acting-out child to come and sit next to the teacher or an aide. The story can then be immediately continued. A reader who is standing can move near the child and involve the child in the story. Involving the child with the reader's presence and the story line will often eliminate the inappropriate behavior. Read some of the words: "The wolf huffed and he puffed, Michael" directly to the child. Ask the child to show how the wolf huffed and puffed. It's difficult to ignore the story when brought back into it in this way.

Sometimes children ignore these signals. As a last resort, they should be removed from the group. It should be done as quietly as possible, without stating

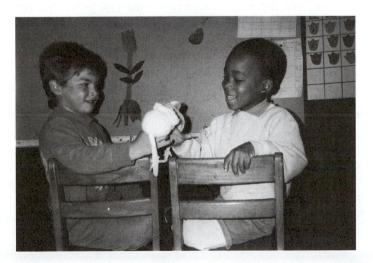

Children come to enjoy each other's company in a shared activity. Courtesy Diana Comer.

anything to them. They can be moved to sit at a table. The teacher should return to the group and continue the story for the others. The less attention given to the situation, the less it disturbs the flow of the story. If there are a couple of stories being read, or if there are appropriate points to pause in the story, the child can be asked to return to the group later.

Ignoring Normal Behaviors

Children stretch and wriggle. Children react verbally to various parts of a story. Children twist their hair around their fingers. Many times, these are unconscious behaviors that harm no one and actually show that children are listening. Adults sometimes mistakenly try to eliminate all motion from the listening child. Since it is normal for children to act in these ways, they should not be penalized for them.

If a child exhibits a behavior that the teacher feels needs to be addressed, it should be done quietly. "No problem" situations can become real problems for both the reader and the child if one attempts to eliminate all movement.

Regaining Attention

It can be difficult to regain a group's attention after a distraction. A dog walking into a room or a call on the intercom can disrupt the momentum of a story. It is best to handle the situation by using intuition and common sense. If it appears to be too late to continue the story, it is best not to attempt it. The children can be told that the story will be concluded later or during the next day. Rushing through the end of a book can be most unsatisfactory for all. It can cause the story to lose its charm. If there is enough time to continue, the children can be regrouped with a quiet fingerplay or song. The reader should repeat some of the past action and resume the story. Better yet, involve the children in the retelling of what has happened in the story prior to continuing the reading.

How Not to Handle Disruptions

At some time in life, everyone has seen the unacceptable way to handle a situation. The "wrong way" refers to a procedure that ultimately may do more harm than good. Humiliating youngsters in front of their peers may quiet them down, but is also likely to bring years of mistrust, resentment, and lowered self-esteem. A variety of other negative, yet common, methods for handling problems at storytime do more harm than good, and should be avoided.

Several of the methods to be avoided merely reveal the adult's frustration. Rolling one's eyes while saying, "Oh, no, not you again," is a good example. Yelling and accusing a child of ruining the reading group, or removing a child with a great deal of visible annoyance also fall into this category.

Threatening actions that will not be taken is foolish. For example, warning, "If you don't settle down, there will be no more stories," is a mistake. It may work for the moment, but it has a better chance of backfiring. In making such a statement, the teacher has surrendered control to the disruptive children, who may enjoy their newly discovered role of deciding the day's schedule—if indeed the stories are discontinued. But children know that there will always be more stories. It is also a grave mistake to link literature and punishment together in such a way. Threatening to tell a child's parents about a behavior is also ineffective. This admits to a child that the teacher cannot handle the problem and is likely to cause more serious problems in the future.

Negative comments, in general, are usually ineffective. It is far better to use positive comments, praising those students who are acting appropriately and offering an alternate activity to those who are not. Positive comments provide attention, build self-esteem, and are effective in managing behavior. Let children hear phrases such as, "I like the way Juan is listening," "I see Beth and Isaac are ready," "I just love the way you look at me with that smile when it is time to read a story." In addition, engage children in clapping, stomping, waving, and naming activities that can be a part of the story.

SUMMARY

Much of the success of reading a story depends on engaging the interest of the children. Armed with a good sense of humor, common sense, and a knowledge of child development, adults can successfully bring magic into storytimes. Creative and whimsical methods of motivation enhance the enjoyment of literature for both the teacher and the children. When adults are motivated to make books an integral and enjoyable part of life, children will respond with delight and a sense of wonder at the world of literature opening before them.

The choice of books and their presentation are critical in enhancing children's interest in books. The atmosphere created in the classroom is important to listening and learning. To create an effective atmosphere, teachers need to be responsive to children and their needs. Magic boxes, stuffed animals, puppets, and interesting objects do more than just motivate children to listen to a particular book. The special ways that adults use them can help children develop an interest in literature in general.

Helping children learn how to adjust to change, interact with literature, and develop listening skills is an important part of the teacher's role. These skills will make children more productive and responsive social beings. But this process does not occur simply by reading a book to children. Carefully plan the readings, taking into account both how literature can be exciting and how problems can occur. Careful planning will prevent many problems from occurring in the first place. When students do exhibit inappropriate behaviors during storytime, a set of sensitive and effective strategies for dealing with them is indispensable to the teacher.

QUESTIONS FOR THOUGHT AND DISCUSSION

1. What are some of the things a storyteller can do to prevent or minimize disruptive interactions between children?
2. How can a storyteller help children increase their listening time spans?
3. Why should teachers develop lesson plans?
4. Why is a motivational procedure important in a lesson plan?
5. Choose a story, and give some examples of motivations that might be used for it.
6. Children should never be read books that are above their age-appropriate level. Defend or refute this statement.
7. Why is it beneficial for children if the teacher prereads a book?
8. Why should the children's interests be part of planning the choice of books?
9. Describe a transitional activity a teacher might use in a classroom.
10. What is meant by the term "wriggle song"?
11. How might a teacher deal with the problem of children sitting too close together during storytime?
12. What steps could one take with a child who disrupts the reading time?
13. What can the teacher do with children who act out during storytime?
14. The aggressive child who starts fighting with another child during storytime should never be removed from the group as it makes him or her feel left out. Defend or refute this statement.

CHILDREN'S BOOKS CITED

Berenstain, S., & Berenstain, J. (1978). *The Berenstain Bears and the spooky old tree.* New York: Random House.

Christiansen, C.B., (1996). *A snowman on Sycamore Street.* New York: Atheneum.

Davison, M. (1992). *Bobby visits the doctor.* New York: Scholastic.

dePaola, T. (1992). *Nana upstairs and Nana downstairs.* New York: Dutton.

Egan, T. (1994). *Friday night at Hodges' Cafe.* Boston: Houghton Mifflin.

Ericsson, J. (1996). *The most beautiful kid in the world.* New York: Tambourine.

Fox, M. (1994). *Tough Boris.* San Diego: CA.

Gliori, D. (1997). *Mr. Bear says peek-a-boo.* New York: Little Simon.

Hoffman, M. (1991). *Amazing Grace.* New York: Scholastic.

Lester, H. (1996). *Listen Buddy.* Boston: Houghton Mifflin.

Payne, E. (1983). *Katy No-Pocket.* New York: Holiday House.

Potter, B. (1902). *The tale of Peter Rabbit.* New York: Warne.

Rockwell, H. (1987). *My dentist.* New York: Mulberry.

Dr. Seuss (pseud. for Geisel, T.) (1960). *Green eggs and ham.* New York: Random House.

Slobodkina, E. (1940). *Caps for sale.* New York: Addison Wesley.

Stieg, W. (1970). *Sylvester and the magic pebble.* New York: Simon and Schuster.

Tafuri, N. (1992). *Early morning in the barn.* New York: Mulberry.

Van Allsburg, C. (1991). *The wretched stone.* Boston: Houghton Mifflin.

Warren, J., & Bittinger, G. (1991). *Piggyback books for school.* Everett, WA: Warren.

Yorinks, A. (1986). *Hey, Al.* New York: Farrar, Straus, Giroux.

SELECTED REFERENCES

Crary, E. (1990). *Pick up your socks . . . and other skills growing children need.* Seattle: Parenting Press.

Dunn, S., & Pamenter, L. (1990). *Crackers and crumbs.* Portsmouth, NH: Heinemann.

Esse, E.L. (1990). *A practical guide to solving preschool behavior problems,* 2d ed. Albany, NY: Delmar Publishers.

Glazer, T. (1988). *Tom Glazer's treasury of songs for children.* New York: Doubleday.

Goldish, M. (1995). *Thematic poems, songs and fingerplays.* New York: Scholastic.

Grant, J.M. (1995). *Shake, rattle and learn.* York, ME: Stenhouse.

Lipson, G.B. (1995). *Manners please.* Carthage, IL: Teaching and Learning.

Saifer, S. (1990). *Practical solutions to practically every problem: The early childhood teacher's manual.* St. Paul, MN: Redleaf Press.

Trelease, J. (1992). *Hey listen to this.* New York: Penguin Books.

Watson, C. (1987). *Father Fox's pennyrhymes.* Madison, WI: DEMCO.

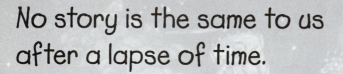

No story is the same to us
after a lapse of time.

– George Eliot

6 How Many Ways Can a Story be Told?

A daily structure provides an important security and reassurance to children. Yet, variations in routine can provide interest and excitement to the day. No matter how enjoyable a routine might be, the sameness can create boredom over time. Thus, good literature can be enhanced with a variety of presentation methods.

Some may be intimidated by the idea of changing the way a story is shared. Others welcome the opportunity to experiment with a variety of presentations. Those who do try a variety of approaches often find the changes refreshing for both the children and themselves. The changes can range from subtle shifts within a familiar presentation style to experimenting with totally new sharing methods. By starting with less obvious changes and proceeding to totally different styles, one can develop a confidence in one's ability to use different styles.

This chapter explores the possibilities of using such diverse methods as oral storytelling, reading aloud, flannelboard stories, theatrical story presentations, and children as authors. Each of these methods has a number of possibilities within it. One may also choose to combine the various presentation methods, making the possible ways of sharing stories endless.

READING ALOUD

Reading aloud to children should begin when they are infants. The close contact and the sounds of a caring voice and the rhythms of the language provide reassurance. The child who is read to grows up with the idea that reading is a normal part of life. As the language becomes meaningful, children can see new worlds constantly opening up before them. Reading stimulates their imaginations and provides a foundation upon which to build new knowledge.

The terms "reading readiness" and "reading readiness skills" give a false impression of what is entailed in learning to read. There really is no clearly defined set of skills that children must master before they are ready to learn to read. Learning to read is a long, ongoing process beginning with being read to as an infant. It culminates in an ability and desire to engage in reading as an enjoyable part of life.

Big books are an excellent tool for sharing stories with larger groups. Courtesy Diana Comer.

Reading aloud to children is a part of helping them to read. According to Jim Trelease, author of *The New Read-Aloud Handbook,* the child who follows the reader's finger across the page will make a natural connection between the sounds of the words and the letters on the page.[1] It is important that this learning not be pushed upon the child. Children will make this connection naturally and in so doing, will experience reading as something that possesses joy, mystery, and excitement.

Jim Trelease compares the planting of a desire to read in a child with the kind of advertising done by McDonald's restaurants. McDonald's has achieved success by advertising so frequently that people become familiar with both the commercials and the characters within the commercials. Trelease is concerned that the "commercials" for reading—frequently reading aloud to children-do not continue during the school years. Reading aloud should be a part of the everyday routine of children throughout their school lives. Yet, the frequency of reading books aloud to children decreases dramatically as children move up though the grades. By the time children graduate from high school, reading aloud has usually ceased to exist as a regular part of the school day.

Using Read-Aloud Books

In planning the read-aloud experience for children, consider how one can make the reading a fascinating and exciting experience. One does not need to be a professional storyteller to read aloud effectively. This skill can be achieved by attention and practice, using voice, pace, and a flexible approach.

---

[1] Trelease, J. (1995). *The New Read-Aloud Handbook.* New York: Viking Penguin.

To begin, one can practice using different voice inflections, pitches, and volume levels. Knowing the story helps to determine when one should vary these elements. For example, one can lower the voice to a whisper at an exciting part of the action. One might even stop reading completely to allow the children to think about what is happening for a moment. Reading slowly helps the children use their imaginations to keep up with the story. Speeding up during certain parts where the action picks up can have them sitting on the edge of their seats.

When the reader is excited about the story, the feeling is usually contagious. An enthusiastic reader provides a good role model for experiencing the fun of literature. Such enthusiasm can be achieved by carefully choosing the books to be read aloud. There is no substitute for selecting books that both the reader and the children like. Humorous books are good beginning choices, as the humor provides a built-in motivation. As reading aloud becomes a practice, varying story themes and plots will provide children with the opportunity to experience all types of literature, possibly including riddle books, poetry, and more serious stories.

TIPS FOR TEACHERS

Invite active or retired police officers, doctors, athletes, and firefighters to read stories aloud to children.
- *A weaver could read* Abuela's Weave.
- *A farmer could read* Barnyard Banter.
- *A police officer could read* Tough Boris.
- *A health-care worker could read* Ten Little Babies.

Use the language of the read-aloud books to promote good language and language growth. Talk about some of the phrases and sentences the author uses. This encourages children to use language provided by good models. While good books can usually be read in their entirety, one should not be afraid to summarize or paraphrase some parts of the story so as to adjust a more difficult book to the audience, to recapture the children's interest, or to better assist the children in understanding a story.

Good Choices for Read-Alouds

Most children's picture books were meant to be read aloud. This does not mean, of course, that every picture book can be read aloud successfully. In addition to the usual criteria for selecting books for children, some additional elements might be considered for books to be read aloud.

The choice of a good read-aloud book will depend somewhat on the age of the children. Infants benefit from books with clear, colorful illustrations and little text. They also enjoy short, simple rhymes and poems. Large pictures and pictures of familiar scenes are enjoyed after the reading is done. Books that encourage the naming of objects, letters, and numbers are also good selections because they often contain familiar sights and sounds.

Author/illustrator Thor Wickstrom. Photo credit: Walter Sawyer.

Toddlers are ready for more sophisticated rhymes and stories. They especially like books with predictable repeated lines. They enjoy the feeling of mastery in joining in and saying the lines after the first couple of repetitions. For example, consider the story of "The Farmer in the Dell." As both a story and a song, its familiar lines are quickly mastered by the young child.

Toddlers also like books that describe mischievous antics of characters to whom they can relate. A sense of the absurd is found in many Dr. Seuss books. This type of humor is often an effective device for involving the independent-two-year old. Lois Lenski and Mercer Mayer have written several small books that toddlers feel are just their size. Many of their books are about toddlers' favorite big people such as cowboys and firemen.

Preschoolers and kindergartners are ready for more involved plots and a wider range of themes. Humor is still a good choice. Arnold Lobel's *Frog and Toad Are Friends* creates a world where the humor is more subtle and where human nature shines through. Adventure stories become an area of interest at this age. An adventure story with a twist is Eugene Trivizas' *The Three Little Wolves and the Big Bad Pig,* an upside-down retelling of the traditional folk tale. The humorous updating includes sledge hammers, pneumatic drills, and steel-reinforced concrete. Using repeated lines and phrases from the original, the tale comes to a harmonious conclusion. *Tough Boris* by Mem Fox is an absolute treasure. It is an easy-to-read tale of Boris, a scruffy pirate who is tender enough to weep when his parrot dies. The book is filled with the pirate lore of buried treasure, thievery, and the adventures of being marooned on an island. Young children will identify with the story development through the illustrations.

In *My Working Mom* by Peter Glassman, readers see what an adventure it would be to grow up in a house where the mother is a kind but mischievous witch.

David Novak, "A Telling Experience." Courtesy David Novak, storyteller.

The setting is an unlikely suburban house full of cauldrons, toads, and bats. An adventure in the big city is featured in *The Big Night Out* by Thor Wickstrom. The author/illustrator's expressive watercolors and bouncy rhyme move the story along at a brisk pace. *Tim and the Blanket Thief* by John Prater uses a dream device to present a mystery with a touch of danger. A mysterious shadowy figure comes in the night and steals Tim's special blanket. Tim gives chase and emerges as a hero at the end. It is a good choice for beginning discussions about imagination and prized possessions. *Dancing with the Indians* by Angela Shelf Medearis creates an adventure that combines African-American and native American cultures. The colorful illustrations and the tale told in verse make it a good selection for reading aloud. An excellent choice for a read-aloud book at bedtime might be Anthony Browne's *Willy and Hugh,* in which lonely Willy's new friendship with High gives him good reason to look forward to tomorrow.

Identifying good read-aloud books is not a difficult task. Knowing the children is the first priority. The next is to use the criteria for good literature in selecting appropriate books. After identifying which books will best lend themselves to an exciting and enjoyable read-aloud experience, the reader must review them to determine just how the story will be read. If this is not done, the reading will not be as effective as it could be, and a good deal of potential will be wasted.

Becoming familiar with a large number of books is the best way to prepare oneself for read-aloud experiences. Having this knowledge of books will enable the

Storytelling connects the generations in a comfortable yet powerful manner.

reader to choose the right book at the right time for a read-aloud activity. The reader should always have a set of well-planned read-aloud books to use when the need arises. The special sharing that will occur as a result will be an effective "commercial" for reading. Read-alouds that do not possess an air of excitement will pose the risk of losing children to some other activity that may seem more interesting. Once their interest is lost, it may be difficult to bring these children back.

STORYTELLING

In most cultures throughout time, the storyteller was a valuable member of the community. In the preliterary world, storytellers were the keepers of the culture. They were both the newspaper of the present and the link to the people's past. They were often the honored guests of kings and queens. As literacy increased, storytellers lost some of their importance. In regions of the world with high illiteracy rates, storytellers continue to hold a position of esteem.

Good storytellers will always hold the power to enchant. They help us to reflect upon our lives, make us laugh, and make us cry. A professional storyteller is both a performing artist and a careful student of literature. Some specialize in a certain type of presentation, using a dialect from a particular region, songs, or costumes. Others focus on certain subject matter such as African tales, humor, or stories of the sea. They may also combine some of these elements to create a new style unique to themselves.

How to Be a Storyteller

The skill and talent of professional storytellers are wonderful to see and hear. However, their services usually cannot be scheduled very frequently. Since almost anyone can become at least an amateur storyteller—the oral sharing of stories is an old tradition—it makes sense to learn some storytelling methods.

One of the best ways to learn the craft of the storyteller is to hear how practicing storytellers go about their work. Aili Paal Singer, a New England storyteller, has a background in teaching, writing, and performing. Along with storytelling, she also works in theater and television. Her presentations include the use of puppetry, mime, and acting. She provides activities and materials designed to involve the children in the stories. Figures 6–1 to 6–4 provide a glimpse into the mind of Ms. Singer as she describes how she approaches her work. Also included are two of her short pieces for sharing.

Another New England storyteller, Doug Lipman, also has a background in teaching, writing, and performing. In addition, he has been involved in music and working with children with disabilities. His presentations include a good deal of active participation and singing. The stories he presents often deal with the themes of African tales, Hasidism, equality of the sexes, and superheroes. He believes that stories should have real content and say something to us as human beings. In Figure 6–5 Doug Lipman shares his ideas for sharing children's stories by using a participatory approach.

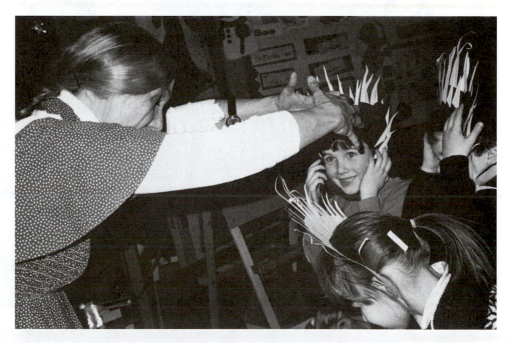

Figure 6–1. Aili Paal Singer demonstrates how to be a tree in a story by using the entire body to play the role. Courtesy Diana Comer.

Figure 6–2. Aili Paal Singer sets the scene for her African story with props such as a drum. Courtesy Diana Comer.

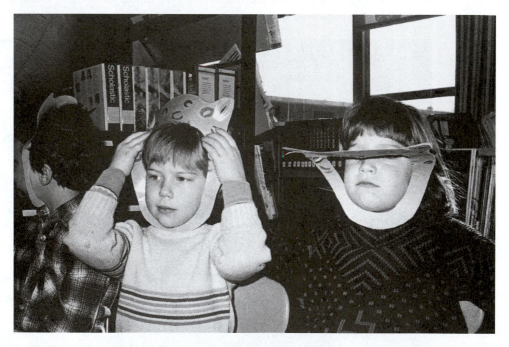

Figure 6–3. Aili Paal Singer uses children with masks as an integral part of her stories. This participation can help the shy child take a more active role in a class. Courtesy Diana Comer.

Figure 6–4. Aili Paal Singer and the children become the story. Courtesy Diana Comer.

I like to tell stories which allow students to join me in acting out the characters and events. Children have often asked me to tell a story in which everyone in the class can participate.

It isn't easy to find a ready made story that could offer parts for 53 people (2 classes of 25 children, 2 teachers, and a storyteller). That is what I was looking for. Fortunately, I found one when I read the African folklore "The King's Drum" in *A Treasury of African Folklore* by Harold Courlander (Crown Publishers, 1975). Though I would retell it and adapt it, I knew it would work well with younger children.

I proceeded to design and construct 53 masks out of various weight colored construction paper: a lion, a monkey, a spider, leopards, giraffes, porcupines, elephants, antelopes. I wanted the children to be able to watch everything without obstruction, so I chose to make the mask surround an opening for the face.

These designs were then adapted to more practical sized masks, for 8 1/2″ by 11″ paper, which I could give out as a follow-up art activity for students.

"What good is it to make a mask if you can't use it?" I asked myself. So, I sat down to write some little stories that could be read and acted out. They contained only the animal characters for which I had masks. These stories were included in my Program Guide for teachers as follow-up material.

Reprinted with permission from NOTES: THE KING'S DRUM © 1988, Aili Paal Singer.

Characters: LIONS LEOPARDS PORCUPINES ANTELOPES GIRAFFES

The neighborhood was quiet and all the animals were asleep.
But the Lions began snoring with sounds loud and deep.

The Leopards woke up and began to complain.
The Porcupines called out, "You sound like a train!"

The Antelopes screamed, "Quiet down, please!"
The Giraffes jumped up startled, and ran to the trees.

They galloped with hooves pounding hard on the ground.
The Lions slept on without hearing a sound.

In the morning, they yawned, smiled and said.
"How nice it is to get a good night's sleep in one's bed."

When the families of Leopard, Porcupine, Antelope and Giraffe
Heard what the Lions said, they had a good laugh.

Reprinted with permission from THE QUIET NIGHT © 1988, Aili Paal Singer

Characters: ANTELOPE FAMILY GIRAFFE

The Antelope family was taking a walk.

Giraffe was standing tall, eating the top leaves of a tree.
Antelope's children pointed to Giraffe.
They giggled and said.
     "What a funny long neck and such skinny legs!"

Giraffe looked down and said,
     "I see Lion coming down the path behind the tree."
He then ran away as fast as the wind.
Antelope's family leaped all the way home.

The next day, the Antelope family again took a walk.

Giraffe was eating the top leaves of a tree.
Antelope's children pointed to Giraffe.
They said, "What a fine long neck, and a great pair of legs!"

Reprinted with permission from ANTELOPE'S CHILDREN, © 1988, Aili Paal Singer.

Figure 6–5. Doug Lipman tells a story through voice, movement, and props.

Any story can be made into a participation story. In general, the audience may participate by joining in with their voices or with their bodies, or by making suggestions.

Join in with the Voice

In the riddle story "In Summer I Die," the audience joins in verbally by repeating rhythmic, chant-like speech: e.g., "Mama, mama, wake up, we're bored." This is the easiest way to join in with the voice, because rhythmic speech has simpler, more predictable rhythms than normal speech.

One step beyond rhythmic speech is singing; the only difference between rhythmic speech and song is the presence of melody. If teller and audience can be induced to sing, it adds to the fun and the mood. If one or the other is too shy, though, or the words are too minor to warrant melody, we may be better to chant than to give up on all rhythm.

Once the audience has heard a story or a phrase several times, they can join in by filling in missing words. To cue an audience for this, we can start a sentence they have heard before, but stop before the end. Our gestures and face indicate that they are to continue. For example, the storyteller begins:

In summer I . . .

and stops, mouth open, gesture stopped mid-air, with an expression of expectancy; and the audience chimes in:

. . . die.

A special case of filling in words is filling in sound effects. For example, "we rang the doorbell, and it went . . . "

Figure 6–5 continued

All these forms of verbal participation can be varied or intensified by saying them in different tones of voice, repeating them, or repeating them with additions, as in a cumulative story.

Join in with the Body

Younger children often find it less threatening to join in with movements than with words; older children and adults often find movements more threatening. Depending on the age of our audience, therefore, movements may become a tool for winning our audience, or a sign that we have already succeeded in gaining their attention and trust.

Rhythmic movements, such as those to accompany the refrain *"Mama, mama, wake up, I'm bored,"* or the rhyme *"In summer I die . . . ,"* are a natural accompaniment to rhythmic speech. Simple miming of a motion, such as knocking on a door or shaking a sleeping person, can be added almost anywhere to snag the wandering attention of preschoolers. These actions become central to the story if they are repeated at different points with different feeling or with a sense of growing urgency or silliness.

Body participation can also include postures. For example, we could ask our audience to "show me how you'd sit if you were bored." Or: "How would you stand if you had just figured out the answer to Grandmother's riddle?" When we say things in a particular posture, by the way, it often affects our tone of voice.

The furthest extreme of body participation is to actually enact a part of the story. Enactment can be done by a whole group at once, all acting out one part after another—or by small groups or individuals taking on separate roles.

Figure 6–6. Doug Lipman brings a story to a dramatic conclusion.

Make Suggestions

Up until now, we, the teller, have made all the choices, and the audience has been invited only to follow along. We can also, however, invite the audience to participate by adding their own point of view, and giving suggestions.

From the teller's perspective, the easiest form of suggestions to manage are "advisory only": suggestions that are not incorporated into the story. For example, we could ask, "What would you do if you were bored and no one else was awake?" After listening to a few answers, our story continues as planned all along. This allows audience members to express their thoughts, and involves them internally in the situation the character faces. It encourages spontaneity from the audience. And yet it allows the teller to preserve the carefully learned and rehearsed sequence of the story.

At the opposite extreme, we can throw open the gate of the story for the audience to find its own way through. A round-robin story is the result. The teller, of course, can still retain the role of shepherd:

"And what do you suppose we did, since we were so bored?"
                    Audience: watched TV.
"So we turned on the TV. What was on?"
                    Audience: Batman!
"Seeing Batman made us think of something in our back yard. What was it?"
                    Audience: our toy Batmobile.
"So we went outside to play in our toy Batmobile. But suddenly we saw something very useful. What do you think it was? . . . "

Between the extreme of no audience control and complete audience control, of course, there are still more middle positions. To give the audience some influence over the story, we can incorporate their suggestions into minor details of the story. For example, we can ask what kind of a house we lived in. Were there steps leading up to the front door? What did we have to cross to get to our friend's house? These details can then be incorporated into the story immediately: "So we climbed down the steps, across the playground, waited for a green light, looked both ways, then crossed the street." But we have to remember these details if they are relevant later: "Then we ran back with the icicles, waited for the green light, looked both ways, crossed the street, ran across the playground, and climbed back up the steps of our house."

The audience suggestions in "In Summer I Die" influence more of the plot than simple details would, but are still contained in a predictable framework. The choice of whom to wake up next stimulates a whole new cycle of waking, chanting, and reacting, but it loops us right back to the same point in the plot: "So we went to find someone else. . . ." The teller decides when to break out of that loop and go on to Grandmother.

A similar loop is repeated later, when the audience suggests what we saw next, and the teller helps compare it to the riddle: "A carrot! What a great idea. So we opened the refrigerator, pulled open the bottom drawer, and took out a carrot. Maybe this is it! Does it die in the summer? . . ." Again, the teller decides when to break out of that loop by taking us outdoors to play with the snow—and when to enter it again to guess outdoor things or the icicle itself.

A Balance of Participation

Any story can be made participatory, by just including some of the techniques described above. The teller's biggest job, though, is to find the right balance: too little participation, and a younger audience loses attention, or we lose an opportunity for fun and feedback; too much, or the wrong kind of participation, and the story itself suffers. A story with too much participation feels "gimicky," and its central triumph becomes obscured. As adapters or creators of stories, we strive to choose the techniques of participation—and the places to use them—that will clarify a story's structure and events, and heighten its emotional impact.

To choose well, we need to be aware of all of our options. Voice, body, suggestions: these three words can remind us of the many choices we have.

Reprinted with permission from General Hints for Making Stories Participatory, *© 1985, Doug Lipman.*

Good Choices for Oral Storytelling

Almost any story that meets the criteria for good literature is a possibility for oral storytelling. It is important to be aware of the fact that this method of sharing is more difficult than reading aloud. In reading aloud, the readers can rely on the book to provide the language. In oral storytelling, readers must put some of themselves and their language into the presentation. The story must be a part of the storyteller's imagination. It would not be effective for one to forget the story at midpoint and to begin reading from the book. The spell of the storyteller would be broken.

It is best to select stories with clear, strong characters. This is especially true if one wishes the children to participate. The setting should be fairly simple in order for children to picture it in their imaginations. Stories with interesting narratives and lines for choral responses by the children are good choices. When children are involved, they are more likely to continue following the story. Finally, the story should be fascinating to the storyteller so that it will generate a natural enthusiasm.

Most storytellers interpret a work before using it. This means that they make some decisions about what the story means, what it is useful for, and how this can be brought out in the telling. They make decisions concerning each character, such as the costumes, voice, and actions to be used. They make decisions about the length of time needed for the story, the portions of the story to be summarized or lengthened, and ways to increase the interest and value of the story. They also make decisions about the audience: the appropriateness of the story for the expected audience, the degree of audience participation planned, and the needs of the audience.

TIPS FOR TEACHERS

Invite members of a community theater group to demonstrate oral storytelling.
- *Show how different animal characters might move and talk.*
- *Combine actors and children in the telling of a story.*
- *Have actors involve children in demonstrating different uses of the voice in telling a story.*

FLANNELBOARD STORIES

A variation of storytelling is the flannelboard story. A flannelboard is a piece of wood or other rigid material covered with felt or flannel. Characters and objects cut from felt are placed on the flannelboard to portray the visual action of the story as it is being told. While the story may be read from a book, the additional task of manipulating pieces on the flannelboard suggests that an oral presentation would be easier.

Flannelboard stories can be easy and fun to make. A small group of adults can cut the necessary pieces for several stories in a short work session. Once made, they are available for years. The story can be adapted to different age groups by simplifying or elaborating on the plot. New pieces can be added for new plot twists.

Making Flannelboard Materials

The basic components for flannelboard stories are the flannelboard itself and the pictures of the characters and other objects involved in the story that are to be placed on the flannelboard.

Flannelboard. Although they can be purchased commercially, flannelboards are relatively easy to make. Constructing one's own allows the board to be made in a variety of sizes and shapes. First, the backing is cut from thick cardboard, plywood, masonite, acrylic plastic, or any other flat, rigid material. It is then covered with either flannel or felt. Several styles are shown in Figure 6–6.

Besides a basic straight design, one might consider a teepee or tent design. Either two separate boards can be joined at the top, or a single board can be folded over. This design provides two flannelboard surfaces, allowing a story scene to remain in place over time if desired. A three-sided design provides even more flexibility. If space is limited, one might wish to consider a window shade flannel board. The shade is covered with the flannel and mounted with brackets on a wall. The wall provides the rigid surface. Animal-shaped flannelboards lend a whimsical touch. They might be used for units using a variety of animal books.

Characters and Objects. As with flannelboards, the pictures used on the flannelboard can come from a variety of sources. Sets of flannelboard objects, characters, letters, and numbers can be purchased commercially. Such a set may be a good basis upon which to build a collection of additional characters and objects. The most common material from which to make the pieces is felt. It is thicker and more sturdy than flannel, though the latter is often used. Other materials, such as clothes dryer softener sheets, sandpaper, velcro, and double-faced carpet tape, can also be used. Pictures hand-colored or cut from magazines can be glued to flannel or felt pieces as well. Or felt pieces can be painted.

A flannelboard story library will eventually emerge. The pieces required for a particular book and a copy of the book can be stored together in a plastic storage bag or a heavy envelope. In this way, flannelboard stories can be used without the collecting or making the necessary pieces each time the story is shared.

How to Share Flannelboard Stories

As with any story sharing procedure, planning is a key element. The story should be carefully selected and known to the teller. It should be reviewed before it is used. Even if the story is familiar, one can momentarily forget the next part of the action. Such a pause can cause a disruption to the flow of the story.

The pieces needed to tell the story should be lined up in the order they are to be used. This will eliminate the need to search for a missing piece halfway through the story. With a flannelboard story, remembering to maintain eye contact with the audience is important. It is easy to forget to do this after adding a piece

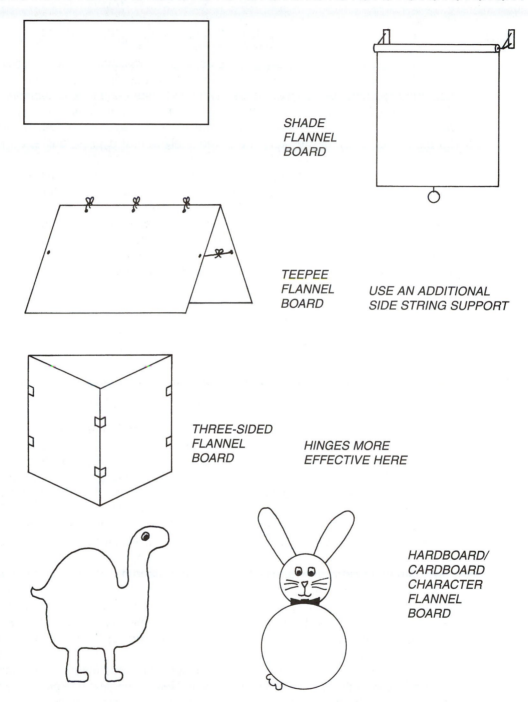

FIGURE 6–7. Flannelboard designs can be simple or complex. Either way, they belong in every early childhood classroom. Courtesy Diana Comer.

to the board. Eye contact is helpful in keeping the attention of the children. It also ensures that the children will hear the teacher's voice.

Telling a flannelboard story a bit slower than normal storytelling speed keeps the story suspenseful and fun. If things occur too quickly, the presentation can become confusing. Children are expected to both listen and look to experience a flannelboard story. By taking one's time, adding sly expressions and poignant pauses, one can increase the impact of the story. However, the pace should not be slow enough to let the story drag; and lively verbal expressions and movements are beneficial only when they are appropriate to the story.

Encouraging interaction will draw the children into the story. Follow the first telling with a retelling of the story by the children. Distribute character and object pieces to children for the retelling. Allow the children to add the correct pieces as the story requires them. A second retelling may be done if the group is larger. Leave the flannelboard up and the pieces out for a time. Allow the children to retell or create new stories after reading time. When children engage in this kind of activity, they are re-creating their learning and experiencing their language.

Good Choices for Flannelboard Stories

The best stories for flannelboards are those in which there is a clear progression of events or characters. This progression allows the teller to add characters and objects as the tale is told. A good example is *The Napping House* by Audrey Wood. The story begins with a sleeping grandmother during a bad storm. As the action progresses, she is joined in the cozy bed by an assortment of other characters. The beautifully illustrated book contains a wonderful surprise ending. One might wish to follow up the reading of the book with an oral retelling using a flannelboard. Children delight in the hands-on fun of adding characters to the bed.

If You Give a Moose a Muffin by Laura Numeroff lends itself to a flannelboard retelling because each page builds humorously on the preceding page. The absurdity of the situation maintains the humor and interest of children. *Traveling to Tondo: A Tale of the Nkundo of Zaire* by Verna Aardema follows a group of four characters as they encounter a series of silly situations that obstruct their trip. A content book on the days of the week that can be done on a flannelboard is *Today Is Monday* by Eric Carle. Using a color copy machine, the distinctive colorful pictures can be copied, cut out, glued onto felt, and used as pictures for the flannelboard. Using an old rhyme, Ted Arnold creates a familiar-sounding story well suited to flannelboard retelling in *No More Jumping on the Bed*. The tale follows a jumper going from apartment to apartment in a series of humorous situations. Turning the flannelboard so that the longer side is vertical for the retelling would add to the foolishness of the situation.

Strega Nona by Tomie dePaola can make a hilarious flannelboard story. In this book, Big Anthony attempts to use Strega Nona's magic pasta pot. Not knowing how to control the magic, he quickly lets things get out of hand. Pasta ends up everywhere. White felt pieces with white yarn "spaghetti" glued on should provide a good picture of the problem on a flannelboard.

Strega Nona *by author/illustrator Tomie dePaola.* (c)1975; reprinted by permission of the publisher, Simon and Schuster Books for Young Readers.

Usually one can tell on a first reading whether or not a book will make a good flannelboard story. The best stories are those where characters and objects are added gradually. Their addition should be closely related to the problem the plot is exploring. If nothing is added or removed as the story goes along, the flannelboard is little more than a still picture.

THEATRICAL STORYTELLING

Everyone likes to see a show performed on stage. The excitement surrounding a performance creates a magic of its own. Even if done on a very small scale, it is a special event. Using a theatrical performance also provides an opportunity to teach children the schema, or procedure, for going to the theater. Before a performance begins, the children can practice the roles of ticket sellers, ushers, announcers, concession stand clerks, and audience.

There are several possible avenues for telling a story using a theatrical framework. The two explored here are puppetry and creative dramatics. Each has strengths and drawbacks. Each works best with a different type of story.

Puppetry

Most children love puppets. They are an enjoyable and easy way to enhance or interpret a story for children. Infants, of course, may not quite know what to make of a puppet the first time they see one. If presented with slow, deliberate movements and a soft voice, however, puppets are usually welcome additions to a young child's surroundings.

Puppets can be safe imaginary friends. Most adults as well as children seem to respond instinctively to them. Shy children will often speak to a puppet before they will speak to an unknown person. Children know that the puppet is not real.

They know that it is the person holding the puppet who is actually speaking. Yet, the puppet has a reality of its own. Children speak to the puppet without reservation. They don't have to talk as though they are talking to the adult holding the puppet.

Puppets are allowed to be all of the things that people might like to be at times. They can be naughty, silly, brave, and mean. Perhaps that is why children speak to puppets so freely; they feel that puppets will accept them because they understand about not being perfect.

TIPS FOR TEACHERS

Ask parents to donate any puppets they may have but are no longer using at home.
• Use a puppet to tell a story with you.
• Have students talk to each other through the puppets.
• Provide puppets during free play to encourage language play and the re-creation of stories.

Since puppets make such good friends, it makes sense to use them in a variety of story sharing activities. Purple monster puppets can help teach the color purple. A monkey puppet can motivate, comment, and ask questions when H.A. and Margaret Rey's books about Curious George the monkey are used. If it seems appropriate, stories can even be told by puppets. This is especially true for fables, since they usually only have two or three characters.

How to Use Puppets. There are no specific rules for using puppets. They can be used to motivate, tell the story, or take part in the story. It is mostly a matter of the teacher trying a variety of procedures and learning what is comfortable. One of the best ways to continue enthusiasm for puppets is to use a variety of puppet types. Although puppets can always be purchased commercially, some of the most interesting ones are homemade. Figure 6–8 illustrates some of the possibilities for making puppets.

Finger puppets are easily constructed from the cut-off fingers of a glove. Facial features can be painted or glued on. Stick puppets are simple and easy to make as well. The puppet can be a photograph or drawing of a character glued onto a stick. Even a story with several characters can be converted to puppets by using child-created pictures or pictures made with a photocopier. The sticks used can be tongue depressors, craft sticks, straws, rulers, or sticks found in the yard.

String puppets are usually made by older children, but even younger ones enjoy making simple versions of these puppets. They are two- or three-dimensional puppets connected with two or more strings to a cross stick or sticks. For more sophisticated designs, the sticks are held above the puppet. The sticks and strings control the puppet's body parts. Rag dolls can be used as well.

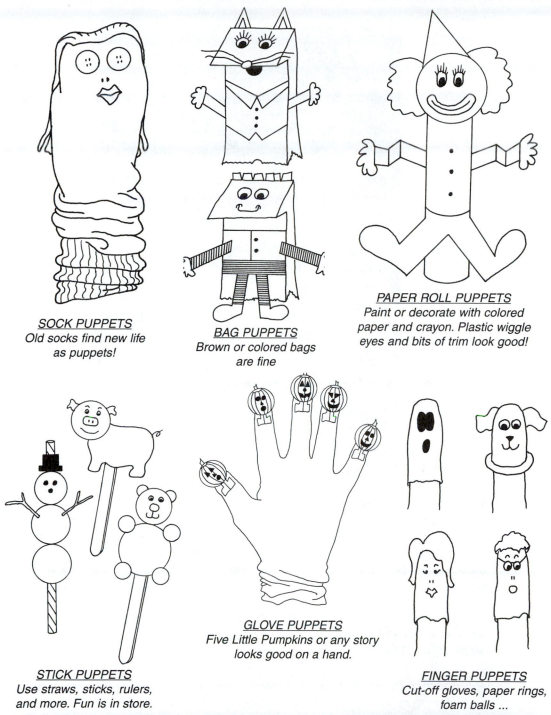

SOCK PUPPETS
*Old socks find new life
as puppets!*

BAG PUPPETS
*Brown or colored bags
are fine*

PAPER ROLL PUPPETS
*Paint or decorate with colored
paper and crayon. Plastic wiggle
eyes and bits of trim look good!*

STICK PUPPETS
*Use straws, sticks, rulers,
and more. Fun is in store.*

GLOVE PUPPETS
*Five Little Pumpkins or any story
looks good on a hand.*

FINGER PUPPETS
*Cut-off gloves, paper rings,
foam balls ...*

*Figure 6–8. Puppet designs do not have to be complicated. A simple puppet can still make
a story memorable. Courtesy Diana Comer.*

Children use toys as puppets as they re-create stories through play. Courtesy Diana Comer.

Effectively using puppets requires a knowledge of things one should not do with puppets. Do not try to be a ventriloquist. When not done expertly, ventriloquism is distracting. Do not use too much body movement. Enthusiasm is important, but too much hand waving detracts from the words of the puppet. Do not distribute puppets to children without planning and guidance. The puppets will simply become toys to fight over. Do not expect puppets to do it all. Most stories require a combination of puppets and a narrator. Do not be afraid to take risks with new and different kinds of puppets. Children tend to be uncritical of puppets, even when one doesn't work out as well as expected. The audience usually loves the show before it begins.

Beginning Puppetry. Trying anything new can make one anxious. Getting accustomed to using puppets is no exception. Start small, build confidence in your ability, and then expand. Encourage children to explore the range of possibilities for using puppets, too.

Finger puppets help to tell a story. Courtesy Diana Comer.

Begin by seating the children in front of a mirror so that they can see both the puppet and themselves. Practice emotions by having the puppet look sad while saying, "I lost my favorite teddy bear." Make the puppet look angry while saying, "I'll NEVER go to bed until I'm two hundred years old!"

Get used to the idea of puppets handling dialogue by using two play telephones. Give one to the puppet, and have the children take turns using the other. Allow the script to emerge spontaneously. Have a puppet on one phone with a child and a puppet on the other. Another way to become comfortable with puppet dialogue is to have the puppet lead a game such as Simon Says. Use motions at first and then follow up with lines such as "Simon says, 'Say meatball' . . . Simon says, 'Say curly caterpillar.' "

The children will expand the possibilities with the right coaching. For example, have several children each hold a puppet at snack time. Explain that each puppet has to take a turn commenting on the snack and answering questions asked by the other puppets. Other scenarios can be used as well: discussions about playground behaviors, getting in line, and so on. When all are comfortable with their skills, it is time to use puppets to tell and re-create stories.

Good Choices for Puppetry. The best kinds of stories for puppet presentations are those with a simple plot and only a few main characters. Since stage settings can be difficult, a few simple props must make the story a reality for the children. *The Carrot Seed* by Ruth Krauss makes a good puppet show. The boy, the sun, the rain, and the ever growing carrot are all that are needed. Any boy puppet would do. A paper-plate sun, a hand-drawn rain cloud, and a real carrot would complete the primary roles. The real carrot can be pushed up from behind the stage as the story unfolds. Cut out shapes of the sun and the cloud, with mouths and eyes drawn on, can become starring characters.

In Gerald McDermott's *Raven,* the main character steals the sun from the sky chief so that it can be given to the earth people. This native American myth from the Northwest can be told with puppets of the raven, the sky chief, and the

Child-staged puppet shows provide both language and sharing opportunities.
Courtesy Diana Comer.

sun chief's daughter. Props such as a bright red ball for the sun could also be used. As a related project, children could make stick puppets so that they could retell the story at home.

Five characters and one machine make *Rain Forest* by Helen Cowcher well suited for puppetry. The bright, colorful rain forest animals flee the approach of the machinery destroying their home. The tale ends on an environmentally appropriate note. Since the rain forest is full of animals, each child can have a part in a whole group retelling. The teacher might need to take the part of the machine, since children might shy away from the role.

Tomie dePaola's *Charlie Needs a Cloak* is a superb story for a puppet presentation. It is the story of a shepherd who finds that his old faithful cloak is too tattered and worn to keep him warm in the winter anymore. He spends the following spring and summer shearing, spinning, weaving, dyeing, and sewing wool into a new cloak. By the following autumn he is ready to face the winter in a new warm red cloak. The story can be told with a boy puppet, one or two sheep puppets, and a few scraps of yarn and fabric. A story that presents similar themes of weaving and making cloth, *Abuela's Weave* by Omar Castaneda, can also be told through puppetry.

Denise Fleming's book, *Barnyard Banter,* will delight you children as an interactive puppet story. In the story, all the farm animals make their unique sounds from the appropriate locations, such as cows mooing in the barn and crows cawing in the cornfield.

Another animal book for puppetry is Nancy Carlson's *Take Time to Relax.* In this tale, Tina the beaver and her parents are always rushing through their busy lives. When they become house-bound by a snowstorm, they come to enjoy the freedom to relax.

◎ Creative Dramatics

Creative dramatics is only a bit more structured than puppetry. This type of drama is not designed for the production of a play for an audience. Rather, it is a more spontaneous process aimed at communicating some message, emotion, or story using dramatic techniques. It seeks to increase sensitivity to the feelings of others, to build positive self-concepts, to increase confidence and concentration, to provide new relationships, and to build an appreciation of the arts.[2] Creative dramatics includes pantomime, mime, and acting to create and re-create ideas and stories.

Why is drama such a powerful tool? Why is it so effective for helping children develop language and an understanding of themselves? Drama is a natural activity for most children. Their play is often a suspension of reality that allows them to explore the possibilities of their environments. When children delve into dramatic play, they cross the line between reality and fantasy. Yet, they are still aware of reality. This allows children to become astronauts, dinosaur hunters, parents, and buildings. Because it is play, children can easily move among the roles of cowboy, firefighter, and medical doctor. They possess a total belief in their roles at the moment they are in those roles. Such an emotional commitment is achieved because of the child's attention and focus when involved in dramatic play.

How to Use Creative Dramatics. The guiding rule for using creative dramatics is to keep things simple. This rule applies to dialogue, characters, setting, and plot. In contrast to puppetry, a creative dramatics format can include everyone. Each child is not a main character, but each can be included as a fourth little pig, another stepsister, or as one of the sheep in a story. Everyone can help move furniture props, paint a chimney for a Santa Claus story, and bring in old clothes for costumes. If everyone is emotionally involved, the effort and enthusiasm will be contagious.

The dialogue may be created or spontaneous. If a chorus line is to be repeated several times, have a group of children do it rather than just a single child. The group will provide security for each of its members. Use a narrator if needed to help the dialogue flow more smoothly.

Costumes can give a feeling of importance to children taking part in the drama. Costumes can be real clothing, old Halloween outfits, yard sale leftovers, and old uniforms. They are relatively easy to collect, and any classroom can quickly accumulate an adequate variety. Help children use their imaginations in using costumes. They do not have to find the entire outfit to play the role. An old army hat and a dark jacket make an airline pilot. A hat with ears attached, brown mittens, and a piece of rope can make a cat. A white shirt and a headband with a round silver foil disc create a doctor's outfit. With just these bits and pieces of costumes available, imagination will do the rest.

[2] Sawyer, W., & Leff, A. (1982). Elementary school creative dramatics: Coming to your senses. In N. Brizendine & J. Thomas (Eds.). (1982). *Learning through dramatics: Ideas for teachers and librarians* (pp. 29–32). Phoenix, AZ: Oryx.

Settings should be simple. If scenery is absolutely essential, a single sheet can be painted or drawn on with markers for a backdrop. Figure 6–9 illustrates two ways to create a scene. Small setting pieces can be cut out of cardboard and painted. They may be free standing or simply leaned against a chair or a wall.

Props are objects needed to help tell the story. They may include pails, brooms, chairs, crowns, and food items. Props should be minimal and need not be real objects. Play telephones or bananas cut from yellow construction paper work just as well as the real thing. Follow the lead of the children. They will spontaneously engage in dramatic play with the barest of props.

Good Choices for Creative Dramatics. Mother Goose stories and nursery rhymes make a great introduction to creative dramatics. They can be portrayed quite easily with a minimum of costumes and props. Poems and songs can be dramatized with a minimum amount of preparation as well.

Good possibilities for dramatization include stories with many parts or groups of characters, enabling varying numbers of children to have an involvement in the experience. Humorous stories and stories with action and suspense make good choices. *Corduroy* by Don Freeman is a wonderful story about a bear searching for a friend. The book has roles that are expandable, since the setting is a department store. It has a great ending and makes a good play.

Cloudy with a Chance of Meatballs by Judi Barrett is a very funny book that could become a very funny play. The story takes place in a land where it rains various kinds of food. Naturally, something goes wrong, and a solution to the problem must be found. In one part of the land, it rains meatballs as big as basketballs. Make-believe meatballs, dropping out of a net from the ceiling, could be made from balloons covered with brown paper. The story would not soon be forgotten.

Legends, fairy tales, and folk tales make good plays because they combine magic, mystery, and action. *A Friend for Dragon* by Dav Pilkey combines elements from fairy tales and ideas important to young children. His unique resolutions to the plots are easily re-created in drama. Julie Lane's *The Life and Adventures of Santa Claus* is a book with a number of dramatic possibilities. Set in the Baltic Sea region of Europe, it recounts the early life of Santa Claus. It captures the old world flavor of early Christmas celebrations. Children are fascinated with knowing more about the life of one of their favorite characters.

Current children's literature has much to offer as well. Many stories meet the requirements for creative dramatics: appropriate numbers of characters, simple plots, memorable dialogue, and few prop requirements. *The Pig in the Pond* by Martin Waddell can be dramatized indoors in the winter using beanbag chairs, or outdoors in summer using a wading pool. The story takes place on the very hottest day of the summer. Mr. Neligan's pig is so envious of the ducks that it decides to jump into the pond as well. The other animals are in an uproar until Mr. Neligan comes home, sees what has happened, sheds his own clothes, and jumps into the pond as well. A bit more challenging a story would be *The Bigness Contest* by Florence Perry Heide, the story of Beasley, a lazy hippopotamus who

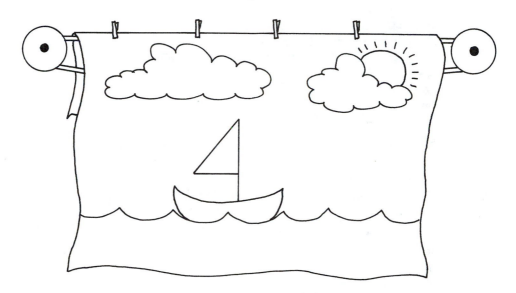

Figure 6–9. Quick and easy stage settings can be created using a sheet placed over a pole (top) or attached to a rope with clothespin. (bottom). Courtesy Diana Comer.

seeks recognition without expending a great deal of effort. The game of Hide-and-Seek is the basis for *Do You See Mouse?* by Marion Crume, featuring a brief narrative and Normand Chartier's endearing watercolor illustrations. The action of the story will be gleefully reenacted by young children. *Ten Little Babies* by Robert Priest is a story told through a poem. The repeating line will have children joining in by the second or third page. It can be done with even young children, since they will be able to participate with only a narrator reading the book.

Content can also be easily incorporated into the dramatization. Many tales set in other cultures provide a natural base to learn about those cultures. *Galimoto* by Karen William, set in Malawi, Africa, is about a boy who wishes to make a galimoto (a car made from wires) for the parade of galimotos. He must trade and work to make his galimoto. Children can create props by crafting their own galimotos from pipe cleaners and other materials. *I Am Eyes, Ni Macho* by Leila Ward is also set in Africa. It incorporates many of the continent's animals. *Tree of Cranes* by Allen Say demonstrates how two cultures, American and Japanese, celebrate Christmas. The friendship tree in the story can be used to expand the story, and can be decorated with the symbols of other cultures as well. For toddlers and preschoolers learning basic concepts and objects, an adaptation of *We're Going on a Bear Hunt* by Michael Rosen and Helen Oxenbury is just the thing. It can be told with or without props and scenery.

TIPS FOR TEACHERS

Respond positively to children's attempts to re-create favorite stories through drama.
- Say, "What a wonderful story you just told."
- Comment, "That was a very scary bear you created."
- Watch and listen attentively as children re-create a scene from a story for you.

Dramatic play is spontaneous. Creative dramatics takes some planning, but it can be done more spontaneously than putting on a play. The line between the two can be wide and hazy. The positive results of a dramatic experience are well worth the effort; this type of drama is supportive of children's efforts and is a

Another Mouse to Feed *by Robert Kraus.* (c)1980; reprinted by permission of the publisher, Simon and Schuster Books for Young Readers.

memorable experience for them. They learn much about life from the pretend situations found in books and made real through creative dramatics. They get to act out their feelings and can experiment with their reactions to situations. Creative dramatics gives a shy child the opportunity to safely take some risks, while allowing the aggressive child to take on the role of a shy character. By seeing themselves in new roles, children ultimately learn more about themselves.

CHILDREN AS AUTHORS, STORYTELLERS, AND ILLUSTRATORS

Children are beginning to write as soon as they begin to draw. They are attempting to make sense of their world through some type of visual process. Some children seem to have more to say than others. Some children seem to be more creative than others. All children, however, do have something to say and have a variety of ways of saying it. Their expression is to be encouraged. Adults must be accepting of children's attempts at writing. If willingness to take risks is destroyed, growth as authors and storytellers will be damaged as well.

Children's creativity is often overlooked. The goal of writing has long seemed to be to have children spell, punctuate, and print correctly. Unfortunately, focusing on the mechanics of writing has had some unfortunate results. Children whose papers are returned full of red correction marks are most likely to write shorter, less interesting pieces in the future. Focusing on mechanics also obscures the more important aspects of writing such as clarity, organization, and a freshness of thinking. Some of this is changing as the whole-language movement makes its way into the country's educational systems.

Stimulating experiences are beneficial to children as authors and storytellers. Exposure to quality art, either through books or in museums and galleries, provides new ideas to think about and talk about. As these opportunities are increased, the potential for intellectual growth is increased as well. Writing and storytelling are thinking activities. The ability to engage in them depends upon one's ability to analyze, question, organize, generate, and reorganize facts and reality. Yet, no two people see things in exactly the same way. The following child-dictated stories illustrate how different children can take a single topic and come up with several different stories about it.

JUNGLE STORY by Marissa and Megan (Becker Day-Care Center)

One day there was an alligator and he was getting a suntan. He got a purple suntan and he put apples on it. His mother got a crab and pinched him. He put a bandaid on it. He laid in bed for a nap. The end.

JUNGLE STORY by Dania and Mellissa (Becker Day-Care Center)

One day we went to the jungle. We saw an elephant. He was eating grass. His mommy said to eat snacks and juice and junk. We also saw a hippo and a lion and they were fighting each other. They scratched and they were licking each other. The end.

JUNGLE STORY by Elizabeth and Bryan (Becker Day-Care Center)

One day we saw a leopard and a snake. They were eating grass. The leopard was jumping and he saw something and he started to roar. It was a bumblebee who stung him and he bit the bumblebee and he ate the bumblebee up. The snake did go in the water to get a drink of water. The end.

How to Encourage Children as Authors

Children usually have something to say that they feel is important, although sometimes they are reluctant to say it. Providing rich experiences will help keep children's minds active and will help them to construct new meanings and new stories. Since many young children will be able to use much more language than they can write, an adult can serve as transcriber and facilitator for their stories. These stories can take a variety of forms. Children tell, expand, respond, and create with paint, clay, puppets, and toys well before they encounter them.

Classroom Books. A classroom book is a good beginning activity. It is particularly appropriate after the class has shared a common experience. The experience could be a walk to the firehouse, a visit from a pet rabbit, or a simple science demonstration. Each child draws a picture depicting the experience. After the picture is completed, the child tells about the picture. The teacher writes, at the bottom of the picture, a brief sentence or key phrase that the child has stated. All of the illustrations and the writing are bound, glued, or stapled together to form a book. The book can be shared over the next few days. This activity conveys the message that children have something important to say and are authors who write books.

A related activity involves the language-experience approach (LEA). The LEA uses the child's own language to teach beginning reading and writing. Using the LEA, the adult encourages the children to generate their own story, which the adult writes for them. The basis for the story might be an experience the class has shared, a story they have heard, or their imaginations. The story usually has a time frame and possesses many of the characteristics of literature.

Frequently LEA stories are written on large sheets of poster paper so that they can be made into "Big Books." Children draw the illustrations for the various pages. They also illustrate their book by pasting pictures on the pages. The story is then shared. The teacher points to each word as it is read. Often the story has a repeated line. When this occurs, children begin to recognize or anticipate the line and join in the reading.

The mechanics of constructing these classroom books are important. The books should be sturdy, so that children will be able to handle them repeatedly. Oaktag or cardboard covers can be used to protect the pages. Clear contact paper on each of the pages protects them over a long period of time. The pages are best bound with yarn or cord to keep them together. Finally, the printing should be done in large manuscript lettering. Typing the words on a computer with a large

Children become both authors and illustrators through their art.

font can produce good lettering. Photo albums with clear magnetic pages are a commercial alternative to having the children construct their own books.

Good Choices for Child-Created Stories

Making books builds self-confidence and a sense of mastery over language. It may be done using the LEA. It may also be done on an individual or small-group basis. While children often have many things to tell about, various themes may be suggested as well. For example, ABC books, counting books, and concept books can be created by individual youngsters or groups of children. The following stories were created, illustrated, and acted out by small groups of children on the concept of spring.

THEME: WHAT HAPPENS IN SPRING?

Charles, David, Jackie, and Marci: "Daffodils grow. It starts to rain. The bees come out and sting you. An elephant at the zoo jumps on you. The Easter Bunny brings eggs and toys. He brings you rabbit candy and chocolate eggs."

Eli, Justin, Erica, and Elizabeth: "In spring, wear spring jackets. Or wear an eagle shirt that says something about a motorcycle. Or wear a Minnie Mouse shirt. Bunnies are funny. I like birds. My favorite is a blue bird. There are blue and white flowers by some trees. I had a dream last night about some yellow flowers that are supposed to grow in spring."

Creating rebus stories with picture stamps is one way to help children experience the creativity of authorship. Courtesy Diana Comer.

Ryan, Danielle, Ben, and Stacie: "Birds eat worms. They love worms. Bunnies and chickies come out. Easter bunnies hide baskets on tables and behind couches. Sometimes you write on paper when it's spring. Yellow flowers grow in sunshine. Sometimes flowers talk. Sometimes birds take care of worms. Trees begin to get food because they're hungry. Leaves grow."

Reprinted with permission by Judy Brown-DuPaul's class.

Creating books that involve the senses can be very successful. For example, a Christmas holiday book might use the senses of sight, smell, and touch. If an activity for the day is baking cookies, cinnamon and other spices can be sprinkled on a spot of glue in the book. In decorating with pine boughs, a twig can be pressed and glued into the book. Sawdust can be added to the page that pictures the tree being cut down. The pictures and stories about the holiday will be greatly enhanced by these additions.

The creation of books can be basic and simple. The goal is not to produce professional-looking books, but to validate the children's thoughts and encourage their creativity and self-expression. If adults are accepting of children's literary attempts, children will begin to see themselves as authors. The correct use of mechanics often comes as children become more familiar with language and books. At this early stage, making sense of language is the most important part of the process.

SUMMARY

There are literally hundreds of fascinating ways to share stories. Taking a new look at some commonsense approaches is helpful. Reading aloud is a most effective way to share stories if it is done with planning and a little bit of acting. Oral storytelling has a long tradition, though it is practiced less today. Certainly it is more difficult than reading aloud, but it is a skill worth mastering. People of all ages can be mesmerized by the spell a good storyteller can cast over an audience. With practice, amateur storytellers can capture some of that magic.

Various materials can be added to the sharing of stories to create diversity and artistic effects. Flannelboards are effective tools for sharing stories. They provide an avenue for both oral and hands-on involvement by children in the telling of the story. Theatrical storytelling takes this one step further. By using puppetry and dramatics, children are given the power to suspend reality and enter a magical world created exclusively for and by them.

The more involved the children are in the storytelling process, the greater their creative and intellectual growth can be. The ultimate goal is, of course, helping children to attain literacy. Involving them early as authors by guiding them in the construction of their own classroom books can be a critical step in this journey. The positive self-concepts they gain by creating stories provide them with confidence to continue on the road to greater literacy.

QUESTIONS FOR THOUGHT AND DISCUSSION

1. Why should a variety of approaches for sharing stories be used?
2. Which method of sharing stories is easiest to begin with?
3. What can one do to prepare to read a story aloud?
4. Why should a teacher read a story aloud to the children every day?
5. What should one consider when choosing a book to read aloud?
6. Why is child involvement important in oral storytelling?
7. What are the characteristics of a good story for oral storytelling?
8. What materials are needed for a flannelboard story?
9. What are some things a teacher telling a flannelboard story should be aware of?
10. What are the characteristics of a good flannelboard story?
11. Why should one use flannelboard stories with children?
12. Why are puppets effective as storytelling tools?
13. Defend or refute this statement: A teacher who uses puppets must learn to be a ventriloquist.
14. What kinds of stories are best to use with puppets?
15. Why is drama a useful tool for telling stories to young children?
16. What should be considered when planning a creative dramatic experience with children?

17. Why should young children use costumes and props when involved in dramatics?
18. Defend or refute this statement: Young children are unable to write stories.
19. What is a classroom book?
20. Is the language-experience approach (LEA) useful for preschool children? Why?

CHILDREN'S BOOKS CITED

Aardema, V. (1991). *Traveling to Tondo: A tale of the Nkundo of Zaire.* New York: Scholastic.

Arnold, T. (1994). *No more jumping on the bed.* New York: Dial.

Barrett, J. (1978). *Cloudy with a chance of meatballs.* New York: Atheneum.

Browne, A. (1991). *Willy and Hugh.* New York: Alfred A. Knopf.

Carle, E. (1993). *Today is Monday.* New York: Scholastic.

Carlson, N. (1993). *Take time to relax.* New York: Puffin.

Castaneda, O. (1993). *Abuela's Weave.* New York: Lee and Low.

Cowcher, H. (1988). *Rain forest.* New York: Farrar, Straus, Giroux.

Crume, M. (1995). *Do you see Mouse?* Parsippany, NJ: Silver Press.

dePaola, T. (1973). *Charlie needs a cloak.* Englewood Cliffs, NJ: Prentice Hall.

dePaola, T. (1975). *Strega Nona.* Englewood Cliffs, NJ: Prentice Hall.

Fleming, D. (1994). *Barnyard banter.* New York: Henry Holt.

Fox, M. (1994). *Tough Boris.* San Diego, CA: Harcourt Brace Jovanovich.

Freeman, D. (1976). *Corduroy.* New York: Puffin.

Glassman, P. (1994). *My working mom.* New York: Morrow.

Heide, F.P. (1994). *The bigness contest.* Boston: Little, Brown.

Krauss, R. (1945). *The carrot seed.* New York: Harper & Row.

Lane, J. (1979). *The life and adventures of Santa Claus.* Orford, NH: Equity.

Lobel, A. (1979). *Frog and Toad are friends.* New York: Harper & Row.

McDermott, G. (1993). *Raven.* New York: Scholastic.

Medearis, A. (1991). *Dancing with the Indians.* New York: Scholastic.

Numeroff, L. (1991). *If you gave a moose a muffin.* New York: HarperCollins.

Pilkey, D. (1991). *A friend for Dragon.* New York: Orchard.

Prater, J. (1993). *Tim and the blanket thief.* New York: Atheneum.

Priest, R. (1989). *Ten little babies.* Windsor, Ontario, Canada: Black Moss.

Rosen, M., & Oxenbury, H. (1989). *We're going on a bear hunt.* New York: McElderry.

Say, A. (1991). *Tree of cranes.* Boston: Houghton Mifflin.

Trivizas, E. (1993). *The three little wolves and the big bad pig.* New York: McElderry.

Waddell, M. (1992). *The pig in the pond.* Cambridge, MA: Candlewick.

Ward, L. (1987). *I am eyes, ni macho.* New York: Scholastic.

Wickstrom, T. (1993). *The big night out.* New York: Dial.

William, K. (1990). *Galimoto.* New York: Lothrop, Lee & Shepard.

Wood, A. (1984). *The napping house.* New York: Harcourt.

SELECTED REFERENCES

Baker, A., & Greene, E. (1987). *Storytelling: Art and technique.* New York: Bowker.

Barton, B., & Booth, D. (1990). *Stories in the classroom.* Markham, Ontario: Pembroke.

Brizendine, N. & Thomas, J. (Eds.). (1982). *Learning through dramatics: Ideas for teachers and librarians.* Phoenix, AZ: Oryx.

Gillard, M. (1995). *Storyteller, storyteacher.* York, ME: Stenhouse.

Glazer, T. (1983). *Music for ones and twos.* New York: Doubleday.

Heinig, R.B. (1993). *Creative dramatics for the classroom* teacher. Englewood Cliffs, NJ: Prentice Hall.

Kelner, L. (1993). *The creative classroom.* Portsmouth, NH: Heinemann.

Koste, V.G. (1995). *Dramatic play in childhood.* Portsmouth, NH: Heinemann.

Lipman, D. (1993). *We all go together.* Phoenix, AZ: Oryx.

MacDonald, M.R. (1993). *The storyteller's start-up book.* Little Rock, AR: August House.

Maguire, J. (1985). *Creative storytelling: Choosing, inventing, and sharing tales for children.* New York: McGraw-Hill.

McCaslin, N. (1990). *Creative dramatics in the classroom.* Studio City, CA: Players.

Polsky, M. (1989). *Let's improvise.* Lanham, MD: University Press of America.

Sierra, J. (1987). *The flannel board storytelling book.* New York: H.W. Wilson.

Trelease, J. (1995). *The new read-aloud handbook.* New York: Viking Penguin.

Vaugh, G., & Torn, S. (1990). *Flannel board storybook.* Atlanta, GA: Humanics.

Remember always that you have
the right to be an individual.

– Eleanor Roosevelt

7 Integrating Literature into the Curriculum

Early childhood programs must include a wide range of topics and activities. This variety is needed to address the total development of each child. Literature is only one of the things that should be provided to children in their formative years. Age-appropriate academics, art, music, free play, nutrition, and other parts of the program must all be addressed as well. One might easily feel overwhelmed by the number of topics and activities that should be provided.

How can all of these parts be provided? Should some be dropped from the program? If so, how can one decide which things to drop? Can anything be combined with something else? These questions can be puzzling. Obviously, one will need to plan carefully in order to avoid leaving out parts of a program that have a truly legitimate purpose. This chapter discusses an innovative strategy for including each of the important aspects of the program. The strategy is the use of a web as an aid to planning activities for young children.

WEBS AS ORGANIZATIONAL TOOLS

Much time has been spent over the past two decades studying how the human brain works. Scientists have examined this field by trying to make computers behave in the same way as a human brain. Since the computer is a machine, and a human being possesses natural intelligence, this concept is known as *artificial intelligence.* From these experiments, it has been concluded that people understand new ideas by relating the new to the known.[1] In other words, they see how the new idea fits with what is already comprehended. The process is likened to fitting new information into a web of the information already possessed.

This idea of a web of knowledge can be applied to planning the various components of an early childhood program. Rather than looking at each part of the program as an isolated activity, visualize each as a piece of the whole. In order to do this, one has to understand how each part fits in with the other parts. As new parts of the program are considered, they can be integrated.

[1] Weaver, C. (1994). *Reading process and practice.* Portsmouth, NH: Heinemann.

A Web for Understanding

Perhaps the best way to explain how a web might work is to use an example. Consider a young child who sees a man walking a dog on a leash down the street. The child might not be familiar with that particular breed of dog prior to this time. Yet, the child points at the animal and proudly exclaims, "Doggy!" How the child knew what the animal was is explained by understanding how the child took the new information (i.e., the dog being walked) and fit it in with the known (i.e., what the child already knew about dogs).

Although the child might not have been able to explain everything about dogs, the child already knew some things about dogs, such as barking, Lassie, a wagging tail, and chasing cats. It is reasonable to believe that a young child would possess most of the information contained in Figure 7–1, which depicts a knowledge web for dogs with information organized under four subheadings. With this web of knowledge, a child could identify several things about an unfamiliar dog that would fit in with what was already known about dogs—for example, the leash, collar, four legs, a tail, walking, and perhaps a bark. Based on these characteristics a child would likely conclude that the unfamiliar animal was a dog even though it did not look like any previous dog the child had seen. Of course, this process doesn't always work out so neatly, which is why children are often heard making errors. The child might just as easily have seen a horse and called it a dog, a false conclusion reached because the child didn't have enough information about horses to clearly identify one.

In any case, it is seen in Figure 7–1 that the information is organized. It is believed that the human mind organizes knowledge in a similar way. That is why one doesn't constantly mistake cats for dogs and vice versa. Upon meeting the new dog, the child could learn its name and add that new name to examples of dogs that are known to the child. The process the child has gone through is an example of relating the new to the known. It is done by all human beings throughout life.

The lines that make up Figure 7–1 are similar to the lines that form the web constructed by a spider, which is the reason for the term. The web is helpful in understanding how children comprehend information and thus how the various components of an educational program can be related and integrated with one another.

TIPS FOR TEACHERS

Become a collector of poems, fingerplays, songs, riddles, and ideas to be used in the future.
• Use songs and fingerplays to connect one activity to the next.
• Identify specific poems to use in themed activities or units.
• Keep several anthologies of poems readily available, and place labeled bookmarks in them to identify the location of poems to be used.

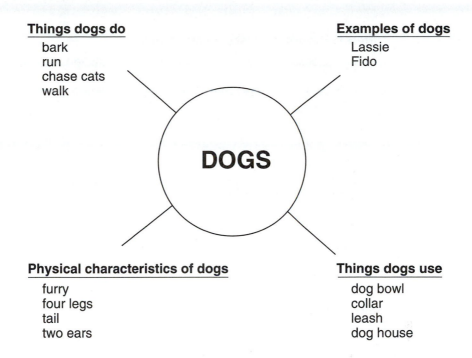

Things dogs do
  bark
  run
  chase cats
  walk

Examples of dogs
  Lassie
  Fido

DOGS

Physical characteristics of dogs
  furry
  four legs
  tail
  two ears

Things dogs use
  dog bowl
  collar
  leash
  dog house

Figure 7–1. A knowledge web for dogs. A web for any other concept is developed through a similar procedure. Courtesy Walter Sawyer.

Planning with a Web

A web is a useful tool in a variety of planning situations. It may be used to visualize or organize a total program or just certain aspects of a program.

To construct a web, begin with a central theme. Using a free-flowing brainstorming approach, list a variety of aspects related to that central theme. The next step might be to select relevant items from the list and organize them under subheadings. The final step is to create a web that visually represents the total picture. Figure 7–2 illustrates the steps one might follow when considering a topic such as toys. Notice that some items appear under more than one subheading. Dotted lines are used to point out this relationship in the actual web. As new ideas or new knowledge is gained, the web grows outward, and the lines showing relationship may increase.

This same process may be used to plan a unit. The central idea might be art, music, literature, science, social studies, nutrition, or math. The teacher might then generate related ideas such as activities or books to use with the theme. The ideas could be organized under subheadings, and a web could be created.

Step 1: Brainstorm a list of related terms:

blocks	cars	trucks	stuffed animals
rattles	pots	pans	teddy bears
clay	crayons	paints	board games
balls	bats	markers	rubber duck

Step 2: Select items and organize under subheadings:

Soft Toys	**Bed Toys**	**Group Toys**	**Art Toys**
stuffed animals	stuffed animals	balls	crayons
teddy bears	teddy bears	board games	clay
clay	rubber duck		paint
balls			markers

Step 3: Create a web and show relationships:

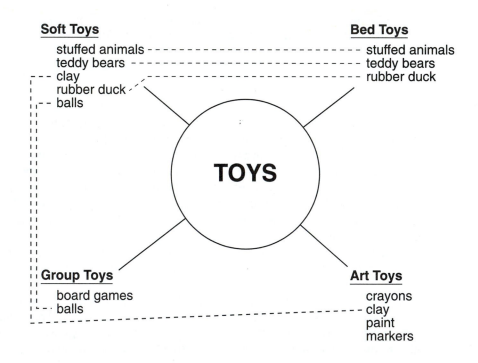

Figure 7–2. Creating a web for toys. Courtesy Walter Sawyer.

Scary stories book display. Courtesy Walter Sawyer.

Literature Web

A web might be constructed for a literature theme as follows. After a topic has been identified, focus mainly on the literature concerning the topic. In this case, the subheadings might include poems, fingerplays, and stories related to a particular literature theme. Under each subheading would be a listing of examples that might be used in the unit.

Figure 7–3 depicts a literature web for the theme of owls. Notice that the web is drawn in a slightly different way than those depicted in Figures 7–1 and 7–2. There is no specific method for designing a web. The design should be one that makes sense to the individual using the web. Using the web in Figure 7–3, the teacher might designate certain pieces of literature to be used at specific times of a day or week. The web requires an overall understanding of each piece of literature to be used throughout the unit so that reference can easily be made to what might be coming in the future or what the class did that morning.

If the teacher doesn't know where the class is heading, chances are the program is lost. Used as a roadmap for the day or week, the web can be a tremendous help in preventing such a situation. Webs can be revised each year. They can be added to or have sections deleted as needed. Keeping the web on file helps reduce planning time in subsequent years.

THEMES FOR DEVELOPING WEBS

Teachers do not need to think of each theme or book around which to develop a curriculum or literature web. Borrowing and learning from others is a teaching tradition that can and should be relied on. Doris Bullock has written a book containing a wealth of ideas for expanding on many of the books commonly used in early childhood education.[2]

2 Bullock, D. (1986). *Designed to delight.* Belmont, CA: Fearon.

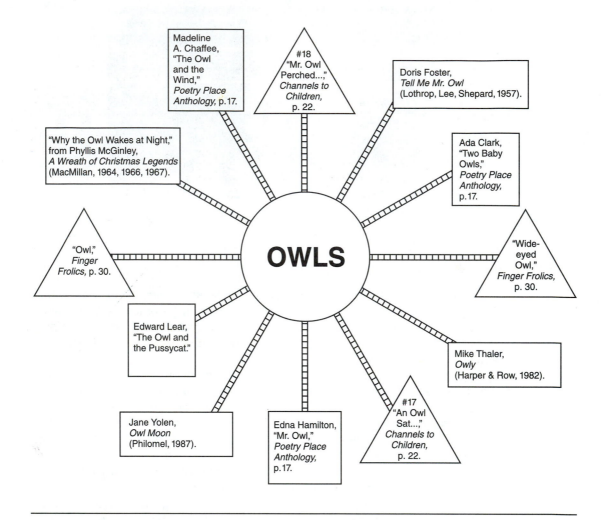

KEY: ▢ POEM △ FINGERPLAY ▭ STORY

Figure 7–3. A literature web. Courtesy Diana Comer.

Webs can be used to plan around one book or a theme using several books. They may be used to plan for a single day or a longer period of time such as a one-week unit. An important use of webs is planning the integration of subject areas around a common theme.

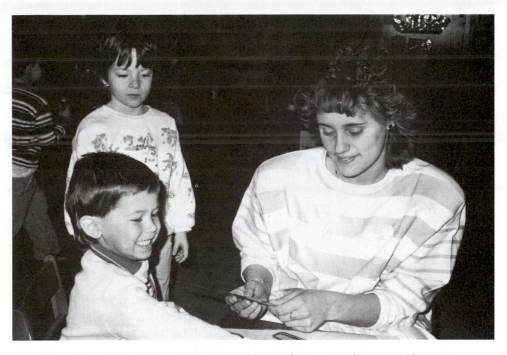

Based on a literature unit on community workers, a teacher created a game that includes both colors and community workers. Courtesy Diana Comer.

Subject Area Themes

Themes may be developed around topics and areas of interest to children. Consider combining areas through related elements or books. Several topic areas will be considered, including science, social studies, mathematics, arts, basic concepts, language, movement, and celebrations.

Science. The most common topic within this area is the study of ourselves. Children are very curious about their bodies. Topics for themes might include the body, teeth, foods we eat, illness, good health, and accident prevention. The study of other living things should also be considered. This subject would include pets and pet care, plants and animals, ocean/pond life, insects, sex differences, and babies. Natural phenomena are also of interest. These include magnetism, bubbles, weather, how things grow, electricity, simple machines (e.g., pulleys, wheels), stars, and planets.

Social Studies. In social studies, the focus is often on the community and neighborhood helpers. Safety issues can be investigated with themes on personal safety, emotions, and families. The focus can expand to other communities as well, in units such as the farm, the city, the desert, the mountains, lifestyles, outer space,

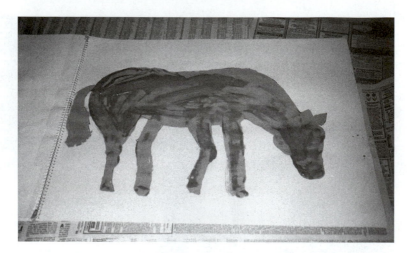

Stories can be extended through the arts. Courtesy Diana Comer.

and climates. A sense of time can be developed in units on history, dinosaurs, and historical figures. The world community can come alive with themes on the differences and similarities of people, cultural heritage, holidays around the world, climates, ethnic celebrations, and geography.

Mathematics. Mathematics in early childhood education includes more than just learning numbers. Themes can be developed on building principles using shapes, blocks, and estimating. Early computation skills include the concepts of counting and adding and subtracting by using concrete objects. Other mathematics themes might include predicting, metrics, graphing, and charting.

The Arts. The arts include music, drama, and the visual arts. Music themes might include songs, fingerplays, instruments, and choral singing. Drama themes include plays, puppetry, fingerplays, costuming, skits, and role playing. Themes in the visual arts could include color, design, collage, painting, markers, clay, 3-D art, junk art, easel art, and ecology art. Book illustrations are a natural springboard for integrating literature and the children's art activities.

Basic Concepts. The term "basic concepts" includes all of the taken-for-granted aspects of life that explain such things as size, proximity, and action. They include spatial concepts such as near, far, in front of, on top of, behind, and so on; actions such as push, pull, open, fast, and close; size and weight concepts such as big, small, heavy, and light; sensory concepts such as color, sound, taste, feel, sweet, soft, and bright. Each can be studied as a separate concept. However, it makes much more sense to integrate their study. One seldom sees just "red" or experiences the concept of "near" in isolation. One sees red crayons, red fire

The arts and literature can be combined by creating story characters from clay.
Courtesy Diana Comer.

engines, and red mittens. One is near a cat, or near a mommy, or near a friend. Each of these concepts is integrated in life. It makes sense to integrate them with other components of a program.

Language. Language, of course, can be easily integrated with any of the other theme areas. Language is used to describe and deal with each of them. When considering language, one is concerned with ABCs, color words, word patterns, sequencing, solving puzzles, rebus writing, labeling, name learning, literature, picture dictionaries, listening, etc. It is often helpful to see language as a device that can be used to link and integrate two or more of the other themes together.

Movement. During the early years, children acquire a great deal of control over their bodies. This aspect of a program can easily be integrated with other themes. Included in a movement theme are such concepts as growth and development, muscle control, body fluidity, coordination, challenging oneself, and group cooperation. After reading a book about colors, one can easily construct a game in which children are asked to take turns placing a number of objects of various colors at different locations around the room. This activity integrates colors and listening (language and art), spatial awareness (basic concepts), and muscle control (movement) with literature (reading of the book).

TIPS FOR TEACHERS

Make an aerobic movement game of "Simon Says" to integrate language and motor skills.
- *Simon says to wave and say, "I'm happy!" three times.*
- *Simon says to hop three times and say, "1 - 2 - 3!"*
- *Simon says to wiggle your fingers and say, "I have two hands!"*
- *Simon says to march in a circle and say, "I'm on a merry-go-round!"*

Nontraditional Celebrations. The category of nontraditional celebrations can cover virtually everything else one wants to do. Nontraditional refers to the idea of times other than holidays or the changing of seasons. In a classroom, the teacher and children are in charge of celebrations. There are many unique celebrations that can be created using professional resources such as Kathy Flagella's resource guide for celebrations.[3] One can give free rein to imagination and a sense of adventure. New celebrations can be created during weeks that do not contain a Thanksgiving, Valentine's Day, or Halloween. Common themes can be given a sense of excitement by creation of a week-long celebration for them. A "Pets in Our World" week might include books on pets, a trip to a veterinarian or pet shop, making pet rocks, and a contest for drawings of favorite pets. A "Teddy Bear Celebration" might include books about teddy bears, a teddy bear picnic, a teddy dance, bring-a-teddy-bear day, and snacks made with honey. These celebrations can easily be molded to include activities and content from each of the other theme areas.

The more that concepts can be integrated into the curriculum, the better the learning will be. If children have had an enjoyable experience, the memories they re-create from that experience will reinforce the concepts learned. Children usually enjoy a multisensory, hands-on approach to learning. Therefore, planning that includes this approach will result in more effective instruction. Literature that provides interest, motivation, and language can be used to integrate many parts of the curriculum.

Books That Don't Fit Themes

Sometimes one plans a unit for which there doesn't seem to be a good book. At other times, one discovers a particularly good book that doesn't seem to fit any of the units being planned. This doesn't mean that either the unit being planned or the wonderful book should not be used. A unit that provides stimulating learning should always be used even if literature cannot be integrated with it. A good book can be read simply for the enjoyment of the story. In fact, many good books can and should be read solely for that reason.

In addition, one might discover a book such as Robert McCloskey's *Time of Wonder* and, knowing that a unit on the sea is planned for a later time, put that

[3] Flagella, K. (1987). *Celebrate every day: Hundreds of celebrations for early childhood classrooms.* Bridgeport, CT: First Teacher Press.

Stories, art, and science can be combined. Courtesy Diana Comer.

book aside until the sea unit is begun. On the other hand, one might be planning to use *Frogs Jump* by Alan Brooks during the month of June, but a child brings in a jar of tadpoles at the beginning of May. Obviously, it makes sense to use *Frogs Jump* immediately, while interest in the subject is high. Saving it until the June unit on pond life would serve no purpose. Common sense and flexibility often go hand in hand in situations such as this.

A few more words on *Frogs Jump* are justified. This is a cumulative counting book that shows the activities of frogs and other animals. It is always the right time for Steven Kellogg's humorous mixed-media illustrations, which portray some ridiculous but explainable scenes.

Adjusting a book or poem to fit a particular purpose should also be considered when an exact match between a book and a theme cannot be found. In telling a story, one can always add characters, change settings, or lengthen the plot. Take, for example, the kindergarten class that wished to do a Christmas play. Since it was difficult to find a story or play with twenty-two parts, the children adapted one using Dr. Seuss's *How the Grinch Stole Christmas*. The play included a group of really rotten rats (five children) with one lead rat (dressed as a ragged Santa) who burst through a cardboard chimney to steal Christmas. The play also included four other children, the real Santa, the nine reindeer, and a mother and father. All twenty-two children had important roles. Reading the Dr. Seuss story helped the children understand the idea that would be created in the play. The Grinch was a superb model for the behavior of the rotten rats. All children had a speaking role through the use of a choral line that was repeated at key points in the play. One of the best parts of the experience was that no child had to play an "added on" part such as a tree or a bush.

FACILITATING INTEGRATION

Webs can be an immense help in developing integrated lessons. They allow one to step back and plan the big picture of a lesson prior to actually using it with children. In addition to planning, there are steps that can be taken within the lesson to further facilitate integration. Some of these ideas require the acquisition of materials to use in the lesson. Others focus on taking advantage of the things that happen within the lesson.

Re-creating the Experience

Providing opportunities for children to re-create the learning enhances their understanding of the lesson. Providing inexpensive or no-cost materials can ensure that the learning or the story will be experienced again. Good health care as illustrated in *Dr. Dog* provides an excellent example. Written and illustrated by Babette Cole, Dr. Dog's unorthodox methods are hilarious, but right on target in terms of good hygiene and health care. Throughout the book, Dr. Dog strives to reform the unhealthy habits of his human owners. Class books can be used here to re-create the experience as well. The common phrase, "If you want to be healthy, be sure to . . ." can be used by all children to form pages for the class book. Each child creates an ending for the phrase and a picture to illustrate the idea. The repetitive phrasing will encourage children to read the class book.

Another example might be Jean Johnson's *Postal Workers A to Z.* After the reading, children could be provided with a pile of old envelopes, stickers, an ink pad, and a rubber stamp. Milk cartons could be made into mailboxes, enabling the children to re-create the story. One of the purposes of free play is to allow children to try out the world from a safe harbor. It may be beneficial to allow children to engage in this activity prior to a field trip to a real post office.

Using Children's Interest

Use the motivation of the children to lead into another activity, even if it isn't the next activity originally planned. A high interest level should be a deciding factor in shifting the order of the day's activities. Suppose the motivating factor is the reading of Donald Crews's book, *Freight Train.* If interest is high, the time is ripe to make different colored train cars as an expansion of the reading. Teaching shapes (of the cars) or counting (the number of cars) are additional expansions of the initial motivation. A variety of fine motor activities could also be included in the construction of the paper train.

Robert McClung's *Animals that Build Their Homes* might provide inspiration for a matching game of animals with their homes. A listening activity could be used as well by having children identify the animals that make a particular sound. Clay or papier-mâché houses and animals might be used to integrate art with the other activities.

Young children are motivated to try new things. Margaret Miller's *Now I'm Big* is right on target for this area. Young children involved in new accomplishments will see themselves in this book about momentous changes in young lives.

TIPS FOR TEACHERS

Take a walk in the neighborhood to discover the nests, buildings, structures, hives, and holes in the ground that animals use as their homes.
• Ask children if they can identify the birds they see, giving the identities of common birds to those who do not know them.
• Find the homes of a bird, squirrel, dog, bee, ant, and so on.

A Sense of Flexibility

It is important to keep a sense of flexibility. Even carefully made plans do not always work out as expected. Being flexible and being willing to capitalize on unexpected opportunities for further learning is an advantage when working with children. Without these skills, one misses the possibilities that are always presenting themselves. Keep the original plan in mind, but don't be a slave to it.

A frustrated reaction to a plan not working is detrimental. Children are quite forgiving when things don't work out. They also notice the reactions of adults, since adults are their role models. It is important for both teacher and children to be willing to take healthy risks. Seeing the negative reactions of adults when things don't work out discourages this risk taking on the part of children. Model a proper response to life's minor disappointments by making calm or humorous remarks and demonstrating that one can always try again or do something else.

LITERATURE USE IN INTEGRATED UNITS

Integrated units are often taught around a general theme or a key idea. These themes include the content for the lesson or unit. One may wish to develop a theme around a specific book. For example, Figure 7–4 illustrates a single-book curriculum web developed around the theme of Ruth Sawyer's classic story *Journey Cake, Ho!* The focus may also be in a content area such as science, social studies, basic concepts, or holidays. Selecting both fiction and nonfiction literature to support these content areas will be discussed. In addition to these, other units might be developed around literature, unique classroom projects, or nontraditional topics.

While Ruth Sawyer's classic story is used in this example, the same web could be revised for use with a number of contemporary titles related to the theme of food. Two stories featuring multicultural characters are *Everybody Cooks Rice* by Norah Dooley and *In the Diner* by Christine Loomis. Preschoolers will howl with delight at the antics of the animal characters in *Elephant Pie,* written and illustrated by Hilda Offen. Three nonfiction titles about food include *Cranberries* by William Jaspersohn, *Siggy's Spaghetti Works* by Peggy Thomson, and *Pasta Factory* by Hana Machotka. The latter title could be paired with a reading of Tomie dePaola's classic story *Strega Nona.*

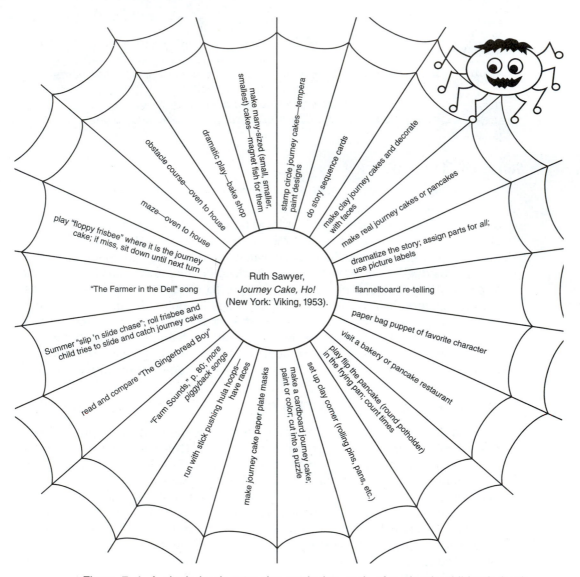

Figure 7–4. A single-book extension-curriculum web of a classic children's book.
Courtesy Diana Comer.

Figure 7–5 provides a similar single-book curriculum web for a contemporary title, *Houses and Homes* by Ann Morris. This nonfiction book presents a wide variety of houses and cultures from around the world. Ken Heyman's crisp clear photographs aid in establishing the similarities and differences of the structures. In addition to the web activities, children can expand on the unit by creating gingerbread houses, designing houses using recycled materials, and learning about houses used in previous centuries.

Figure 7–5. Single-book cross-curriculum web. Courtesy Diana Comer.

Science Units

When developing a unit on science, it is important to possess current information. This need for up-to-date information should be included as a specific criterion when selecting books for use in the unit. The teacher should read each of the books to be used ahead of time. Anticipating the questions that might be asked by

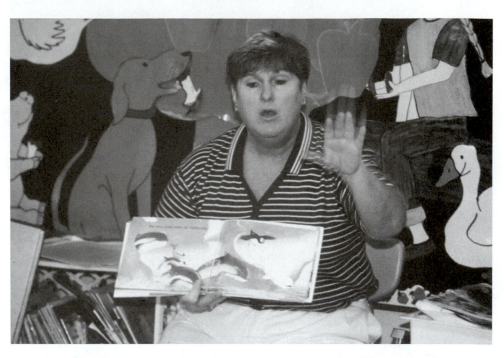

Learning language through nonfiction picture books can be integrated into the study of science.

children will help the teacher provide better responses. Careful planning will help to make a content area theme a success. Webs can be particularly helpful. Figure 7–6 illustrates an integrated-curriculum web used to plan a unit on the ocean.

Various authors and some commercial publishing companies specialize in science-related books. The books should, and usually do, contain an abundance of age-appropriate photographs and illustrations. Certain field guides, if they are written at an appropriate level, can be useful as well. A *field guide* is a book used

Everybody Cooks Rice *by Norah Dooley.* Reprinted by permission of Carolrhoda Books.

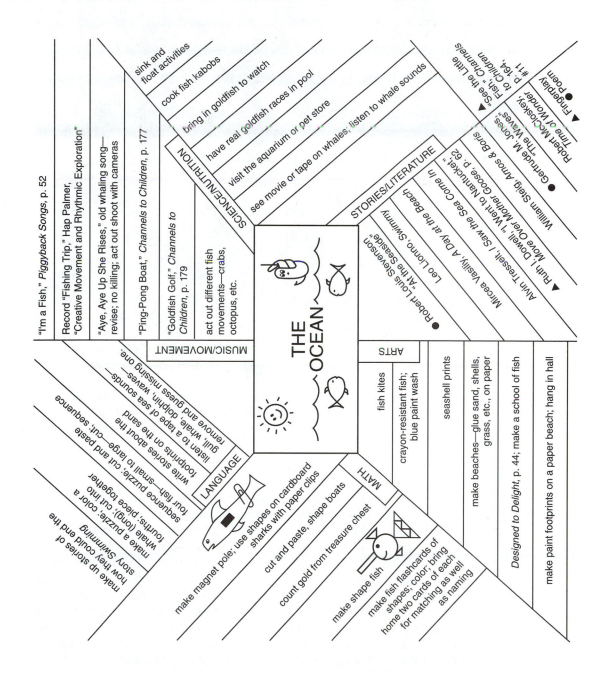

Figure 7–6. Integrated-curriculum web. Courtesy Diana Comer.

Illustration by Robert McCloskey from Journey Cake Ho! *by Ruth Sawyer.*
(c)1953 by Ruth Sawyer and Robert McCloskey. Copyright renewed 1981 by
David Durrand and Robert McCloskey. All rights reserved. Reprinted by permission of Viking Penguin, a division of Penguin Books USA, Inc.

to identify things such as plants, birds, insects, trees, animals, and clouds. It contains clear pictures and brief, descriptive paragraphs of information.

The sparse text and soft pastel hues of Petra Mathers's watercolor illustrations in Marry McKenna Siddals's *Tell Me a Season* reveal the scientific reality of
the changing seasons. There is a highly successful merging of text and illustrations that allows children to use the illustrations, the text, or both to understand
the changing seasons. In Pat Hutchins's *Shrinking Mouse,* science and math
combine to help children learn about both animal behavior and the mathematical
concept of spatial perspective. Children will be captivated by the story line; they
come to discover that the animals are becoming smaller because they are moving away rather than shrinking. A rhythmic prose-poem of the water cycle is combined with lustrous oil paintings in Thomas Locker's *Waterdance.*

Cats, dogs, and other animals are familiar as pets to many children. As
such, they represent a good starting point for exploring the animal world. Stories

about cats for use in this area include *Nobody's Cat* by Barbara Joosse, *When the People Are Away* by Ann Jungman, and *The Big Storm* by Rhea Tregebov. *Wag Wag Wag* by Peter Hansard is a good nonfiction choice to introduce the topic of dogs. Stories about dogs include *He's Your Dog!* by Pat Schories and *Pole Dog* by Tres Seymour. Although most of these selections are fictional stories, the dogs and cats portrayed are true to their nature, enabling young readers to develop an understanding of these animals.

Finding animals and other natural objects has never been as fascinating as in Caron Lee Cohen's, *Where's the Fly?* The youngest readers will enjoy the large print and detailed illustrations that require us to change our way of looking at things with each turn of the page. Dee Dee Duffy's *Forest Tracks* is a visual treat for the readers of this book, as they use the words and Janet Marshall's cut-paper illustrations to help them name the animals making different tracks in the landscape.

Steve Metzger has created a series of dinosaur books in which the characters are four-year-old dinosaurs who behave just like four-year-old humans. In *Dinofours: It's Time for School!*, Brendan and Albert miss their mommies on the first day of school. Steve Metzger and illustrator Hans Wilhelm magnificently capture the body language, words, and feelings of four-year-olds. In *Dinofours: I'm Super Dino!*, Brendan discovers that acting like a superhero gets in the way of making friends. In *Dinofours: It's Class Trip Day!*, Tara grudgingly agrees to go on a class trip and unexpectedly turns out to be a hero. An important lesson about the meaning of friendship is learned by Tracy and Danielle in *Dinofours: I'm Not Your Friend!* Finally, younger children will appreciate the clear and understandable information in C.E. Thompson's nonfiction book, *How Big Were the Dinosaurs?* It comes with a snap-together Tyrannosaurus rex skeleton.

Commercial publishers often provide a variety of books in science-related areas. Usborne Publishing includes a nature series in its offerings. Topics addressed by its books include birds, butterflies, moths, flowers, and trees. Troll Publishing includes a wide assortment of science books appropriate for young children. They address many topics including the ocean, fish, clouds, trees, ponds, wind, alligators, crocodiles, whales, dolphins, and more. Books are grouped in a series aimed at particular age levels. As read-alouds, many of the books aimed at ages seven and up can be shared with younger children.

Goldencraft is another publisher that presents its books in age-related groups. The focus tends to be on animals and habitats. Included are topics such as animal homes, jungles, birds, and mammals. Using some of the books from Goldencraft's higher series can be useful as well. The completeness and ease of use of these books will allow the teacher to quickly answer a wide range of questions on a given scientific topic. National Geographic, Franklin Watts, and Mister Rogers' Neighborhood Books are other publishers that provide books related to science. They each offer features that enable a teacher to explore the topic more easily. Care has been taken in all these books to provide excellent photographs and clear illustrations on important points.

Social Studies Units

In selecting books related to social studies, one must consider other criteria than those discussed so far. Social studies at the early childhood level generally consists of developing an understanding of self, family, community, health/nutrition, and social skills. These are all critical areas that demand that authors be perceptive and sensitive observers of humanity. It may be unwise to use a series of books on one of these sensitive topics without examining each book in the series individually. Books in a series are often written by a number of authors. As a result, each book is only as good as the author who wrote it. Since the literature about early childhood social studies concepts is often fictional, the writer becomes the critical component. Identifying authors who write with empathy and understanding on these issues becomes helpful in selecting these books.

Some writers seem to gravitate toward the concepts of family, relationships, and the community in most of their books. Among the writers with multiple titles in these areas are Martha Alexander, Stan and Jan Berenstain, Nancy Carlson, Barbara Cooney, Russell Hoban, Angela Johnson, Mercer Mayer, Helen Oxenbury, and Rosemary Wells. Helen Buckley also explores these areas and includes some excellent work on grandparents in her writings.

Norman Bridwell's Clifford books explore the nature of love, even in the face of imperfections. Michael Bond uses an animal, Paddington Bear, to portray social concepts. Children enjoy exploring the mishaps Paddington encounters in doing things in an individualistic manner.

There are, of course, many other authors and books that can be used to address these areas. Some are intended to address a specific problem, while others are not. Many books can be used simply to make a point or to begin a discussion about a social problem. Selecting such books is facilitated by a clear sense of the purpose of the overall unit.

Basic Concept Units

Basic concept units address some aspect of mathematics, language, the alphabet, and so forth. The purpose of literature in these units is to reinforce the learning of the concept, whether it be counting, spatial relationships, or a letter of the alphabet. Many of the books that would be effective for such a unit might not appear to have been written for that purpose. For this reason, it is important to have a wide knowledge of books and authors.

Tana Hoban is an author who uses photographs to illustrate her texts. Her books have long been used to reinforce such concepts as pushing, pulling, and counting. Eric Carle's books are each imaginatively different. They are also quite effective in reinforcing concept learning with children. *My Very First Book of Colors* and *1, 2, 3 to the Zoo* are two of his books that have been used by early childhood educators for years. Motor skills and movement are topics of some enjoyable and interactive books. Zita Newcome, in *Toddlerobics,* uses catchy rhythms to have everyone swaying and bouncing to the tempo of the text, which encourages spontaneous movement by reader and listeners alike. *Marie in Fourth Position: The Story of Degas' "The Little Dancer,"* by Amy Littlesugar takes a unique perspective. Marie is a "rat" in the Paris Opera. Her mother agrees to let Marie model for Degas, the famous artist with a frightening reputation. Under Degas's magical guidance, however, Marie is transformed from a clumsy, unattractive dancer to a model of inspired grace. Ian Schoenherr's impressionist illustrations recall the well-known work of Degas. Young children will snap their fingers, clap their hands, and drink in Pat Dybold's stimulating collage illustrations in Linda Lowery's *Twist with a Burger, Jitter with a Bug,* which simply demands movement and involvement.

Donald Crews has made a substantial contribution to children's concepts with his books about buses, trains, and transportation. Mitsumasa Anno, Arnold Lobel, Tana Hoban, Gail Gibbons, Brian Wildsmith, Richard Scarry, Tomie dePaola, Ed Emberly, and Dr. Seuss are all authors who have made innumerable contributions to this area of children's learning. Their books cover topics such as ABCs, planting a garden, shapes, numbers, seasons, and categorizing.

Holiday Units

Holidays are a celebration of life. They bring with them a sense of warmth, tradition, culture, and history. Each has the potential to increase understanding of our mutual humanity. While no one wishes to offend children and families with holidays not celebrated in each child's home, learning that our culture is multiethnic and multireligious is important. Since most holidays have some religious connotation, perhaps it is best to inform parents about which holidays will be celebrated. If it is stated that the celebrations will not be religious but rather explanatory in nature, there is less likelihood of a problem.

Parental involvement can be used to help with holiday celebrations. Parents can provide explanations of various celebrations to children from their knowledge of the holiday. This will help to integrate all children and their families in the educational process. It will strengthen the parent-child bond in each involved family as well.

TIPS FOR TEACHERS

Invite parents in to share a holiday tradition from their cultural ancestry.
* *Ask parents to go back several generations if necessary to identify specific countries in their heritage.*
* *Show children that there are many different countries in Africa, Asia, and the Hispanic world, and that their individual cultures can differ.*
* *Share traditions that appeal to the senses, such as foods, songs, dances, and decorations.*

It makes sense to become aware, early in the year, of the cultural diversity of pupils in a class. This will enable the teacher to plan the holiday units to be celebrated throughout the year. Parents can be requested to explain the customs and traditions of particular holidays early in the year to the class so that children unfamiliar with those holidays can gain an understanding of them and perhaps participate in some aspects of their celebration.

December is a major holiday season. It is advisable to combine Christmas, Kwanzaa, Hanukkah, New Year's Day, and Las Pasadas into a single-unit "friendship" celebration. The activities can include decorating a friendship tree, playing with a dreidel, making candles and gifts, breaking a piñata, and perhaps a social activity. The social activity could be a gift to the community. Visiting a nursing home to sing songs or collecting donations for a food pantry would be appropriate.

Tomie dePaola has written several books about Christmas. They include *An Early American Christmas; Baby's First Christmas; Christmas Pageant; Strega Nona;* and *Tomie dePaola's Book of Christmas Carols.* Margaret Wise Brown's *Christmas in the Barn* is another title that would complement the stories by Tomie dePaola. Titles devoted to Christmas abound. They can often be used to develop important themes across cultures. In Cyndy Szekeres's *Yes, Virginia, There Is a Santa Claus,* a darling kitten assumes the role of Virginia in a retelling of Virginia O'Hanlon's story. Stephen Gammell, in *Wake up, Bear . . . It's Christmas,* presents the reader with a bear who is determined not to hibernate right through Christmas again this year. Not only does the bear succeed, but he also meets a very special guest. A father and son search for a Christmas tree in William George's *Christmas at Long Pond* while the reader is treated to a spectacular celebration of the natural environment. Mary Pope Osborne, in *Rocking Horse Christmas,* follows the lives of a boy and his rocking horse as they move through adventures together, grow older, and part company. Ned Bittinger's rich oil paintings enhance the message of longing, hope, and the wonder of childhood.

The Christmas Star *by Marcus Pfister. Copyright* (c)1993 by Nord-Sud Verlag A.G. Gossau Zurich, Switzerland. Used by permission of North-South Books, Inc.

Halloween book display. Courtesy Walter Sawyer.

Several contemporary titles reflect the traditional values that surround the holiday season. *The Christmas Star* by Marcus Pfister re-creates the story of the star that guided shepherds, kings, and animals. The author illustrates the book with intriguing holographic foils. *Good King Wenceslas* by John Neale takes the reader beyond the story told in the popular carol, the words of which are included in the book. Christopher Manson's exquisite hand-painted woodcuts of medieval scenes give a powerful dramatic feeling to the story. Trina Schart Hyman uses the search theme, common in folk tales, as the premise for a wonderful tale about discovery in *How Six Found Christmas.* Alan Benjamin provides the perfect way to acquaint young children with the festival of lights in *Hanukkah Chubby Board Book and Dreidels.* The package comes with everything needed to play "Spin the Dreidel." *Christmas in Other Lands* by Janet Riehecky tells how Christmas is celebrated in Mexico, Sweden, Greece, Zimbabwe, and the Philippines. Finally, the cultures of East and West are combined in a Japanese story of a mother helping her son learn about Christmas in Allen Say's *Tree of Cranes.*

Easter and Passover might be celebrated together as well. Activities might include an Easter parade, creating mosaics with colored eggshells, an Easter Bunny visit, sharing a meal, hatching baby chicks, and making Easter bonnets. Easter books and books about bunnies that might be used include James Stevenson's *The Great Big Especially Beautiful Easter Egg,* *The Bunny Who Found Easter* by Charlotte Zolotow, *The Runaway Bunny* by Margaret Wise Brown, *Zomo the Rabbit* by Gerald McDermott, *Clifford's Happy Easter* by Norman Bridwell, *Cranberry Easter* by Wende and Harry Devlin, and *The Easter Surprise* by Janet McDonnell.

A Mardi Gras festival might be just the thing to liven up a program toward the end of a long winter. A costume parade and samples of Cajun cooking could be included. Other popular holidays to consider include

St. Patrick's Day–March 17
April Fools Day–April 1

Arbor Day–April 28
May Day–May 1
Rosh Hashanah (Jewish New Year)–September/October
Harvest Festival—(Jewish, Chinese, Asian)–fall
Halloween–October 31
Thanksgiving–November

Some less well-known holidays that might also be considered include

Purim (Jewish Festival of Happiness)–March
Hina Matsuri (Japanese Doll Festival)–March 3
Now-Ruz (Iranian New Days)–March 21–23
Holi (Hindu Spring Festival)–spring
Song Kran (Buddhist New Year)–mid-April
Tangonosekku (Japanese Boy's Festival)–May 5
St. Lucia Day (Candles and Lights)–December 13
Kwanzaa (African Harvest Festival)–last week of December

Other festivals and celebrations may include such themes as Groundhog Day, Dental Health Week, and Fire Safety Week. Resources from the references at the end of this chapter can be used to provide ideas for celebrating festivals and holidays. Valentine's Day can be celebrated with *Comic Valentine* by Stan and Jan Berenstain, while Thanksgiving can be the occasion for Eve Bunting's *A Turkey for Thanksgiving*. Passover stories include *Matzo Ball Moon* by Leslea Newman, *The Four Questions* by Lynne Schwartz, and *Matzo Ball: A Passover Story* by Mindy Portnoy.

Halloween books, like Christmas books, abound. They include counting books, scary books, and stories that can be used to deal realistically with fears. Top choices include Deborah Lattimore's hilarious *Cinderhazel, On Halloween Night* by Ferida Wolff and Dolores Kozielski, *By the Light of the Halloween Moon* by Caroline Stutson, *Old Devil Wind* by Bill Martin, Jr., *James in the House of Aunt Prudence* by Timothy Bush, and *A Job for Wittilda* by Caralyn Buehner. Two non-fiction books for Columbus Day are *Christopher Columbus* by Stephen Krensky and *A Picture Book of Christopher Columbus* by David Adler.

SUMMARY

Starting with literature and then expanding on its themes will enhance the whole curriculum. Literature can serve as a solid foundation that permits the teacher to have flexibility with planning while lending stability, an important component of early childhood education. Integrating each of the content areas with literature brings a cohesiveness to the program and the classroom, yet still allows wonderful things to happen in the classroom.

To achieve integration in the program requires careful planning. A planning process using webs helps the teacher choose the best activities for teaching var-

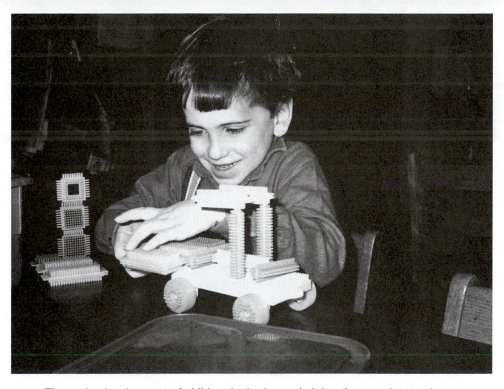

The active involvement of children is the key to helping them understand new information. Courtesy Diana Comer.

ious concepts, allows the consideration of many choices, and affords time to gather the materials and ideas needed for creative and effective learning activities. Planning webs can be used in a variety of ways. Three types of planning webs discussed in this chapter were the literature web, the single-book web, and the integrated-curriculum web.

Both beginning and experienced teachers should frequently visit a children's library and spend substantial time reading the books. Keeping notes of those books that are enjoyable and helpful is a good way to be organized for upcoming units. Watch children interact with the books and the library. This is the most effective way to remember a child's level of thinking about literature, which will aid in planning creative lessons for children. Simply browsing through books can generate ideas, thoughts, and memories as the illustrations, words, and characters pass by. Old friends jump out from some books, and delightful new ones draw the reader into others. Planning and integrating a program using webs can be a fascinating process.

QUESTIONS FOR THOUGHT AND DISCUSSION

1. Explain the term *web* as it is used in program planning.
2. What is the difference between a literature web, a single-book web, and an integrated-curriculum web?
3. Defend or refute the following: It is better to create your own ideas for units than to rely on someone else's.
4. What are the reasons for using an integrated curriculum with children?
5. Are there times when a teacher should not use an integrated approach with literature? Explain your reasons.
6. When might a teacher change or adapt a poem or rhyme for class use?
7. How can a teacher facilitate the integration of the curriculum?
8. Defend or refute the following: The use of a book series is never an appropriate approach because the quality is poor.
9. How might a field guide be helpful in early childhood education?
10. Which writers have written several books dealing with either family life or peer relations?
11. Identify a general theme and create an integrated-curriculum web for that topic. Identify the level of the children for whom the unit is being planned.
12. Choose a topic and develop a literature web for it.
13. Develop a single-book web for the preschool or kindergarten level.

CHILDREN'S BOOKS CITED

Adler, D. (1991). *A picture book of Christopher Columbus.* New York: Holiday House.

Benjamin, A. (1997). *Hanukkah chubby board book and Dreidels.* New York: Little Simon.

Berenstain, S., & Berenstain, J. (1997). *Comic valentine.* New York: Cartwheel Books.

Bridwell, N. (1994). *Clifford's happy Easter.* New York: Scholastic.

Brooks, A. (1996). *Frogs jump.* New York: Scholastic.

Brown, M.W. (1949). *Christmas in the barn.* New York: Crowell.

Brown, M.W. (1977). *The runaway bunny.* New York: Harper.

Buehner, C. (1993). *A job for Wittilda.* New York: Dial.

Bunting, E. (1991). *A turkey for Thanksgiving.* New York: Clarion.

Bush, T. (1993). *James in the house of Aunt Prudence.* New York: Crown.

Carle, E. (1985). *My very first book of colors.* New York: Crowell.

Carle, E. (1969). *1, 2, 3 to the zoo.* New York: Collins World.

Cohen, C.L. (1996). *Where's the fly?* New York: Greenwillow.

Cole, B. (1997). *Dr. Dog.* New York: Alfred A. Knopf.

Crews, D. (1985). *Freight train.* New York: Penguin.

dePaola, T. (1988). B*aby's first Christmas.* New York: Holiday House.

dePaola, T. (1978). *Christmas pageant.* Minneapolis, MN: Winston.

dePaola, T. (1987). *An early American Christmas.* New York: Holiday House.

dePaola, T. (1986). *Strega Nona.* New York: Harcourt Brace Jovanovich.

dePaola, T. (1987). *Tomie dePaola's book of Christmas carols.* New York: Putnam.

Devlin, W., & Devlin, H. (1993). *Cranberry Easter.* New York: Aladdin.

Dooley, N. (1991). *Everybody Cooks Rice.* Minneapolis, MN: Carolrhoda.

Duffy, D.D. (1996). *Forest tracks.* Honesdale, PA: Boyds Mills Press.

Gammell, S. (1990). *Wake up, Bear . . . It's Christmas.* New York: Mulberry Books.

George, W. (1996). *Christmas at Long Pond.* New York: Mulberry Books.

Hansard, P. (1994). *Wag Wag Wag.* Cambridge: MA: Candlewick.

Hutchins, P. (1997). *Shrinking mouse.* New York: Greenwillow.

Hyman, T.S. (1991). *How Six found Christmas.* New York: Holiday House.

Jaspersohn, W. (1991). *Cranberries.* Boston: Houghton Mifflin.

Johnson, J. (1987). *Postal workers A to Z.* New York: Walker.

Joosse, B. (1992). *Nobody's cat.* New York: HarperCollins.

Jungman, A. (1993). *When the people are away.* Honesdale, PA: Boyds Mills Press.

Krensky, S. (1991). *Christopher Columbus.* New York: Random House.

Lattimore, D. (1997). *Cinderhazel.* New York: Blue Sky.

Littlesugar, A. (1996). *Marie in fourth position: The story of Degas' "The Little Dancer."* New York: Philomel.

Locker, T. (1997). *Waterdance.* San Diego, CA: Harcourt Brace.

Loomis, C. (1991). *In the diner.* New York: Scholastic.

Lowery, L. (1995). *Twist with a burger, jitter with a bug.* Boston, MA: Houghton Mifflin.

Machotka, H. (1992). *Pasta factory.* Boston: Houghton Mifflin.

Martin, Jr., B. (1993). *Old devil wind.* San Diego, CA: Harcourt Brace Jovanovich.

McCloskey, R. (1957). *Time of wonder.* New York: Viking.

McClung, R. (1976). *Animals that build their homes.* Washington, DC: National Geographic Society.

McDermott, G. (1992). *Zomo the Rabbit.* San Diego, CA: Harcourt Brace Jovanovich.

McDonnell, J. (1993). *The Easter surprise.* Chicago: Children's Press.

Metzger, S. (1997). *Dinofours: I'm not your friend!* New York: Cartwheel Books.

Metzger, S. (1997). *Dinofours: I'm Super Dino!* New York: Cartwheel Books.

Metzger, S. (1997). *Dinofours: It's class trip day!* New York: Cartwheel Books.

Metzger, S. (1997). *Dinofours: It's time for school!* New York: Cartwheel Books.

Miller, M. (1996). *Now I'm big.* New York: Greenwillow.

Morris, A. (1992). *Houses and homes.* New York: Lothrop, Lee & Shepard.

Neale, J. (1994). *Good King Wenceslas.* New York: North-South.

Newcome, Z. (1996). *Toddlerobics.* Cambridge, MA: Candlewick.

Newman, L. (1998). *Matzo ball moon.* New York: Clarion.

Offen, H. (1993). *Elephant pie.* New York: E.P. Dutton.

Osborne, M.P. (1997). *Rocking horse Christmas.* New York: Scholastic.

Pfister, M. (1993). *The Christmas star.* New York: North-South.

Portnoy, M. (1994). *Matzo ball: A Passover story.* Rockville, MD: Kar-Ben.

Riehecky, J. (1993). *Christmas in other lands.* Chicago: Children's Press.

Sawyer, R. (1953). *Journey cake, ho!* New York: Viking.

Say, A. (1991). *Tree of cranes.* Boston: Houghton Mifflin.

Schories, P. (1993). *He's your dog!* New York: Farrar, Straus, Giroux.

Schwartz, L. (1989). *The four questions.* New York: Dial.

Dr. Seuss (pseud. for T. Geisel), (1957). *How the grinch stole Christmas.* New York: Random.

Seymour, T. (1993). *Pole dog.* New York: Lothrop, Lee & Shepard.

Siddals, M.M. (1997). *Tell me a season.* New York: Clarion.

Stevenson, J. (1996). *The great big especially beautiful Easter egg.* New York: Mulberry Books.

Stutson, C. (1996). *By the light of the Halloween moon.* New York: Puffin.

Szekeres, C. (1997). *Yes, Virginia, there is a Santa Claus.* New York: Cartwheel Books.

Thompson, C.E. (1997). *How big were the dinosaurs?* New York: Cartwheel Books.

Thomson, P. (1993). *Siggy's spaghetti works.* New York: Tambourine.

Tregebov, R. (1993). *The big storm.* New York: Hyperion.

Wolff, F., & Kozielski, D. (1994). *On Halloween night.* New York: Tambourine.

Zolotow, C. (1998). *The bunny who found Easter.* Boston, MA: Houghton Mifflin.

SELECTED REFERENCES

Alexander, S. (1996). *Art for all seasons*. Huntington Beach, CA: Teacher Created Materials.

Barkin, C., & James, E. (1994). *The holiday handbook.* New York: Clarion.

Bayless, K., & Ramsey, M. (1991). *Music: A way of life for the young child.* New York: Macmillan.

Bromley, K.D. (1991). *Webbing with literature.* Boston: Allyn & Bacon.

Cerullo, M. (1997). *Reading the environment.* Portsmouth, NH: Heinemann.

Cliatt, M.P., & Shaw, J.M. (1992). *Helping children explore science.* New York: Macmillan.

Herr, J., & Libby, Y. (1990). *Creative resources for the early childhood classroom.* Albany, NY: Delmar Publishers.

Kucer, S., Silva, C., & Delgado-Larocco, E. (1995). *Curriculum conversations.* York, ME: Stenhouse.

Lipke, B. (1996). *Figures, facts, & fables.* Portsmouth, NH: Heinemann.

Mayesky, M.E. (1995). *Creative activities for young children.* Albany, NY: Delmar Publishers.

McKinnon, E. (1989). *Special day celebrations.* Everett, WA: Warren.

Oppenheim, C. (1995). *Science is fun.* Albany, NY: Delmar Publishers.

Pica, R. (1995). *Experiences in movement with music, activities and theory.* Albany, NY: Delmar Publishers.

Rubright, L. (1995). *Beyond the beanstalk.* Portsmouth, NH: Heinemann.

Short, K.G., & Burke, C.L. (1991). *Creating curriculum: Students and teachers as a community of learners.* Portsmouth, NH: Heinemann.

Van Manen, M. (1986). *The tone of teaching.* Portsmouth, NH: Heinemann.

Whitin, D., & Wilde, S. (1995). *It's the story that counts.* Portsmouth, NH: Heinemann.

I seldom think about my limitations,
and they never make me sad.

– Helen Keller

8 Bibliotherapy: Using Books to Heal

The first part of the term *bibliotherapy* is *biblio*, a derivation of a Greek word referring to books. The second part, *therapy*, is a derivation of a Greek word referring to procedures used to treat bodily disorders. Thus. literally, *bibliotherapy* means the treatment of bodily disorders using books. However, the term has come to mean the use of books, and the subsequent discussions about those books, to address a variety of psychological concerns.

In order to make full use of bibliotherapy, it is necessary to have an understanding of the concerns possessed by young children and an awareness of some of the books that may be helpful in addressing those concerns.

UNDERSTANDING BIBLIOTHERAPY

The use of bibliotherapy as a tool for teachers and librarians was recognized over a quarter of a century ago by educators David Russell and Caroline Shrodes.[1] They described bibliotherapy as a process in which the reader and the literature interacted. Taking a clinical approach, they felt bibliotherapy was a promising tool for assessing personality and monitoring adjustment and growth in individuals.

Years later Patricia Cianciolo published her beliefs using a less clinical perspective on how books can help the child.[2] She identified six areas in which books could provide positive help to children. Two of these areas addressed education and learning issues. Books could help children acquire information about human behavior, including areas that were a current concern to them. Books could also help children come to an understanding of the phrase "heal thyself." That is, children could learn that the answer to some problems must come from within. Two of the areas identified focused on the need to extend oneself. Through books, one can find interests outside oneself. Also, stories can be used to relieve stress in a controlled manner. The last two areas focused on the use of books as problem-solving tools. Books provide individuals with an opportunity to identify and

[1] Russell, D., & Schrodes, C. (1950, September). Contributions of research in bibliotherapy to the language arts program. *School Review, 58,* 335–392.

[2] Cianciolo, P. (1965, May). Children's literature can affect coping behaviors. *Personnel and Guidance Journal, 43,* 897–901.

compensate for personal problems. That is, it is often easier to talk about a problem if it is someone else's problem. Finally, stories can illuminate personal difficulties and help one acquire insight into personal behavior. That is, a problem can be clarified by seeing it described by another person in a story.

Books as Therapy

Charlotte S. Huck and Doris Young Kuhn provide a picture of how bibliotherapy can be used with children experiencing a variety of fears, anxieties, and worries associated with everyday life.[3] They identify the three processes of psychotherapy and suggest that they can parallel three stages of bibliotherapy. The first process is *identification,* in which there is an association of oneself with an individual found in literature. Second, there is *catharsis*, meaning the releasing of emotion. It is believed that by observing and identifying with a character in a story with a similar problem, one can gain some degree of relief from the stress and emotion caused by the same problem in one's own life. The third process is *insight*, in which one develops an emotional awareness of one's own motivations in dealing with a problem. That is, by observing and understanding how a character in a story deals with an emotion, one can better deal with the same emotion in real life.

This view can be helpful, since it provides a step-by-step procedure for using bibliotherapy with children. Teachers, parents, and others attempting to use bibliotherapy should use some caution, however. It is an appropriate tool for helping children approach minor anxieties associated with everyday life. But when children have deeper psychological problems, they should be referred to other professionals who possess the appropriate training to deal with those difficulties.

The Chronically Ill Child

Bibliotherapy is an effective tool to use with children who are physically ill. Hospitals, clinics, and treatment centers throughout the country frequently use such an approach with their young patients. Regina Houston describes the special considerations which one must have in using bibliotherapy with chronically ill children. At one point, she was the "Story Lady" in the pediatrics ward at the University of Massachusetts Hospital. She shares these thoughts:

Stories give readers experiences they haven't had in life. Books also acquaint the reader with different ways of looking at life. Watty Piper's *The Little Engine that Could* has inspired many young listeners to try their very best. It has given confidence to children even during the most difficult of times and in the face of the most adverse situations. The stories can help release tension and develop values. They can show one how to evaluate situations and how to solve problems. They do so by allowing us to observe the solutions reached by the characters in both ordinary and unusual situations. In so doing, books extend both a child's experience and world.

[3] Charlotte S. Huck and Doris Young Kuhn, *Children's Literature in the Elementary School* (New York: McGraw-Hill, 1993).

All people share the basic needs for food, clothing, shelter, and safety. Other needs which everyone has include the need for love, being part of a group, a positive self concept, and an understanding of what makes each of us special. Many of these needs can be partially met in books. Stories nurture the hopes and dreams of the child. They reinforce each child's uniqueness and provide courage and friendship.

Hospital-confined children have a special need for bibliotherapy. Children struggling with long-term illnesses find peace and solace in stories. Stories are comforting to the chronically ill child. The association lessens some of the trauma they are dealing with. Justin, a three year old, found a safe refuge in stories after his painful weekly injection. Another child, Benjamin, has used stories to come to an understanding that life has a beginning, a middle, and an end. Part of his regular out-patient visits to the hospital include a visit to the "Story Lady." It is an enjoyable and nonthreatening part of his visit. The story sessions are not an escape from pain for Benjamin. Rather, they are an important part of Benjamin's total medical program as explained to him by his doctor and his mother.

Pediatric physicians have observed children as being more relaxed during examinations after they have shared and experienced a story. The stories provide a therapeutic vehicle through which the child can deal with fears and doubts. They can both educate the child and facilitate the procedures which the child must endure. One of the greatest benefits, however, comes from the human interaction of the child and the reader. Through voice and body language, the reader can communicate a calmness and a warmth. This acceptance of children and their fears is invaluable to both the pediatric patient and the well child.

Parents, teachers, and others who share stories with the chronically ill child must have certain understandings. Such children have special needs which go beyond that of well children. Medications, phases of an illness, and healing processes can all affect behavior. One should take care to not misread or misunderstand these changes in behavior. Knowledge of a child's physical needs and problems is necessary for anyone using bibliotherapy with a chronically ill child. It requires interest and caring on the part of the reader. That is true for all children, of course. With the chronically ill child, it is critical.

BENEFITS OF BIBLIOTHERAPY

Bibliotherapy can address a number of different needs a child may have in dealing with a difficulty. Obviously, some needs can be addressed better than others. The success of bibliotherapy depends on the child, the problem, and the situation in which bibliotherapy is used. The benefits discussed here include information, mutuality, empathy, options for action, and reaffirmation of life.

Information

The first benefit of bibliotherapy is the providing of information. Using books that address a particular problem often enables the child to gather accurate and reliable information in a subtle, nonthreatening manner. Educating children to the

Comfort can be found in sharing a book with a friend and a teddy bear.
Courtesy Diana Comer.

realities of the world and its problems provides a base of knowledge that they can rely on.

Many times children develop anxiety over a problem because they do not see the problem in its proper perspective. Education and the gaining of the truth that can come from books is helpful in destroying myths, misconceptions, and untruths. Problems often become much more solvable when they are seen.

Mutuality

Mutuality refers to the experience of sharing. When children are confronted with a problem that is affecting them deeply, they often feel alone. They are frightened by the sense of isolation they feel. Discovering, through books, that others share the same problem reduces this sense of isolation. Realizing that one isn't the only person in the world with a particular problem is helpful in coping with that problem.

Empathy

Empathy refers to the ability to share the feelings of another individual. Children are not necessarily born with empathy. A visit to most schoolyards will support the fact that children can be both cruel and thoughtless toward those they perceive to be different. Often this cruelty is based on ignorance or fear. It may be that the other child dresses, looks, or acts differently. The development of empathy is one of the most important things children can achieve. It places them firmly within the highest circle of humanity.

Books share the thoughts and feelings of others with their readers. Through books, children learn not only of their own worth but of the worth of others, even others who may not be like themselves. One might question whether this is truly the role of the educator. It cannot, of course, be otherwise. Achievement in academics without the development of character is of limited worth.

TIPS FOR TEACHERS

Ask librarians and book store employees if they have new titles that address children's fears and concerns.
* *Let these people know the age group you are interested in.*
* *Mention specific issues of interest.*
* *Communicate with librarians and bookstore employees on a regular basis.*

The caregiver is in a unique position to address both character development and academic achievement. As a matter of fact, how can one ignore the importance of each within a classroom? One cannot meaningfully teach a group of children while some in the group are shunned and hurting. Group cooperation is impossible if some children avoid the child with cerebral palsy for fear of "catching it." The social relationships within a class have a direct influence on the productivity of the class. Addressing or ignoring these issues determines whether or not the group will have a heart and a soul. Bibliotherapy is most effective when used by an adult who is committed to addressing the whole child. Building empathy begins with seeing others as human beings with needs similar to our own.

Options for Action

When faced with a difficult problem, adults can often feel in a bind with no solution. Children are no different. They may be so focused on the problem that they are incapable of stepping back and seeing the situation in a larger framework.

Books provide opportunities to observe how others view a problem. They explore various attempts by characters to resolve that problem. Through books, children come to realize that there are alternative ways for dealing with a problem. In discussing a story with an adult, children can learn that choices can be made in regard to most things in life. It is an important and healthy life skill to be able to cultivate options in problem solving.

◎ Reaffirmation of Life

When a person is faced with what appears to be a tremendous problem, the world can seem a cold and frightening place. It is true that some bad things do happen in life. The world will never be perfect. Yet, there are many wonderful and beautiful things about life. There are some truly caring and loving people on this earth. There are flowers, birds, songs, and gorgeous sunsets. Children need to understand this when faced with problems. They need to be able to affirm that there are some truly beautiful things about life. This does not eliminate the problem; it merely helps put it in perspective.

Children are exposed to many of life's grim realities through television and the media. Unfortunately, the good things aren't deemed as newsworthy as the more sordid aspects of life. Children need to talk about the fears they have regarding some of the things they have seen. They often look to adults to help them affirm the positive aspects of their existence as people.

USING BIBLIOTHERAPY

Bibliotherapy can be a powerful and effective tool for addressing the problems and concerns of young children. As with any activity or lesson to be used with children, though, planning will increase the effectiveness of bibliotherapy. In order to plan effectively, one must be aware of several factors surrounding the use of bibliotherapy: (1) develpmental appropriateness, (2) accuracy of content and effectiveness of style, (3) strategies for presentation, and (4) awareness of the limitations of bibliotherapy.

◎ Developmental Appropriateness

The criteria for choosing developmentally-appropriate books for bibliotherapy are similar to those used for choosing books for other purposes. Be aware of the understanding children have at different developmental levels. Be aware also of the types of concerns they have at different ages. These can vary, of course, but one can reasonably expect three-year-olds to have night fears, for example.

Adults need to realize that the fears children experience are very real to them. The best way to respond is with honesty and empathy. Children's fears need to be addressed without ridicule. While children's fears may not be totally overcome, coping skills and management of the fears can be established. A powerful aid to overcoming fear is an adult who is consistently accessible to the child and reinforces the concept that things are under control. This is true whether the child's fears are real or imaginary.

There are a variety of possible sources of concern for the young child. Some things such as parental separation, divorce, adoption, death, AIDS, pregnancy, or the birth of a new sibling are centered around the family. Other concerns are more closely related to the child's ability to deal with the immediate environment. These may include friendship, illness, death, bullies, school, animals, moving, foster care, and self-worth. Still other fears may focus on world events. These may include nuclear war, crime, terrorism, and drugs. If the child initiates a discussion about one of these fears, chances are it is very real in the mind of that child.

In determining whether a book or an activity is developmentally appropriate, the National Association for the Education of the Young (NAEYC) (1997) warns against seeing the concept as a polarizing "yes/no" issue. That is, there is no single characteristic that defintely makes something developmentally appropriate or not. NAEYC illustrates the complexity of the concept through a set of statements which can be used as a guide to making decisions concerning the developmental appropriateness. Some NAEYC comments that are particularly relevant to book selection observe that children

- Develop their own individual understanding of the world and profit from teaching by peers and adults.
- Benefit from knowing their boundaries and from opportunities to make choices within those boundaries.
- Grow through practicing new skills and knowledge in realistically challenging situations.
- Develop a sense of competence by being treated as individuals and by having opportunities to collaborate with their peers.
- Need to develop a sense of respect for themselves and for others who may be different from themselves.

◎ Choice of Books

There are many good books for meeting needs within most problem areas. The illustrations and text must be analyzed with the same criteria used to select books for any use. Particular attention should be paid to the accuracy of the content and the style of delivery. A book that trivializes the problem or solves it in an oversimplified manner might not help a child to deal with reality. In bibliotherapy, the concept of reality is extremely important even though the books may be fictional.

Books that use either animals or people can be appropriate. Even though children know that bears don't talk, the books by Stan and Jan Berenstain are effective in dealing with problems because the issues are realistic. The use of talking bears simply allows the child to look at a problem through another's eyes. Using books with animal characters can be especially appropriate when dealing with topics that are embarrassing to children. It is easier to talk about an embarrassing problem in the context of an animal character.

To be effective, a book must communicate with children on their level. Children, like adults, do not like to be talked down to. They often react in anger to such an approach or at least end the communication. The story should also have a clear appeal. At an early point in the book the child must be able to relate to the character and the solution. A good message or theme is worthless if the story is not captivating.

Strategies for Presentation

Planning ahead will make bibliotherapy a more powerful tool. Using effective strategies for presentation will help as well. The most helpful strategies deal with such things as (1) informing parents; (2) making decisions about when and how to use bibliotherapy; and (3) planning how to share the experience with children.

Research the Facts. It is important to have a good grasp of the information to be used. Only facts and real information should be used. Half truths and lies will only destroy credibility, no matter how well-intended they are. This is true whether the information comes from the literature or other sources. If the information is known ahead of time, it can be better tailored to the audience. Review books and articles on the topic for ideas on the best ways to introduce the subject and how much to introduce at each level.

Be Sensitive. When using bibliotherapy, one is providing help to both the child and the family. A child with a problem does not exist in a vacuum; such a child exists within a family, and the family is most likely aware of the problem as well. Therefore, it makes good sense to let parents know how the problem is being addressed. This can be done through meetings, telephone calls, or newsletters. The method of communication will depend on the type of problem. When working with children, it is helpful to anticipate all of the possible reactions children could have prior to beginning the lesson. By doing this, one can plan responses to these reactions. Such planning can help ensure that bibliotherapy will be carried on in a nonthreatening and supportive manner. As a result, children will be more likely to feel empowered by the experience.

Use Good Timing. Introducing bibliotherapy prior to the time that children are ready for it can mean failure. Make certain that trust has been established. Trust is something that builds up over time. It is inadvisable, therefore, to discuss anything more than minor concerns during the first week of school. Another aspect of good timing is to ensure an adequate amount of time for fully exploring the issue. It is inappropriate to begin a session on new babies or racial issues at the end of the day or in the middle of a free-play period. A time must be chosen when the class-room is quiet and there will be enough time to talk, to listen, and to internalize.

Integrate the Topic. No problem exists all by itself. Likewise, no solution exists in isolation. All the various parts of our existence are integrated on our life. It is both logical and efficient to integrate the use of bibliotherapy with other parts of the curriculum. Many of the books one would use in a bibliotherapy session would be appropriate for other aspects of the curriculum as well. By integrating the understandings and issues, the learning is reinforced for children.

Plan for the Long Term. In planning a long-term integrated curriculum, it makes sense to plan bibliotherapy in a logical progression of steps. For example, one might begin with self-concept, followed by family concerns, school concerns, and personal safety. Each topic builds on the previous one. A child's understanding increases when a logical order such as this is followed.

Remember the Role. There will always be the temptation to deal with issues that should be left to others. The teacher using bibliotherapy should keep in mind that the purpose is to shed light and understanding on some of the normal problems and fears children encounter as they are growing up. Serious mental and psychological problems should be referred to others with the appropriate training as soon as they are discovered. If a child is observed reacting with agitation or acting-out behavior when a topic is discussed, the child should be talked to privately. A calm and supportive manner in posing gentle, nonthreatening questions is the most productive way to deal with a frightened child. If the child is not able to participate and continues to exhibit reactions that are noticeably different from those of other children, a parent conference is suggested. In meeting with the parents, it is important to listen to their understanding of the problem. When a mutual understanding of the problem is achieved, the best decision for the child can be made.

Maintain Flexibility. When working with young children it is important to be flexible. With bibliotherapy, it is particularly important. Be ready to shift gears, take an unexpected turn, or back up as the situation demands. While discussing a problem in a bibliotherapy session, it is a good idea to restate any questions a child might ask. This restating makes sure that everyone understands what is being asked. Then provide just enough information to answer the question. Too detailed an answer could lose the children's interest. One should always respond to a question, however. Choosing to ignore a question that was honestly asked is a poor response. If an appropriate answer cannot be given, one needs to say so rather than fail to respond. Be aware, too, that children often ask simple and general questions prior to asking the real question that addresses a current problem or difficulty. Allow children time to build up to discussing their real concerns.

TIPS FOR TEACHERS
Be ready for children to bring up unexpected concerns.
- *A worry about a parent who smokes.*
- *A scary dream from last night.*
- *A fear of the loud dog next door.*

ADDRESSING THE CONCERNS OF CHILDREN

Young children often have different concerns than those of older children, adolescents, and adults. Sometimes what adults perceive to be the concerns of children actually cause them little difficulty. The best way to learn of children's concerns is to ask them or listen to their general conversation. Sometimes adults forget to do this, but it is a technique that really does work. Indirect means such as reading a book and discussing it can also bring out the true concerns children possess. There is no one best way to learn of a child's concern. Each individual sees things differently. Each child will use different approaches and coping strategies for dealing with problems.

In general, however, there are certain themes that address the concerns and problems of children: self, family, friends, other people, illness and death, and the world. This is not the only way of grouping these areas, of course. It is used here because it serves as an easily understood frame of reference.

Self

Am I as pretty as Jane? Does my ball bounce as well as the ball that Joe has? Will I always be short? Will Mom have time for me when the new baby arrives? These are only a few of the possible concerns of young children. While adults may see some issues as foolish, they are quite real to the child who wants to fit

Children often see a bit of themselves in the characters they meet in stories.

in with the rest of the world. The problems can be increased if other children learn about them and taunt the child. Such teasing can be the beginning lesson on the dark side of human nature.

Children need adults to bring light to this dark side of life. Sharing a book related to the situation can enable everyone to think about their actions and the effect they have on others. Such a book can help to bring out the importance of feeling good about oneself.

A variety of books can be used to explore this topic. Tomie dePaola's *Oliver Button Is a Sissy* explores the idea of being true to yourself and trying to do your best in your areas of interest. In *Talking Walls* and *Who Belong's Here? An American Story*, Margy Burns Knight explores the difficult concepts and implication of hate, peace, and world friendship. The emotion of personal fear is examined in such favorites as Patrice Aggs' *The Visitor*, Debbie Harter's *Walking Through the Jungle*, Tudor Humphrie's *Hiding*, Tony Johnston's *The Chizzywink and the Alamagoozlum*, and William Joyce's *George Shrinks*.

In *Go Away, Big Green Monster*, Ed Emberly uses a clever series of die-cut pages that enable the child or reader to construct and deconstruct a big green monster. Vivid language is used to create the monster in a friendly way so that fears of monsters and nightmares can be lessened. A blue monster is dealt with by a plucky princess in Paul Borovsky's *The Strange Blue Creature*. Still another monster is presented in *Alistair Underwater* by Marilyn Sadler. Libba Moore Gray tells the story of how a nearsighted frog overcomes a fear of jumping to the next lily pad in *Fenton's Leap*. Timothy learns how knowledge can help overcome fear in *Timothy Twinge* by Florence Perry Heide and Roxanne Pierce Heide. Using less than forty words, Chris Raschka presents a powerful lesson on fear in *Yo! Yes?* A frightening loud noise creates a climate of fear for Savi the elephant and Harold the bird until they learn what made the noise, in Judith Richardson's *Come to My Party*. A child's fear for a lost pet is touchingly shared by Uli Waas in *Where's Molly?* Concerns about being a competent person both at home and at school are

Alistair Underwater *by Marilyn Sadler.*
Illustrations by Roger Bollen. © 1988; reprinted by permission of the publisher, Simon and Schuster Books for Young Readers.

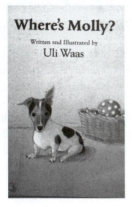

Where's Molly? *by Uli Waas.* Copyright © 1993 by Nord-Sud Verlag AG, Gossau Zurich, Switzerland. Used by permission of North-South Books, Inc.

addressed in Robert Kraus's *Leo the Late Bloomer,* Tomie dePaola's *Andy, That's My Name*, Richard Edwards's *Moles Can Dance*, Helen Lester's *Three Cheers for Tacky*, David Mereveille's *Thomas the Circus Boy*, Mike Thaler's *Hippo Lemonade*, Pili Mandelbaum's *You Be Me, I'll Be You*, Debra Hess's *Wilson Sat Alone*, Watty Piper's *The Little Engine That Could*, Patricia Reilly Giff's *Happy Birthday, Ronald Morgan*, Mick Inkpen's *Nothing*, and Miriam Cohen's *When Will I Read?* In *That Bothered Kate*, Sally Noll explores the themes of jealousy and guilt. Finally, Jane Yolen's wonderful book, *Sleeping Ugly,* does an exceptional job of dealing with the concept of physical attractiveness.

Family

The family continues to be seen as the basic social unit of society, but the twentieth century has brought many changes to it. Families are getting smaller and tend to be more spread out geographically. Separation, divorce, single parenthood, and extended families are more and more common. Children sometimes do not understand these changes, causing them to develop fears. Children wonder if they caused the divorce, whether Dad will ever come back, and whether they will be divorced by their families. They also worry about the mortality of parents, grandparents, and themselves.

The traditional causes of stress in families have never left. New babies, deaths, illness, sibling rivalry, unemployment, poverty, and homelessness continue to create pressures on the young child. These aspects of family life put pressure on the entire family with a variety of results. The young child is the least able member of the family to deal with the fears these changes bring. These fears overwhelm the verbal and coping skills of the very young. Bibliotherapy can help. It will not solve all of the problems, but it will provide both a framework and some of the language necessary for children to understand the stresses.

Books dealing with family issues include Russell Hoban's *A Baby Sister for Frances*, Tony Bradman's *A Goodnight Kind of Feeling*, Marc Brown's *Arthur's*

TIPS FOR TEACHERS

Listen to the concerns and worries of children and their families in a nin-judgmental manner.
• Know in advance which issues you need to refer to a professional.
• Listen to the whole story the child is telling you.
• Don't invade or usurp the parents' authority.

Birthday, Tres Seymour's *Too Quiet for These Old Bones*, Cynthia Rylant's *When I Was Young in the Mountains*, Charlotte Zolotow's *Something Is Going to Happen*, Martha Alexander's *Nobody Asked Me if I Wanted a Baby Sister*, Tom Birdseye's *A Regular Flood of Mishap*, Brian Mangas's *Sshaboom!*, Valeri Reddix's *Dragon Kite of the Autumn Moon*, Tricia Tusa's *The Family Reunion*, and Charlotte Zolotow's *The Quiet Lady*. Fathers are the focus of Robert Munsch's *50 Below Zero*, and Susan Patron's *Dark Cloud Strong Breeze*. Mothers are the focus of Judith Casely's *Mama, Coming and Going*, Rebecca Emberly's *My Mother's Secret Life*, Caitlin Dundon's *The Yellow Umbrella*, and Marisabina Russo's *Trade-in Mother*. Nick Butterworth demonstrates the special relationships that can develop between children and their grandparents in *My Grandma Is Wonderful* and *My Grandpa Is Amazing*. Using a peaceful reassuring approach, Robin Ballard examines the sensitive topic of separation and divorce in *Gracie*. The issue of illiteracy in the family is addressed in Eve Bunting's *The Wednesday Surprise*. Children have concerns about gender, sex, and where babies come from. The best answers to questions children raise are, of course, honest explanations. There are

Andy, That's My Name *by Tomie dePaola. © 1973;* reprinted by permission of the publisher, Simon and Schuster Books for Young Readers.

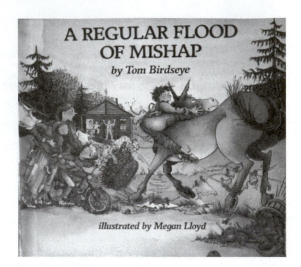

A Regular Flood Mishap *by Tom Birdseye.* Reprinted by permission of Holiday House, New York.

Herman the Helper *by Robert Kraus.* © 1974; reprinted by permission of the publisher, Simon and Schuster Books for Young readers.

several books to help address some of the issues and provide information as well. They include *It's Perfectly Natural* by Robie Harris and two books by Joanna Cole, *My Puppy Is Born* and *How You Were Born.* Siblings and sibling rivalry are the issue in books such as Jane Cutler's *Darcy and Gran Don't Like Babies,* Holly Keller's *Geraldine's Baby,* Addie Lacoe's *Just Not the Same,* Julia McClelland's *This Baby,* Susan Bonners's *Just in Passing,* Marc Brown's *Arthur's Baby,* and Judy Cox's *Now We Can Have a Wedding.* Showing that sibling rivalry transcends time and culture are Ashley Wolff's modern tortoise-and-hare tale *Stella and Roy* (multiethnic), *Por Los Aires* by Asun Balzola (Spain), and *The Crane Girl* by Veronika Charles (Japan).

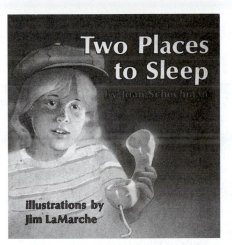

Two Places to Sleep *by Joan Schuchman.* Reprinted by permission of Carolrhoda Books.

Issues affecting the family can be explored in books as well. Poverty is the focus in Barbara Shook Hazen's *Tight Times*. For a related problem, *Hotel Boy* by Curt and Gita Kaufman uses real photographs to illustrate the story of impending homelessness. Two excellent books on grandparents suffering from Alzheimer's disease are worth noting: Vaunda Micheaux Nelson's *Always Gramma* and Jonah Schein's *Forget Me Not*. The stresses and worries of a child whose parents are divorced is addressed in *As the Crow Flies* by Elizabeth Winthrop and *Two Places to Sleep* by Joan Schuchman. Finally, imaginary fears are expertly dealt with in *Arthur Goes to Camp* and *D.W.'s Lost Blankie* by Marc Brown, *Come Along, Daisy* by Jane Simmons, and Judith Viorst's *My Mama Says There Aren't Any Zombies, Ghosts, Vampires, Creatures, Demons, Monsters, Fiends, Goblins or Things*.

Friends

As children grow, they move from a focus on themselves to the need to be a part of a group. They want to extend their social interactions beyond their families. They seek friendships. This is a long process along a path that can have many obstacles and pitfalls. Since humans are social beings by nature, it is a path that all must somehow travel.

Adults often wince at what young children sometimes say and do to their friends. They can be alternatively very loving and very hostile. Toddlers may hug each other one minute and bite each other the next. Preschoolers change best friends as though they are participating in a card game. Kindergarteners announce the beginnings and endings of best friendships as publicly as political campaigns announce endorsements. As a result, childhood friendships possess a combination of happiness, pain, and chaos. One can deal with these issues through discussion, understanding, and the use of bibliotherapy. It is through the reading of a story that sounds familiar to the real situation that the best and most sensitive discussions will emerge.

Books that can be used to generate bibliotherapy discussions include Miriam Cohen's *Will I Have a Friend?*, Marc Brown's *Arthur's Birthday*, Nancy Carlson's *How to Lose All Your Friends*, Lindsay Camp's *Keeping Up With Cheetah*, Nancy White Carlson's *Blow Me a Kiss, Miss Lilly,* Lucille Clifton's *Three Wishes*, Berlie Doherty's *Willa and Old Miss Annie*, Elisa Kleven's *The Lion and the Little Red Bird,* and Dianne Wolkstein's *Little Mouse's Painting*. Two superb books on the subject of sleeping over at a friend's house are Jacqueline Rogers *Best Friends Sleep Over* and Bernard Waber's *Ira Sleeps Over*. The joys of friendship are celebrated in *You and Me* by Salley Mavor and *Beezy Magic* by Megan McDonald. The sadness of moving away is explored in *Faraway Drums* by Virginia Kroll. In this touching story about an urban black family, Jamila is very unhappy in the new apartment her family has moved to. Having to come home right after school to babysit her little sister Zakiya makes things even worse. Zakiya is even more unhappy, because the new nighttime sounds frighten her. Floyd Cooper's gritty but striking illustrations lend an air of realism to the story. This book will help stimulate young people to talk about the difference between a building and a home. The ups and downs of friendship are addressed in Arnold Lobel's *Frog and Toad Are Friends*, Nancy Carlson's *Witch Lady*, and Patricia Reilly Giff's *The Beast in Ms. Rooney's Room.*

Other People

Children try to make sense of the world. When things don't fit neatly into place in the child's mind, fear can arise. "Other people" is a grouping that refers to people who for one reason or another may cause stress and fear in a child. Any unfamiliar person may fall into this category. The stress and fear are usually caused by ignorance on the part of the child. Children with disabilities and children of different ethnicity who may appear to be different can cause anxiety. Children often exhibit fear toward people with disabilities because they are afraid that they will "catch it." Skin color, dress, and language that are not familiar can cause anxiety for both minority and nonminority children. Through bibliotherapy, children can learn that despite the differences, people are all human beings. Bibliotherapy can help decrease ignorance and focus discussions on the common humanity of all people.

There are many books that explore the concept of other people. Physical disabilities are clarified and explained in stories such as Barbara Dugan's *Loop the Loop*, Susan Jeschke's *Perfect the Pig*, Ken Kesey's *The Sea Lion,* Margaret Mahy's *The Three-Legged Cat*, and Berniece Rabe's *The Balancing Girl*. Visual disabilities are dealt with in Jack Ezra Keats's *Apartment Three*, Virginia Kroll's *Naomi Knows It's Springtime*, Miriam Cohen's *See You Tomorrow, Charles*, and Patricia MacLachlan's *Through Grandpa's Eyes*. Hearing disabilities are the focus of such books as *Mandy* by Barbara Booth. This story has the added advantage of demonstrating the special grandparent-and-grandchild relationship. Other disabilities and differences are addressed in Miriam Cohen's *When Will I Read?*, Tomie dePaola's *Oliver Button Is a Sissy*, Charlotte Zolotow's *William's Doll*,

Charles Amenta's *Russell Is Extra Special,* Mitchell Sharmat's *Sherman Is a Slowpoke*, Berniece Rabe's *Where's Chimpy?*, Virginia Fleming's *Be Good to Eddie Lee*, Ada Litchfield's *Making Room for Uncle Joe*, and Daniel Pinkwater's *Uncle Melvin.*

TIPS FOR TEACHERS

Use books about other cultures and about characters who have a disability so that children will know that these diefferences are a natural part of life.
- *Use multicultural books throughout all aspects of the day.*
- *Treat characters with disabilities matter of factly, making the disability only a single aspect of the character.*
- *Invite people with disabilities to read books with children, not to discuss their disabilities, enabling children to focus on the reader as a person.*

Books are also available that can help educate children about minority groups. Black Americans are the focus of books such as Debbi Chocolate's magical and musical *The Piano Man*, Angela Johnson's *Daddy Calls Me Man*, Jack Ezra Keats's *The Snowy Day*, Lucille Clifton's *The Boy Who Didn't Believe in Spring*, David Adler's *A Picture Book of Sojourner Truth*, Elizabeth Howard's *Aunt Flossie's Hats (and Crab Cakes Later)*, Patricia McKissack's *A Million Fish . . . More or Less*, and Cecile Schoberle's *Morning Sounds, Evening Sounds.* Three delightful books by Angela Johnson featuring African-American families are *Joshua by the Sea*, *One of Three*, and *When I Am Old With You.* Books involving Hispanic Americans include Omar Castaneda's *Abuela's Weave*, Alejandro Cruz Martinez's *The Woman Who Outshone the Sun/La Mujer Que Brillaba Aun Mas Que el Sol*, Arthur Dorros's *Abuela*, Monica Gunning's *Not a Copper Penny in Me House, Poems from the Caribbean*, Juanita Havil's *Treasure Nap*, and Linda Jacobs's *Amelia's Road.* All of these stories are superb tales that transcend cultures.

Illness and Death

Illness and death are a part of life that most people fear to some extent. For children, who have less understanding of these events than adults, the anxiety may be greater. The topics of illness and death can trigger powerful emotions, particularly in a child who is close to someone who is seriously ill or who has just died. For this reason, it is important to be particularly sensitive when dealing with these topics. The death of a classroom pet may provide an opportunity to explore this concept on a less emotional level. On the other hand, the fears associated with medical and dental visits can be addressed quite readily with bibliotherapy.

The topic of illness and death are addressed in Jonathan London's *Gray Fox,* Tomie dePaola's *Now One Foot, Now the Other*, and H.A. and Margaret Rey's *Curious George Goes to the Hospital.* Medical visits and illnesses are dealt

A Picture Book of Sojourner Truth *by David Adler.* Reprinted by permission of Holiday House, New York.

Storyteller Marilyn Omifunke Torres uses her multiethnic background to illustrate the connections of all the world's people through her stories. Courtesy Marilyn Omifunke Torres.

with in Lillian Hoban's *Arthur's Loose Tooth*, Jo Carson's *Pulling My Leg*, Tomie dePaola's *Strega Nona Meets Her Match*, Patti Boyd's *My Doctor's Bag*, Harriet Ziefert's *When Daddy Had the Chicken Pox*, and Susan Kuklin's *When I See My Dentist*. The topic of death is explored in a sensitive manner in Libby Hathorn's *Grandma's Shoes*, Amy Ehrlich's *Maggie and Silky and Joe*, Mem Fox's *Tough Boris*, Robert Munsch's *Love You Forever*, Mavis Jukes's *I'll See You in My Dreams*, Pirkko Vainio's *The Snow Goose*, Winfried Wolf's *Christmas with Grandfather*, and Judith Viorst's *The Tenth Good Thing about Barney*. Tomie dePaola deals with the death of a grandparent in an honest and straightforward manner in *Nana Upstairs, Nana Downstairs*.

Children can bring personal knowledge and experience to storytime. Courtesy Diana Comer.

The Snow Goose *by Pirkko Vainio. Copyright © 1993 by Nord-Sud Verlag AG, Gossau Zurich, Switzerland.* Used by permission of North-South Books, Inc.

A fine contemporary book for young children on the topic of HIV/AIDS is *Too Far Away To Touch* by Leslea Newman. In this story, Zoe's Uncle Leonard is dying from AIDS. With touching sensitivity, Uncle Leonard provides reassurance to Zoe that he will always live in her memories. Catherine Stock's watercolor illustrations support the compassionate focus of this significant book.

The World

The world of children is technically the same as the world of adults, but children often perceive it differently. They have lived a shorter time, have not had the opportunity to study our world, and have not developed the mental capacities to comprehend the intricacies of modern life. However, children watch the news, listen to adults as they express their fears, and observe such things as pollution, crime, and homelessness in many neighborhoods.

Childhood Fears. Children have reason to have fears. In fact, some fear can be a healthy thing. Fear keeps one from engaging in dangerous activities and reminds one to use common sense. On the other hand, fear can be overwhelming if it produces stress beyond the point that children can effectively cope. Many children develop fears about the great unknowns of the world. Adult explanations of the problems of the world are very often too complex and sophisticated for young children to comprehend. When children are without satisfactory understandings of a major societal problem, they may turn to the solutions offered in the media of their childhood world, and the media, particularly television, often stress a violent solution to problems. In addition, many of the toys aimed at children encourage violent and warlike play. Such play often makes adults uncomfortable, but there is a reluctance to interfere because it is just play.

TIPS FOR TEACHERS

Accept the fears of children as genuine and real to those children.
* *Ask children why they have a certain fear so that they can share their feelings.*
* *Agree that something can be scary when it is a legitimate fear, and beware of ridiculing a fear that seems foolish.*

Doug Lipman, a New England storyteller, has studied the issue of violent play modeled after the superheroes children observe on television. He conducts workshops on this topic for parents and teachers. He contends that one should look at the issue from the child's point of view in terms of the needs that the play is meeting. As those needs are met in other ways, the superhero play will diminish. It is not necessarily desirable to totally eliminate this type of play. After all, there are many admirable heroes in life, song, and literature.

Causes of Pressure. According to Doug Lipman, there are six underlying emotional causes to superhero play. Since the play is usually a result of stress or pressure, children are affected in different degrees. The first stress is the fact that children sometimes feel powerless. Children need to possess a certain amount of power to feel competent. Adults can avoid power struggles and use the need for power to build independence skills. A second cause is a feeling of incompetence. Children need to constantly be made aware of the fact that they are loved and have much worth. Boys especially feel the expectation to be "super competent." Children need to be told that they can do many things well.

The third cause of pressure applies to boys: it is the subtle societal understanding placed on boys that they may have to take command at any time. They often feel that they might not be able to meet the challenge. The fourth cause also applies mostly to boys, who quickly learn that they, more often than girls, will be the agents and objects of violence. While there has been some enlightenment in

Faithful Elephants *by Yukio Tsuchiya.* Reprinted by permission of Houghton Mifflin Co., Boston.

society's attitude toward sex roles over the past decades, boys are aware that they are more likely than girls to kill and be killed in wars and that they will be involved in most of the violent crimes. The fifth cause is again applicable to boys, who are discouraged from dealing with their feelings. They are aware of the expectation that they "must be strong" and "not show that they are afraid." It is a tremendous burden, and one that is both unhealthy and unfair. The sixth and final cause relates to girls. Girls learn that they are often expected to remain dependent on males and that they will be treated as objects by males. Part of this message is given by the superhero play of boys. Girls learn that such play is the proper role for boys. The role of girls is different. Each of these pressures is unhealthy. Unforunately, society has not yet succeeded in eliminating violence and sexist attitudes.

Books on World Stresses. The world can be a highly complex and frightening place. To address some of the needs of children in trying to understand the world's complexity and danger, bibliotherapy can again be a powerful tool. Through books, children can learn facts and begin to deal with those facts through discussions with caring and sensitive adults. Books that address the issues of war include Matt Novak's *The Pillow War*, Tres Seymour's *We Played Marbles*, and Dr. Seuss's *The Butter Battle Book*. Another powerful book on the subject of war is the newly reissued *Faithful Elephants* by Yukio Tsuchiya. It is a somber reminder of the inhumanity and irrationality of war. Children and adults will both be moved by its message.

The long-term effects of war, often horrifying, are dealt with in some books. In *The Wall* by Eve Bunting, a boy and his father travel to the Vietnam Memorial in Washington, D.C., to locate the name of the boy's grandfather. Not a pretty book, *My Hiroshima* by Junko Morimoto recounts the immediate and long-lasting effects of the first nuclear bomb used in war. In *The Lilly Cupboard* Shulamith Oppenheim tells the story of a Dutch family whose members risked their lives to save a young Jewish girl from Hitler's madness.

Books on pollution include Dr. Seuss's *The Lorax* and Sheila MacGill-Callahan's *And Still the Turtle Watched*. The issue of crime is confronted in *Miss Penny and Mr. Grubby* by Lisa Ernst, *I'm the Real Santa Claus* by Ingrid Ostheeren, and *Tim and the Blanket Thief* by John Prater. Self-concept is the topic in *Peeping Beauty* by Mary Jane Auch, *My Body Is Private* and *Who Is a Stranger and What Should I Do?* both by Linda Girard, *Kalinzu: A Story from Africa* by Jeremy Grimsdell, and *Nathaniel Willy, Scared Silly* by Judith Matthews and Fay Robinson. A fine story overthrowing both age stereotypes and sex stereotypes is *Old Turtle* by Douglas Wood. Other books suggested in other areas may be applicable for issues here as well.

SUMMARY

Bibliotherapy is a powerful tool to be used with children at all age and grade levels. It can be effective with even very young children. Educators cannot ignore the emotions and feelings of children as they attempt to be a part of their environment. The understandings of children need to be clarified and expanded. It is only through that process that children will decrease their ignorance and gain confidence in their ability to deal with the world.

There are many benefits to using bibliotherapy. The use of books to clarify misconceptions and to encourage discussion can lead the way to understanding and self-confidence. When children feel safe and competent, achievement in academics will be enhanced. The benefits of bibliotherapy are likely to be long-term ones. Caution should, of course, be exercised when dealing with highly emotional topics and with children with severe psychological needs.

A variety of childhood concerns can be addressed with bibliotherapy, including those related to self, family, friends, other people, illness, death, and problems of the world in general. Many books that can be for bibliotherapy. In addition to the regular criteria for choosing books, particular care should be taken with the content and presentation of books used in this way.

QUESTIONS FOR THOUGHT AND DISCUSSION

1. What is bibliotherapy?
2. How does one know whether or not a book is age appropriate for a child?
3. Why is it important that a book dealing with an issue be first and foremost a good story?
4. Briefly describe some of the emotional causes of superhero play.
5. If superhero play is not all bad, what is the role of the educator regarding this type of play?
6. Why should a teacher use caution with bibliotherapy?
7. What are some of the benefits of bibliotherapy?

8. What are some of the concerns of young children?
9. Fear can be both a benefit and a liability. When does it become a liability? When is it a benefit?
10. Briefly explain some of the strategies one should utilize with bibliotherapy.
11. List three different books for young children that deal with any of the following topics: divorce, poverty, war, sibling rivalry, death, illness, minority groups, and the handicapped.
12. Is parental notification and involvement important when using bibliotherapy? Why or why not?
13. Why expose a child to a book that deals with war?

CHILDREN'S BOOKS CITED

Adler, D.(1994). *A Picture book of Sojourner Truth*. New York: Holiday House.

Aggs, P. (1998). *The visitor*. New York: Orchard.

Alexander, M. (1971). *Nobody asked me if I wanted a baby* sister. New York: Dial.

Amenta, C. (1992). *Russell is extra special*. New York: Magination Press.

Auch, M.J. (1993). *Peeping beauty*. New York: Holiday House.

Ballard, R. (1993). *Gracie*. New York: Greenwillow.

Balzola, A. (1991). *Por Los Aires*. Madrid: Ediciones SM.

Birdseye, T. (1994). *A regular flood of mishap*. New York: Holiday House.

Bonners, S. (1989). *Just in passing*. New York: Lothrop, Lee, & Sheperd.

Booth, B. (1991). *Mandy*. New York: Lothrop, Lee, & Sheperd.

Borovsky, P. (1993). T*he strange blue creature*. New York: Hyperion.

Boyd, P. (1994). *My doctor's bag*. Los Angeles: Price/Stern/Sloan.

Bradman, T. (1989). *A goodnight kind of feeling*. New York: Holiday House.

Brown, M. (1998). *Arthur's baby*. Boston, MA: Little Brown.

Brown, M. (1998). *Arthur's birthday*. Boston, MA: Little Brown.

Brown, M. (1998). A*rthur's family vacation*. Boston, MA: Little Brown.

Brown, M. (1998). *Arthur goes to camp*. Boston, MA: Little Brown.

Brown, M. (1998). *D.W.'s lost blankie*. Boston, MA: Little Brown.

Bunting, E. (1990). *The wall*. New York: Clarion.

Bunting, E. (1989). *The Wednesday surprise*. New York: Clarion.

Butterworth, N. (1991). *My grandma is wonderful*. Cambridge, MA: Candlewick.

Butterworth, N. (1991). *My grandpa is amazing*. Cambridge, MA: Candlewick.

Camp, L. (1993). *Keeping up with cheetah*. New York: Lothrop, Lee, & Shepard.

Carlson, N.W. (1990). *Blow me a kiss, Miss Lilly*. New York: Harper.

Carlson, N.W. (1994). *How to lose all your friends*. New York: Viking.

Carlson, N.W. (1985). *Witch lady*. New York: Viking Penguin.

Carson, J. (1990). *Pulling my leg*. New York: Orchard.

Casely, J. (1994). *Mama, coming and going*. New York: Greenwillow.

Castaneda, O. (1993). *Abuela's weave*. New York: Lee & Low.

Charles, V. (1993). *The Crane girl*. New York: Orchard.

Chocolate, D. (1998). *The piano man*. New York: Walker.

Clifton, L. (1973). *The boy who didn't believe in spring*. New York: E.P. Dutton.

Clifton, L. (1992). *Three wishes*. New York: Doubleday.

Cohen, M. (1983). *See you tomorrow, Charles*. New York: Dell.

Cohen, M. (1977). *When will I read?* New York: Dell.

Cohen, M. (1967). *Will I have a friend?* New York: Macmillan.

Cole, J. (1993). *How you were born*. New York: Mulberry.

Cole, J. (1991). *My puppy is born*. New York: Mulberry.

Cox, J. (1998). *Now we can have a wedding!* New York: Holiday House.

Cutler, J. (1993). *Darcy and Gran don't like babies*. New York: Scholastic.

dePaola, T. (1973). *Andy, that's my name*. New York: Simon and Schuster.

dePaola, T. (1973). *Nana upstairs, Nana downstairs*. New York: Simon and Schuster.

dePaola, T. (1981). *Now one foot, now the other*. New York: G.P. Putnam.

dePaola, T. (1979). *Oliver Button is a sissy*. New York: Harcourt Brace Jovanovich.

de Paola, T. (1993). *Strega Nona meets her match*. New York: Putnam.

Doherty, B. (1994). *Willa and Old Miss Annie*. Cambridge, MA: Candlewick.

Dorros, A. (1991). *Abuela*. New York: Scholastic.

Dugan, B. (1992). *Loop the Loop*. New York: Greenwillow.

Dundon, C. (1994). *The yellow umbrella*. New York: Simon and Schuster.

Edwards, R. (1994). *Moles can dance*. Cambridge, MA: Candlewick.

Ehrlich, A. (1994). *Maggie and Silky and Joe*. New York: Viking.

Emberly, E. (1993). *Go away, Big Green Monster!* Boston: Little, Brown.

Emberly, R. (1998). *My mother's secret life*. Boston, MA: Little, Brown.

Ernst, L. (1991). *Miss Penny and Mr. Grubby*. New York: Bradbury.

Fleming, V. (1993). *Be good to Eddie Lee*. New York: Philomel.

Fox, M. (1994). *Tough Boris*. San Diego, CA: Harcourt Brace Jovanovich.

Giff, P.R. (1984). T*he beast in Miss Rooney's room*. New York: Dell.

Giff, P.R. (1986). *Happy Birthday, Ronald Morgan*. New York: Viking Penguin.

Girard, L. (1984). *My body is private*. Morton Grove, IL: Albert Whitman.

Girard, L. (1985). *Who is a stranger and what should I do*? Morton Grove, IL: Albert Whitman.

Gray, L. M. (1994). *Fenton's leap*. New York: Simon and Schuster.

Grimsdell, J. (1993). *Kalinzu: A story from Africa*. New York: Kingfisher.

Gunning, M. (1993). *Not a copper penny in me house, poems from the Caribbean*. Honesdale, PA: Boyds Mills.

Harris, R. (1994). *It's perfectly normal*. Cambridge, MA: Candlewick.

Harter, D. (1997). *Walking through the jungle*. New York: Orchard.

Hathorn, L. (1994). *Grandma's shoes*. Boston: Little, Brown.

Havil, J. (1992). *Treasure nap*. Boston: Houghton Mifflin.

Hazen, B.S. (1979). *Tight times*. New York: Viking Penguin.

Heide, F.P. & Heide, R.P. (1993). *Timothy twinge*. New York: Lothrop, Lee & Shepard.

Hess, D. (1994). *Wilson sat alone*. New York: Simon and Schuster.

Hoban, L. (1985). *Arthur's loose tooth*. New York: Harper and Row.

Hoban, R. (1960). *A baby sister for Frances*. New York: Harper and Row.

Howard, E. (1991). *Aunt Flossie's hats (and crab cakes later)*. New York: Clarion.

Humphries, T. (1997). *Hiding*. New York: Orchard.

Inkpen, M. (1998). *Nothing*. New York:: Orchard.

Jacobs, L. (1993). *Amelia's road*. New York: Lee & Low.

Jeschke, S. (1980). *Perfect the pig*. New York: Scholastic.

Johnson, A. (1997). *Daddy calls me Man*. New York: Orchard.

Johnson, A. (1994). *Joshua by the sea*. New York: Orchard.

Johnson, A. (1991). *One of three*. New York: Orchard.

Johnson, A. (1990). *When I am old with you*. New York: Orchard.

Johnston, T. (1998). *The chizzywink and the alamagoozlum*. New York: Holiday House.

Joyce, W. (1985). *George shrinks*. New York: Harper and Row.

Jukes, M. (1993). *I'll see you in my dreams*. New York: Knopf.

Kaufman, C. & Kaufman, G. (1987). *Hotel boy*. New York: Atheneum.

Keats, J.E. (1983). *Apartment three*. New York: Macmillan.

Keats, J.E. (1962). *The snowy day*. New York: Vanguard.

Keller, H. (1984). *Geraldine's baby*. New York: Greenwillow.

Kesey, K. (1995). *The sea lion*. New York: Puffin.

Kleven, E. (1992). T*he lion and the little red bird*. New York: Dutton.

Knight, M.B. (1992). *Talking walls*. Gardiner, ME: Tilbury House.

Knight, M.B. (1993). *Who belongs here? An American story*. Gardiner, ME: Tilbury House.

Kraus, R. (1971). *Leo the late bloomer*. New York: Simon and Schuster.

Kroll, V. (1998). *Faraway drums*. Boston, MA: Little, Brown.

Kroll, V. (1993). *Naomi knows it's springtime*. Honesdale, PA: Boyds Mills.

Kuklin, S. (1988). *When I see my dentist*. New York: Bradbury.

Lacoe, A. (1992). *Just not the same*. Boston: Houghton Mifflin.

Lester, H. (1994). *Three cheers for Tacky*. Boston: Houghton Mifflin.

Litchfield, A. (1984). *Making room for Uncle Joe*. Morton Grove, IL: Albert Whitman.

Lobel, A. (1970). *Frog and Toad are friends*. New York: Scholastic.

London, J. (1995). *Gray fox*. New York: Puffin.

MacGill-Callahan, S. (1996). *And still the turtle watched*. New York: Puffin.

MacLachlan, P. (1980). *Through Grandpa's eyes*. New York: Harper and Row.

Mahy, M. (1995). *The three-legged cat*. New York: Puffin.

Mandelbaum, P. (1990). *You be me, I'll be you*. Brooklyn, NY: Kane/Miller.

Mangas, B. (1993). *Sshaboom!* New York: Simon and Schuster.

Martinez, A.C. (1991). *The woman who outshone the sun/La mujer que brillaba aun mas que el sol*. San Francisco, CA: Children's Book Press.

Matthews, J. & Robinson, F. (1994). *Nathaniel Willy, scared silly*. New York: Bradbury.

Mavor, S. (1997). *You and me*. New York: Orchard.

McClelland, J. (1994). *This baby*. Boston: Houghton, Mifflin.

McDonald, M. (1998). *Beezy magic*. New York: Orchard.

McKissack, P. (1992). *A milliom fish...more or less*. New York: Knopf.

Mereveille, D. (1993). *Thomas the circus boy*. New York: Holt.

Morimoto, J. (1987). *My Hiroshima*. New York: Viking Penguin.

Munsch, R. (1986). *50 below zero*. Toronto, Ontario, Canada: Annick.

Munsch, R. (1988). *Love you forever*. Scarborough, Ontario, Canada: Firefly.

Nelson, V.M. (1988). *Always Gramma*. New York: G.P Putnam's Sons.

Newman, L. (1998). *Too far away to touch*. New York: Clarion.

Noll, S. (1993). *That bothered Kate*. New York: Puffin.

Novak, M. (1998). *The pillow war*. New York: Orchard.

Oppenheim, S. (1992). *The Lilly cupboard*. New York: Harper Collins.

Ostheeren, I. (1994). *I'm the real Santa Claus*. New York: North-South.

Patron, S. (1994). *Dark cloud strong breeze*. New York: Orchard.

Pinkwater, D. (1989). *Uncle Melvin*. New York: Macmillan.

Piper, W. (1954). *The little engine that could*. Eau Claire, WI: Hale.

Prater, J. (1993). *Tim and the blanket thief*. New York: Atheneum.

Rabe, B. (1991). *The balancing girl*. New York: E.P. Dutton.

Rabe, B. (1988). *Where's Chimpy?* Morton Grove, IL: Albert Whitman.

Raschka, C. (1993). *Yo! Yes?* New York: Orchard.

Reddix, V. (1991). *Dragon kite of the autumn moon*. New York: Lothrop, Lee & Shepard.

Rey, H.A. & Rey, M. (1966). *Curious George goes to the hospital*. Boston: Houghton Mifflin.

Richardson, J. (1993). *Come to my party*. New York: Macmillan.

Rogers, J. (1993). *Best friends sleep over*. New York: Scholastic.

Russo, M. (1993) *Trade-in mother*. New York: Greenwillow.

Rylant, C. (1982). *When I was young in the mountains*. New York: E.P. Dutton.

Sadler, M. (1988). *Alistair underwater*. New York: Prentice Hall.

Schein, J. (1988). *Forget me not*. Toronto, Ontario, Canada: Annick.

Schoberle, C. (1994). *Morning sounds, evening sounds*. New York: Simon and Schuster.

Schuchman, J. (1979). *Two places to sleep*. Minneapolis: Carolrhoda.

Dr. Seuss. (pseud. T. Geisel) (1984). *The butter battle book*. New York: Random House.

Dr. Seuss. (pseud T. Geisel) (1971) *The lorax*. New York: Random House.

Seymour, T. (1997). *Too quiet for these old bones*. New York: Orchard.

Seymour, T. (1998). *We played marbles*. New York: Orchard.

Sharmat, M. (1988). *Sherman is a slowpoke*. New York: Scholastic.

Simmons, J. (1998). *Come along, Daisy*. Boston, MA: Little Brown.

Thaler, M. (1986). *Hippo lemonade*. New York: Harper.

Tsuchiya, Y. (1988). *Faithful elephants*. New York: Houghton Mifflin.

Tusa, T. (1993). *The family reunion*. New York: Farrar, Straus, Giroux.

Vainio, P. (1993). *The snow goose*. New York: North-South.

Viorst, J. (1977). *My mama says there aren't any zombies, ghosts, vampires, creatures, demons, monsters, fiends, goblins, or things*. New York: Atheneum.

Viorst, J. (1971). *The tenth good thing about Barney*. New York: Atheneum.

Waas, U. (1993). *Where's Molly?* New York: North-South.

Waber, B. (1972). *Ira sleeps over*. Boston: Houghton Mifflin.

Winthrop, E. (1998). *As the crow flies*. New York: Clarion.

Wolf, W. (1994). *Christmas with Grandfather*. New York: North-South.

Wolff, A. (1993). *Stella & Roy*. New York: E.P. Dutton.

Wolkstein, D. (1992). *Little Mouse's painting*. New York: Morrow.

Wood, D. (1992). *Old turtle*. Duluth, MN: Pfeifer-Hamilton.

Yolen, J. (1981). *Sleeping Ugly*. New York: Coward McCann.

Ziefert, H. (1991). *When Daddy had the chicken pox*. New York: HarperCollins.

Zolotow, C. (1992). *The quiet lady*. New York: Macmillan.

Zolotow, C. (1988). *Something is going to happen*. New York: Harper and Row.

Zolotow, C. (1972). *William's doll*. New York: Harper and Row.

SELECTED REFERENCES

Barbiei, B. (1995). *Sounds from the heart: Learning to listen to girls*. Portsmouth, NH: Hienemann.

Brazelton, T.B. (1997). *Touchpoints*. Reading, MA: Addison Wesley.

Coody, B. (1992). *Using literature with young children*. Dubuque, IA: William C. Brown.

Derman-Sparks, L. (1989). *Antibias curriculum: Tools for empowering young children*. Washington, DC: NAEYC.

Giangreco, M.F., Cloninger, C.J., & Iverson, V.S. (1993). *Choosing options and accommodations for children: A guide to planning inclusive education*. Baltimore: Paul H. Brookes.

Katz, L.G. & McClellan, D.E. (1991). *The teacher's role in the social development of young children*. Urbana, IL: University of Illinois.

Kostelnik, M.J., Stein, L., Whiren, A.P., & Soderman, A.K. (1993). *Guiding children's social development: Classroom practices*. Albany, NY: Delmar Publishers.

Lang, G., & Berberich, C. (1995). *All children are special*. York, ME: Stenhouse.

Leff, P.T. & Walizer, E.H. (1992). *Building the healing partnership: Parents, professionals and children with chronic illnesses and disabilities*. Cambridge, MA: Brookline.

National Association for the Education of Young Children. (1997). *Developmentally appropriate practice in early childhood programs serving children from birth through age 8*. Washington, DC: National Association for the Education of Young Children.

Shure, M. (1994). *Raising a thinking child*. New York: Pocket Books.

Smilansky, S. (1992). *Children of divorce: The roles of the family and school*. Rockville, MD: BJE Press.

Taylor, D. (1991). *Learning denied*. Portsmouth, NH: Heinemann.

Trelease, J. (1995). *The new read-aloud handbook*. New York: Viking Penguin.

The press, like fire, is an excellent servant but a terrible master.

– James Fenimore Cooper

9 Using Commercial and Educational Media

There have been many debates and arguments concerning the relationship of children with television, tape recordings, computers, films, and other media. Since these media are here to stay, some of the arguments are moot. American families usually own at least one television set. Many of the programs depict violence, greed, and unrealistic pictures of life. Many households, and the number is increasing daily, also own videocassette recorders (VCRs), computers, tape players, and compact disc (CD) players. More families also own personal computers and are connected to the Internet. Families receive newspapers and magazines in the home, go to movies, go online, and see billboards along the highways. Because much of the media is presented for the purpose of earning revenue for advertisers, the quality is not always appropriate for children. The role of teachers and parents is to use the media effectively and to help children begin to make critical choices concerning the media.

MEDIA AND LITERATURE

There are two relationships between the media and literature, one friendly and the other adversarial. The friendly relationship is the blending of literature and media to provide more powerful learning experiences for children. Literature can give depth to the superficial aspects of media presentations by allowing children to learn more about a concept or an event. Media can be used to enhance a child's involvement with literature. For example, expand on the experience of reading a book. Media can also be used as a springboard for further discussion of a book or to instill a desire to read a certain book or books in a certain subject.

The adversarial relationship occurs when the media overwhelm and take the place of literature in the lives of children. Media will always be present in children's lives. It is up to parents and educators to control the media rather than letting the media control their children and themselves. If it is going to be a positive force in children's lives, the use of media must be planned so that the best qualities of each type of media can be used to enhance the lives of children. Media can be valuable as an experience in their own right, but care should be taken to see that they do not replace literature, play, adult supervision, or the development of friendships.

Categories of media seem to be increasing rapidly. Hardly a day goes by without a new interactive video, laser disc, or innovative FAX machine being used. However, the predominant media used with young children are television, audio tapes, filmstrips, magazines, newspapers, and computer programs. Criteria for selecting these materials will be suggested. The focus will be on effectively using each medium in conjunction with literature for the purpose of enhancing the experience of a story.

TELEVISION: SEEING THE WORLD FROM A CHAIR

There is no doubt about it: television can be a fantastic medium. From the comfort of an easy chair one can go on an African safari, explore the oceanic coral reefs of Australia, take a shuttle into space, or participate in a bloody military skirmish in a third world country. The seemingly endless variety of experiences available through television is part of the problem. We simply watch too much television.

Negative Aspects of Television

By the time children enter kindergarten, they have watched over 5,000 hours of television. Between the ages of three and seventeen, the average American child watches 15,000 hours. This is 2,000 hours more than that same child will spend in a classroom during those years. Prior to age seventeen, that child will watch 350,000 commercials and 18,000 acts of violence on television.

Television viewing is a passive activity. Little thought or mental activity is required by viewers as they are bombarded by a steady stream of sounds and images. This fact is a particularly important one in regard to young children, who expand their language skills through active interaction with their environment.

TIPS FOR TEACHERS
Increase awareness by having parents keep a log of every minute of television viewing for a period of one week.

The shows offered and the commercials embedded within these shows are another problem area. The quality of television shows seems to have decreased. Our society appears to be more and more drawn to the flashy and the violent. Many good-quality shows have been removed and replaced with violent fare, mostly because of rating points and advertising dollars.

During the past few years, a new low has been reached in which those advertising dollars have become the controlling factor in much children's programming. Previously, children's toys depicting characters from a television show were created and marketed after a show had become popular. Currently, new shows are being programmed based upon the successful marketing of a toy. These include robots, dolls, and action toys. In effect, children who watch the shows are merely watching an ongoing half-hour advertisement based on greed and violence.

Controlling Television Viewing

Most adults know that children watch far too much television. For that matter, most adults spend too much time watching television. There is a need to be aware of this problem and consider its effects. Following awareness and understanding, an appropriate response can be launched.

Awareness. To become aware of the seriousness of the problem requires closer study. Literature from groups such as the National Education Association (NEA), Action for Children's Television (ACT), and the International Reading Association (IRA) is helpful. So is collecting information on children's television viewing. Distribute television-viewing recording charts with boxes for half-hour time slots and days of the week to parents. By blackening a box for each half-hour time slot a child watches a television show, parents will have a weekly picture of their child's television viewing. A chart with large areas of blackened time slots representing all of the time spent in front of a television set will have far more impact on parents than anything that might be said.

Understanding. Young children need to develop an understanding of some of the basic facts about television in order to make decisions about it. An effective approach to this is the use of a videocassette recorder (VCR) to tape various commercials and television shows. The tapes can be played and stopped at various critical points for discussion of what is happening. For example, advertising uses a wide variety of propaganda tricks to get consumers to buy certain products. By stopping to discuss the commercial, you can help children to understand this advertising ploy. Such an understanding will not lessen their trust in people. Rather, it will increase their trust in people who care about them. The understanding will also make them more aware of their own intelligence and their ability to make decisions. In addition, using language to discuss a problem will enhance their command of language.

Children can usually understand the concept of excess. What would happen if it rained all the time? What would it be like if we ate only apples? The comparison can be made with television. What would it be like if we watched television all of our waking hours? What would it be like if there were no television? Children can learn that watching television, like any other activity, can be a part of their life without being the sole focus. Television can help us learn to cook, to draw, and to understand many things. It can be a wonderful machine. However, television is only a part of life. There are many other important parts as well.

Response. Awareness accomplishes nothing without a response. One response is to simply eliminate or drastically reducing television viewing, but this will only partially solve the problem. When one activity is decreased, it is important to have healthy alternatives. Otherwise, the replacement activity will probably be one of children pleading to return to the original habit of watching television.

More than anything else, parental involvement and modeling are the most effective means for teaching children the skills needed to develop reasonable television viewing habits. Parental involvement would include helping children to understand what they are doing with their lives when they spend excessive amounts of time watching television. However, it may be unrealistic to totally eliminate all television viewing for young people. It may not accomplish all of the things one might hope for anyway. For example, most people are aware of the violence exhibited on television and the reports of its effect on young children. Yet, eliminating all television violence will not eliminate all the fears, nightmares, and aggression children might experience.

This does not mean, of course, that unmonitored and indiscriminate viewing of television is acceptable. Rather, one's response should be to talk to and listen to children more. By attempting to understand the perspective of children, one can help them come to a better understanding of themselves. Better understanding leads to better control. This is true whether the topic is a story being read or a television program being viewed. Empowered this way, children become more able to make critical choices, including what and how much television programming they will watch. In addition, they will be better able to make choices about alternatives to television viewing.

Positive Aspects of Television

There have always been good-quality television programs for children, and there are still some wonderful programs. In the past, such shows as "Ding Dong School," "Howdy Doody," "Captain Kangaroo," and "Kukla, Fran and Ollie" were favorites. Later came "Mr. Rogers' Neighborhood," which celebrates the joys of children learning about the world. Fred Rogers, the show's main character, uses language, humor, and stories as integral parts of the program. He has also published a series of books for sharing between child and parent. These informative books, which do not talk down to children, cover such topics as day care, doctors, and new babies.

"Sesame Street" evolved when the Children's Television Workshop turned market research into productive children's programming. Using Jim Henson's muppet characters and a diverse cast, "Sesame Street" provides learning experiences through a series of short segments that take into account the attention span of young children. This was one of the first programs for children to feature a multiethnic cast. Women, minorities, and individuals with disabilities are all featured with realism and dignity.

"Reading Rainbow" focuses directly on literature. During each program, one or more books are shared with the audience. The format expands on the book with dramatization, animation, music, and personal responses to the story. After each book is presented, it is reviewed by children, who share their personal responses to the book. The program has presented a variety of books from classical to contemporary. Among some of the selections are Jack Ezra Keats's *The Snowy Day*, Aliki's *How a Book Is Made*, Jane Yolen's *Owl Moon*, Chris Raschka's *Charlie Parker Played Be Bop*, Brian Pinkney's *Max Found Two Sticks*, Jeanette Winter's *Follow the Drinking Gourd*, Megan McDonald's *Is This a House for Hermit Crab?*, Eve Bunting's *Wall*, Lynne Cherry's *The Great Kapok Tree*, and Bill Martin Jr.'s *Knots on a Counting Rope*. "The Magic School Bus" show explores science concepts based on the popular book series of the same name.

Commercial networks have also adapted several well-known children's books for television. The quality of the presentations is uneven; some of the presentations ring remarkably true to the original story, whereas others have been disturbingly altered. Cable television, through the Disney and Discovery channels, has tied several of its programs to literature. Again, the quality of the adaptations varies.

Using Elements of Television

Because television can be a vehicle for learning, parents and educators can harness its power. By using selected television programs, parents and educators can reinforce basic concept skills, socialization skills, and self-esteem. Some of the thousands of commercials children watch can be used to teach about nutrition and critical decision making. By critically analyzing food commercials, children can learn about alternative snacks and nutrition. By analyzing toy commercials, children can make better decisions about whether they really need a particular toy.

The concept of developing their own programs can be appealing to children. A large cardboard box can become a television set on which children put their own shows and commercials. The spontaneous acting that will result during free play periods can reinforce language development. Brief skits and commercials, some based on stories they have read, will help children to re-create the experience of the story. The emphasis should not be on the excellence of the production. The main focus should be on the use of language within the experience.

Author Bill Martin, Jr. Courtesy Bill Martin, Jr.

AUDIOVISUAL MATERIALS

Audiovisual materials include cassettes, photographs, CDs, VCR tapes, slides, films, and the equipment needed to use them. Each can be used effectively to enhance the curriculum. A wide range of literature related to them is available as well. As a result, audiovisual materials can be used to extend and enhance the literature used in the curriculum.

When using any audiovisual material to enhance a story, more planning time is needed to organize the presentation. The children may need more help in understanding what is happening than was apparent in the reading of the book. The reason for this is that the teacher may be less involved in the presentation. The machine may set the pace. Of course, a tape recorder cannot detect a puzzled look on a child's face. Audiovisual materials should never replace the teacher, the parent, or the book. They should be used only as a supplement.

Many sources exist for audiovisual materials. Public libraries and elementary school libraries are both good sources. They usually have a variety of literature-related materials. New materials may be purchased from various of commercial sources. Educational supply companies usually have catalogs offering their materials.

The use of audiovisual materials should be an occasional rather than a regular activity. There are two very important reasons for this. First, nothing can replace the warmth of the live human voice and the caring eye of a sensitive storyteller or reader. Audiovisual materials should be used mainly as a support for a live reading. Second, the range of audiovisual materials related to children's literature is quite limited. Very few books reach this format. Those that do reach it do so only after they have proved themselves effective in the print market. As a result, the majority of titles available will be limited to older classics and a few recent titles that have been commercially successful.

Criteria for Selecting Audiovisual Materials

Audiovisual materials that bring a book to another medium need to be carefully screened. The videotape version of a story should neither diminish nor replace the original story. The illustrations, flow, and feeling of the story should create the same impact as the initial reading of the story. Effective use of an audiovisual presentation should extend the reading and re-create the story for the child.

Disney Studios has successfully produced animated versions of stories for years. The Disney stories, however, are often not faithful to the original texts. As a result, many of them seem to be new stories with lives of their own. It is still important for children to see and hear the original stories. This will add to the magic of the literature and broaden children's understanding of the story.

Infusing a desire to read and nurturing an enjoyment of literature in young children are two very important objectives for parents and educators. Audiovisual materials should be selected with these criteria in mind: The materials should enhance the original version of the story. They should be clear and coherent to the child. They should re-create or extend the magic of the original story and should never be used to replace it.

Using Audiovisual Materials

Videotapes, audiotapes, and CDs may present stories, music, or stories that include music. Videotapes contain a visual and sound re-creation of a story. The selection of materials should depend mainly on how well they fit into the overall objective for sharing or experiencing a story in the first place. When that is clear, a wide range of possible activities can be used in conjunction with the audiovisual materials.

Compact Discs and Audio Tapes. Designating a specific quiet area of the room is helpful for using CDs and tapes. The area can serve for both instructional purposes and free play listening. Providing additional headsets enables several children to listen to a story at one time without filling the room with sound. Using a copy of the book with the recording is usually beneficial. Most recordings have a signal indicating the need to turn the page. Even if the children cannot read the words, they will become accustomed to the concept of reading words and the idea that language flows by turning the pages as the story proceeds. In addition to using tapes of well-known books such as Ann McGovern's *Stone Soup,* classroom tapes can be created whenever the teacher reads a book. Children can relisten to these tapes as well.

Some companies specifically distribute audio tapes of children's books. Scholastic distributes titles such as *Alexander and the Terrible, No Good Very Bad Day, Jamberry, Over In the Meadow, Clifford's Family, Make Way for Ducklings, Noisy Nora, A Pocket for Corduroy,* and *The Very Hungry Caterpillar.* The titles that Sundance distributes include *Anno's Counting Book, Frog and Toad Are*

Friends, Goodnight Moon, The Berenstain Bears and Too Much TV, and *Miss Nelson Is Missing*. Random House distributes *Richard Scarry's Bedtime Stories*, *How the Grinch Stole Christmas*, *The Night Before Christmas*, and *Sing With Me Mother Goose*.

Story tapes played at naptime can help children both relive the story and settle down for a quiet time. Consider making some of the tapes available for parents to sign out. In this way, parents can share the story with their children and enhance the experience with further discussion.

Videocassettes. A videocassette is similar in function to a film, with the story shown on a television screen or monitor. Troll Associates publishes a variety of classic stories on videocassette including "The Brementown Musicians," "Little Red Riding Hood," "The Ugly Duckling," and "The Three Little Pigs." Costs vary greatly. Some classic and current books are also available on VCR tapes. Several Berenstain Bears titles, along with *The Paper Bag Princess*, *Abuela's Weave*, *The Rainbow Fish*, *The Very Hungry Caterpillar*, and *Strega Nona*, are available from Sundance. Random House distributes videotape versions of *Hop On Pop*, *Abel's Island*, and *Swimmy*. Titles available from Scholastic/Weston Woods include *The Snowy Day*, *Time of Wonder*, and *Where the Wild Things Are*.

Audio tapes can be used to re-create the experience of the original reading of a story.

These presentations should not replace the use of a book for the telling of stories. Rather, the presentation can and should be used to extend and enhance the story. For example, if fairy tales are being used in the classroom, their concepts can be extended with a re-creation of some of the original stories on videotape. If a camcorder can be used, children in costume can re-create the stories as well.

Photographs and slides can be used to create books about any topic. Both original pictures and photographs of pictures from books and magazines can be starting points for original stories. Photographs of children enacting a story could also be used with a language-experience approach (LEA).

When creating with audiovisual equipment, it is best to consider a few things prior to the activity. Parents should always be informed. This is particularly true if the pictures will be used by the press. If parents don't wish their child to be included, the request should be honored without comment. Letting parents know ahead of time also gives them the opportunity to have their children look their best. If costumes or props are to be used, it allows parents enough time to create them.

Planning for the unexpected is recommended. Practice with the equipment beforehand so that sufficient skill will have been achieved. Obtain additional lighting and extra extension cords as needed prior to the activity. Finally, a backup plan should always be ready. Equipment may get lost or malfunction. Children get sick. An alternate plan can help achieve the goals of the project even when these problems occur.

MAGAZINES AND NEWSPAPERS

Magazines and newspapers abound in our culture. It is challenging, however, to find quality magazines that appeal to the interest of children. Likewise, it requires some creativity to develop appropriate uses for newspapers with young children. Figure 9–1 contains a summary of quality magazines appropriate for young children.

Magazines and newspapers have a low cost, are filled with print, and contain many superb illustrations. They are also up to date, have short pieces, and contain a variety of topics to cater to different interests. It makes sense to use them as a resource for developing literacy with young children. To do this in conjunction with a literature program requires two things: First, one must have certain criteria for deciding to include newspapers and magazines. Second, one must develop a set of activities and strategies for effectively using them.

Criteria for Selecting Magazines and Newspapers

First, determine whether the magazine, article, story, or illustration supports the objective or purpose of the lesson or activity. Does it fit into the curriculum web for this lesson? Does it reinforce a concept that is being learned? Does it clarify the meaning of something the class is doing? Does it extend the learning in some way? The answers to these questions will help to determine how well the print media will support the purpose of the lesson.

Babybug, P.O. Box 300, Peru, Illinois 61354 includes brief stories, poems, and rhymes for infants and toddlers.

Ladybug, P.O. Box 330, Peru, Illinois 61354 includes stories, read alouds, songs, and poems for toddlers and preschoolers.

Spider, P.O. Box 300, Peru, Illinois 61354 features stories and poems on all topics for preschoolers and kindergartners.

Turtle, 1100 Waterway Blvd., Indianapolis, Indiana includes fiction, poems, and activities for toddlers and preschoolers.

Ranger Rick, National Wildlife Federation, 1412 Sixteenth Street NW, Washington, D.C., includes material on nature and ecology (preschool to grade 2).

Scienceland, 501 Fifth Avenue, Suite 2102, New York NY 10017, features vivid photography on science (preschool to kindergarten).

Sesame Street Magazine, P.O. Box 52000, Boulder, Colorado, features basic concept activities and stories (preschool to kindergarten).

Surprises. P.O. Box 236, Chanhassen, Minnesota 55317, includes activities for parents and children to do together (ages four to twelve).

Turtle, Children's Better Health Institute, P.O. Box 567, Indianapolis, Indiana 46206, includes poetry, stories, and games on health (preschoolers).

Your Big Backyard, National Wildlife Federation, 1412 Sixteenth Street NW, Washington, D.C. 20036, includes nature stories, activities, photographs, and recipes (toddlers and preschoolers).

Let's Find Out, Scholastic, 2931 East McCarthy Street, Jefferson City, Missouri 65102, includes activities and games for holidays, seasons, and other topics (preschool to kindergarten).

Figure 9–1. Magazines for young children. Courtesy Walter Sawyer.

TIPS FOR TEACHERS

Make use of early childhood journals, activities magazines, and computer software for planning activities for children.
- *Read the issues of journals at the public library if you are not a subscriber.*
- *Photocopy and file pages of journals and magazines you plan to use.*
- *Use computer software by yourself before having a child use it in order to identify the places the child may become confused.*

Second, determine the suitability of the piece for children. Try to see it through the eyes of a child. What might be a stunning photograph to an adult, or even an older child might be too complex and vague to a younger child. A written text that might be fascinating to an adult or older child might be too abstract and confusing to a younger child.

Using Magazines and Newspapers

In addition to the magazines listed in Figure 9–1, other magazines might be useful as well. Although the texts might be inappropriate, the titles and photographs from many different magazines might be helpful in reinforcing or extending a story or a concept. For example, sports magazines might contain illustrations and photographs appropriate for a unit on books dealing with sports and motor skills. Family magazines might include pictures of foods mentioned in the stories children are reading. Newspaper advertising headlines may contain words and phrases used in language development and story activities.

A variety of hands-on activities related to a story can be done with pictures and words cut from the pages of magazines and newspapers. Collages can be made from pictures of animals, foods, and shapes. Category charts can be constructed from pictures of houses, trucks, animals, or parts of the body. Sequences of a sports activity, a plant growing, or a cake being made can be cut out and mounted as a project. A series or set of related pictures can be displayed to children so that they can create their own story about the pictures. Games (e.g., "War," "Old Maid") can be created by mounting various types of pictures on index cards. Laminating any of these projects can protect them for long-term use.

COMPUTERS AND SOFTWARE

There are many arguments for using computers with young children: computers are a part of the increasingly technological society that children live in. Children will have to know about computers when they enter school. Computers can give them a head start on reading. On the other hand, there are several arguments against the use of computers with young children: they take children away from social interactions. The software is often of poor quality. Children aren't ready to use a computer at a very young age. Each of the arguments on both sides of the issue may have some truth. One's decision on computer use might vary depending on the age of the child.

It is important to have a clear idea of the issues involved here in determining the amount of computer use in a literacy development program for young children. The position taken in this chapter is that computers can be an effective tool to supplement and enhance literacy with young children. They must be used, however, as part of a carefully thought out plan that considers the child's development, the purpose for using the computer, and the software that will be used.

Criteria for Computer Use

The criteria for using computers must address child development, the purpose of the computer use, and the software selected for use.

Child Development. The child's development will have an effect on his or her ability to use the keyboard and other peripheral devices of a computer. Parents and caregivers may also be concerned about the possibility of eyestrain in children who look at a computer screen for lengthy periods of time. One might, therefore, question the appropriateness of having children work independently at a computer terminal.

On the other hand, if the teacher manages or guides the use of the keyboard while the children view the screen, there may be ample reason for using certain programs. Teacher management of the keyboard does not mean that children are not allowed to touch it. Opportunities to experiment and manipulate parts of the computer environment can and should be provided. Realistic expectations are necessary, however, when children are given control of a computer, as development takes place over a period of time.

TIPS FOR TEACHERS

Seek family and community assistance to schedule effective use of computers in programs and classrooms.

Purpose. The purpose of using a computer should be legitimate in terms of literacy goals. One might have as a purpose the simple notion of exposing children to a powerful technology. While that may be a valid purpose, it is not necessarily part of a literacy program. If the purpose is to drill young children on letter and number identification, it would be at odds with current thought on developing such skills. Computer drills tend to take children away from the social interactions and the opportunities to re-create stories and events that are important to language development. These drills can also lead to a belief that language and reading are monotonous and boring activities.

Computer use can harmonize with a contemporary view of literacy development when it is used to reinforce and enhance the development of literacy in a social context. This can be done in several ways. As noted earlier, the teacher can control or guide the use of the keyboard while children interact with each other and the program on the screen. The teacher guides the group so that the technology is used as a means to create and re-create language and stories in meaningful ways. The teacher can also provide opportunities in which pairs of students interact with each other as well as the computer in order to accomplish a task. Guidance is a key to providing effective opportunities for computer use with young children.

Software. A great deal of poor-quality software is available. This type of software tends to require little more than rote responses from children. In effect, it does little more than duplicate a ditto sheet or a workbook page on an electronic screen. One should seriously question using an expensive piece of electronic equipment for a task that can be accomplished just as easily with a pencil and paper.

The software selected might better be used to encourage the development of original stories or to re-create stories the child has experienced. Creative art programs and simplified word processing programs are available for this purpose. They better reflect contemporary thought on literacy development. They also provide an experience for the child that is much more meaningful than the simple recall of rote information.

Methods of Computer Use

It is best to use the computer as a means rather than an end. Learning about computers is important for nearly everyone, but it is not absolutely essential that children acquire this familiarity in early childhood. The focus in an early childhood education program should be on using the computer as a means to enhance literacy development. While children might be allowed to actually use the computer, it can be a more powerful tool when the teacher guides children in a language development activity using the computer.

For example, a computerized version of a previously read story can be explored through a computer program either on diskette or in CD-ROM format. Titles available on computer media such as disc and CR-ROM include Janell Cannon's *Stellaluna*, Dr. Seuss's *Green Eggs and Ham*, Dr. Seuss's *ABC*, Kevin Henkes's *Sheila Rae the Brave*, Marc Brown's *Arthur's Teacher Trouble*, Mercer Mayer's *Just Grandma and Me*, and Laura Numeroff's *If You Give a Mouse a Cookie*. Companies such as Scholastic, Broderbound, and National School Products distribute these and other titles in both IBM and Apple's Macintosh format versions. Literature-related computer products also include Sierra's "Mixed Up Mother Goose," Edmark's "Bailey's Book House," and Queue's database resources for children's poems, stories, songs, and nursery rhymes.

A language-experience approach (LEA) story can be created as an original piece on the computer. A previously read story can be re-created on the computer using the words of the children. "Scholastic's Wiggle Works" program includes a word processing program appropriate for young children. This title is also an interactive computer-based program designed to encourage reading, listening, and speaking skills for three levels of emergent literacy development. An alternative word processing program that could be used is "Muppet Slate" by Sunburst Communications. Designed for young children, it combines words and pictures in a word processing format. Sunburst also markets a multisensory interactive alphabet program called "A to Zap." The major point with these approaches is that the language and the understanding of the story are the focus rather than the computer. Thus these approaches coincide with the major purposes and objectives of a literacy curriculum for young children.

Useful Websites

The information superhighway, that is, the Internet, which includes the World Wide Web (WWW), is fast becoming a useful resource for parents and early childhood caregivers. It is particularly useful in linking children and adults with literacy resources beyond the classroom and community. Useful websites for emergent literacy include

> **http://www.crocker.com/**—This site provides book reviews and ideas for using picture books in all subject areas.
>
> **http://www.knowledgeadventure.com/**—This site, which profiles children's authors and illustrators, is helpful for selecting the best children's books.
>
> **http://www.mindspring.com/**—This site includes book reviews, interviews with authors and illustrators, and tips for using picture books with children.
>
> **http://www.amazon.com/**—This site identifies itself as "Earth's Biggest Bookstore." If you can't find the titles found in this book at your local bookstore, you will almost always be able to order them through this website.
>
> **http://www.ipl.sils.umich.edu/youth/Ask Author/**—This site serves as a question-and-answer site for numerous authors.
>
> **http://www.inkspot.com/**—This site contains a directory and links to numerous children's book authors.
>
> **http://www.cbcbooks.org/**—This is the Children's Book Council website, containing valuable ideas for teaching with children's books year round.
>
> **http://www.janbrett.com/**—This is author/illustrator Jan Brett's website.
>
> **http://www.eric-carle.com/**—This is author/illustrator Eric Carle's website.
>
> **http://www.itpubs.ucdavis.edu/richard/tcles/**—This website is an excellent source for multicultural stories and folk tales from around the world.
>
> **http://www.bookwise.com/**—This website contains texts of many classic children's books for searching, reading, and printing.

SUMMARY

The commercial media is a major influence in the lives of young children. It brings forth a constant stream of new ideas and images. Children, however, need to grow at their own pace. They are often not able to discriminate between the important, unimportant, truthful, and deceptive images they find before them. They are exposed to television, audiovisual materials, newspapers, magazines, and computer software. The question isn't whether children should or should not be exposed to this; it will happen anyway. The question for teachers and parents is how to control the amount, the timing, and the use of that media exposure.

Appropriately introduced and used, commercial media can support the development of literacy in young children. Introduced too soon and in inappropriate amounts, they can leave a child confused about many aspects of reality. Teachers and parents need to decide how to use the media for their own purposes rather than for the purposes the media may have developed. While television can be a tremendous problem if overused, there are constructive purposes that it can support. The same is true for audiovisual materials, magazines, newspapers, and computers. Adults must develop appropriate structures for their effective use. The key ingredients include understanding the development of the child, developing clear purposes for media use, and carefully selecting the appropriate media for those uses.

QUESTIONS FOR THOUGHT AND DISCUSSION

1. What are some of the dangers of overusing the media?
2. What are some of the positive aspects of television?
3. What are some of the negative aspects of television?
4. Why is it important to have alternative activities available when television viewing is decreased or eliminated?
5. What are the criteria for effectively using television with young children?
6. Describe an activity in which television can be used to support the development of literacy.
7. What are the criteria for effectively using audiovisual materials with young children?
8. Describe an activity in which audiovisual materials can be used to support the development of literacy.
9. What are the criteria for effectively using print media with young children?
10. Describe an activity in which print media can be used to support the development of literacy.
11. What are the criteria for effectively using computers with young children?
12. Describe an activity in which computers can be used to support the development of literacy.
13. Although television viewing is not the sole cause of nightmares and childhood fears, how can violence on television affect a young child?
14. What is the appropriate role of computer technology in the early childhood program?

CHILDREN'S BOOKS CITED

Aliki (Brandenburg), (1986). *How a book is made.* New York: Crowell.

Allard, H. (1977). *Miss Nelson is missing.* Boston, MA: Houghton Mifflin.

Anderson, H.C. (1979). *The ugly duckling.* Mahwah, NJ: Troll.

Anno, M. (1975). *Anno's counting book.* New York: Harper Collins.

Berenstain, S., & Berenstain, J. (1984). *The Berenstain Bears and too much TV*. New York: Random House.

Bridwell, N. (1984). *Clifford's family*. New York: Scholastic.

Brown, M. (1986). *Arthur's teacher trouble*. Boston: Little Brown.

Brown, M.W. (1975). *Goodnight moon*. New York: Harper and Row.

Bunting, E. (1990). *The wall*. New York: Clarion.

Cannon, J. (1993). *Stellaluna*. San Diego, CA: Harcourt Brace Jovanovich.

Carle, E. (1981). *The very hungry caterpillar*. New York: Philomel.

Castaneda, O.S. (1993). *Abuela's weave*. New York: Lee and Row.

Cherry, L. (1990). *The great kapok tree*. San Diego, CA: Harcourt Brace Jovanovich.

Degen, B. (1983). *Jamberry*. New York: Harper Collins

Delacre, L. (illustrator) (1987). *Sing with me Mother Goose*. New York: Random House.

dePaola, T. (1975). *Strega Nona*. Englewood Cliffs, NJ: Prentice Hall.

Freeman, D. (1978). *A pocket for Corduroy*. New York: Viking.

Galdone, P. (1986). *Over in the meadow*. Englewood Cliffs, NJ: Prentice Hall.

Grimm. (1979). *The Brementown musicians*. Mahwah, NJ: Troll.

Grimm. (1979). *Little Red Riding Hood*. Mahwah, NJ: Troll.

Henkes, K. (1996). *Sheila Rae the Brave*. New York: Mulberry.

Keats, E.J. (1996). *The snowy day*. New York: Viking.

Lionni, L. (1963). *Swimmy*. New York: Alfred J Knopf.

Lobel, A. (1970). *Frog and Toad are friends*. New York: Harper and Row.

Martin, Jr., B. (1987). *Knots on a counting rope*. New York: Holt.

Mayer, M. (1985). *Just Grandma and me*. Racine, WI: Western.

McCloskey, R. (1985). *Time of wonder*. New York: Viking.

McCloskey, W. (1991). *Make way for ducklings*. New York: Puffin.

McDonald, M. (1990). *Is this a house for hermit crab?* New York: Orchard.

McGovern, A. (1986). *Stone soup*. New York: Scholastic.

Moore, C. (1975). *The night before Christmas*. New York: Random House.

Moore, E. (1981). *The three little pigs*. Mahwah, NJ: Troll.

Munsch, R. (1980). *The paper bag princess*. Scarborough, Ontario, Canada: Annick.

Numeroff, L. (1985). *If you give a mouse a cookie*. New York: Harper and Row.

Pfister, M. (1992). *The rainbow fish*. New York: North-South.

Pinkey, B. (1997). *Max found two sticks*. New York: Simon and Schuster.

Raschka, C. (1992). *Charlie Parker plays be bop*. New York: Orchard.

Scarry, R. (1989). *Richard Scarry's bedtime stories*. New York: Random House.

Sendak, M. (1963). *Where the wild things are*. New York: Harper and Row.

Seuss, D. (1991). *Dr. Seuss's ABC*. McHenry, IL: Follett.

Seuss, D. (1988). *Green eggs and ham*. New York: Random House.

Seuss, D. (1991). *Hop on Pop*. McHenry, IL: Follett.

Seuss, D. (1985). *How the grinch stole Christmas*. New York: Random House

Stieg, W. (1976). *Abel's island*. New York: Farrar, Straus, and Giroux.

Viorst, J. (1972). *Alexander and the terrible, no good, very bad day*. New York: Atheneum.

Wells, R. (1997). *Noisy Nora*. New York: Dial.

Winter, J. (1988). *Follow the drinking gourd*. New York: Knopf.

Yolen, J. (1987). *Owl moon*. New York: Philomel.

SELECTED REFERENCES

Haughland, S. & Shade, D. (1990). *Development evaluations of software for young children*. Albany, NY: Delmar Publishers.

Haughland, S.W. & Wright, J.L. (1997). *Young children and technology: A world of discovery*. Boston: Allyn and Bacon.

Kopperman, P. (1980). *The literacy hoax: The decline of reading, writing, and learning in the public schools and what we can do about it*. New York: Morrow.

Lifton, M. & Adams, M. (1997). *Kid pix for terrified teachers*. Huntington Beach, CA: Teacher Created Materials.

Postman, N. (1980). *Teaching as a conserving activity*. New York: Delacorte.

Ray, J. & Warden, K. (1995). *Technology, computers, and the special needs learner*. Albany, NY: Delmar Publishers.

Student achievement in California schools, 1979–80 Annual report. Sacramento, CA: California Department of Education.

Trelease, J. (1995). *The new read-aloud handbook*. New York: Viking Penguin.

Winn, M. (1987). *Unplugging the plug-in drug*. New York: Penguin.

The axis of the earth sticks out visibly through the center of each and every town or city.

– Oliver Wendell Holmes

10 Involving the Community

Every community, large and small, contains a wonderfully rich variety of resources. Young children can and should learn about these resources. From infancy through the kindergarten years, children are fascinated by the world around them. Use this intrinsic motivation to enrich the lives of children by focusing attention on the people and places found in the community. Make a visit to a library, auto repair shop, or a bank. Invite a visit from a farmer, a nurse, or a bookstore owner. Whatever the occasion, community involvement can be combined with literature and the educational program for children. Recent reform movements at the national, state, and local levels have made it a point to stress the need for much greater involvement of families and communities in education programs and decision making.

In viewing a community, it may be helpful to see it in more than one way. First of all, a community contains people and places. The people have many different jobs, and the places have many different roles. The buildings have been constructed to serve a variety of purposes. Some buildings are like big empty boxes that can be used for a variety of things such as a store, an office, or a business. Other buildings have specific designs and contain specialized equipment so that they can be used as a police station, church, or hospital. Another way of viewing the community is to determine how it can best be used to benefit children's education. Is it best to bring the children to the community? Or should the community be brought to the children? Actually, both approaches can be effective depending on the situation. Each approach will be explored here.

PLACES TO GO: EXPLORING THE COMMUNITY

A field trip is always exciting for children. Since it can be such a powerful learning experience, it makes good sense to plan a field trip within an integrated program. Literature can easily be correlated with such parts of the program. Depending on the community, the possibilities are wide and varied. Each place visited will be important in developing the schemas that children will use to continue to make sense of the world. Libraries, museums, parks, zoos, banks, theaters, and municipal service buildings are all appropriate field trip destinations. Before attempting such a visit, a sound field trip plan should be developed.

Field Trip Planning

In order to have a successful and effective field trip, attend to both the trip details and the learning details. Ignoring either of these can result in an experience that is less meaningful or even one that is unsafe for the children.

Trip Details. When taking a group of children into the community, safety has to be a constant thought. If it is planned ahead of time, the trip will go more smoothly. Always make arrangements with the people at the destination, and have an understanding of what the experience will be like for the children. Planning trips for warmer weather eliminates the need to focus on extra clothing, weather-related closings, and driving conditions. Parental permission slips, children's name tags, and car assignments are all details that must be attended to as well. A walking field trip presents safety concerns for crossing streets and not getting lost. Always make parents feel welcome in the program and on field trips. Parental participation should extend beyond chaperoning duties. Mothers, fathers, and grandparents can participate in the planning, implementing, and extension activities of the filed trip.

Learning Details. Question a field trip to the firehouse if the trip is being planned simply because it is only a block away. If closeness is the main reason for the field trip, it may be more of an entertainment experience than an opportunity for learning. With careful planning of integrated units, it is not difficult to choose both appropriate field trip destinations and appropriate literature to share before, during, and after the trip. Appropriate literature will help children anticipate, enjoy, and re-create the experience, bringing them the greatest benefit.

Libraries

In any program that views books and literature as important to child development, visits to libraries quickly come to mind. Nearly all communities have libraries with long visiting hours. Those that don't may offer a weekly bookmobile. Library visits can have important outcomes: First, children learn that libraries are one of the few places that have a major focus on books. Second, they become aware of the enormous variety of books. Finally, children learn that libraries are places of learning that go well beyond books. Good stories to introduce the library to children might include Gail Gibbon's *Check It Out!* or Marilyn Sadler's *Alistair in Outer Space*. Gail Gibbons provides a factual introduction to the library. Marilyn Sadler shares another of Alistair's adventures, this one taking place as he is returning some books to the library.

Learning to Love Books. From late infancy on, it is possible for children to understand the rules of book friendship. The librarian, as an expert in books, can reinforce the understandings that children have been taught about books and reinforce the modeling of their parents' and teachers' use of books. Other concepts, such as not writing or coloring in books, can also be reinforced. Children often do not distinguish between coloring books other books.

TIPS FOR TEACHERS

Invite the local librarian to a parent meeting to issue cards and explain library programs.

A World of Books. Libraries are special places within the community. One will see many different kinds of people in the library: young, old, rich, poor, men, women, and children. Those people are all there because libraries have books and resources for everyone.

Gone are the days when librarians tried to make the library a place of absolute silence. Today, children talk quietly about a project in the library and even listen to the librarian reading a story out loud. There are programs for toddlers and preschoolers. Libraries sponsor films and puppet shows related to children's books in order to encourage children to use the library. Summer reading programs,

Introducing children to the library is an important milestone in the development of literacy. Courtesy Diana Comer.

craft hours, cooking, singing, and dramatic storytelling are all a part of a modern library program.

Adults can model the benefits of using the library and knowing the librarian. By having a library card, children can take home wonderful stories to be read during the week. By asking the librarian, children can find out about new books by a favorite author or about a favorite topic.

More Than Just Books. Libraries house more than books. They contain videotapes, filmstrips, audio tapes, CDs, magazines, and historical records. Local historical information can be most interesting to children, particularly those whose families have been living in the community for a long time. By using the historical records, one can find the answers to many fascinating questions: What was it like to live in the community one hundred years ago? Were there native Americans? Was it unsettled land or a village? Were there buildings? Was our school here then? Posters, maps, and photographs can often be found in the library to answer many of these questions. This activity can be a springboard to future field trips and for developing language-experience approach (LEA) stories about this topic.

Out of a search of historical records, heroes can emerge. The library can help children learn about the sacrifices and accomplishments of people who lived and worked in the community many years ago. Once this knowledge emerges, it can lead to other activities. The children might be able to visit the childhood home of the individual or have a descendant of the individual visit them.

The library is a very versatile place. It has a tremendous variety of resources about nearly any topic. Librarians are willing to assist visitors and groups in locating information and materials. The library is a place that children can use for many purposes. Libraries now contain CD-ROMs, videotapes, computerized databases, and Internet-access computer terminals for patrons.

TIPS FOR TEACHERS

Use different locations for story sharing.
- *INDOORS: firehouse, restaurant, clothing store, railroad station, flower shop, pet store, bank, shopping mall, etc.*
- *OUTDOORS: pond, farm, park, zoo, playground, college campus, farmer's mrket, etc.*

Museums, Parks, and Zoos

Museums, parks, and zoos offer opportunities to extend and enrich the lives of children. They are special places that compress much of life into a framework that one can experience in a matter of hours. Each of these places has a character of its own. Museums may focus on art, science, natural history, technology, and so forth. Some specialized museums may re-create colonial villages. Parks may feature different terrains, trees, and gardens. Different zoos may contain some similar animals. However, many zoos specialize in birds, monkeys, reptiles, or large cats. Planetariums and aquariums are two other places that can be used to create powerful learning experiences for young children. Most of these resources have a designated education coordinator who can help make a field trip a most beneficial experience for young people.

TIPS FOR TEACHERS

Bring a chart with related pictures and name words on field trips to draw attention to the connection between language and the environment.

Literature can be used before, during, and after a field trip. As a way of encouraging students to stay together as a group on a field trip, one might read Miriam Cohen's *Lost in the Museum* prior to the trip. While going through an art museum with a group of children, one may wish to pause for a story about a visit to an art museum. Laurene and Marc Brown's *Visiting the Art Museum* describes a family visit to an art museum. The idea of paintings in an art museum coming to life is explored in two different books. A Renoir and a Rousseau are among five old masterpieces that come to life in James Mayhew's *Katie's Picture Show*. This theme is explored further in *The Incredible Paintings of Felix Clousseau* by Jon Agee. A natural history museum field trip might include dinosaur books by Aliki. A related fiction work on museums is Chris Babcock's hilarious book, *No Moon*. The plot of the story involves Martha, a histrionic cow, refusing to give any more milk until she becomes a "cowsmonaut." Following a stampede through New York City, Martha finds a creative solution at the Museum of Natural History. A more subdued work is Eric Rohmann's *Time Flies*, a surreal journey back in time as the museum artifacts dissolve to prehistoric time.

The books used do not have to be set in a museum or a park. Rather, books should be selected with the aim of learning in mind. For example, one might simply wish for children to learn about some of the animals, insects, and plants found in the area. Two books that could be used for this purpose are *Lulu Crow's Garden* by Lizi Boyd and *This is Your Garden* by Maggie Smith. Another good example of this type of book is Bianca Lavies's *Lily Pad Pond*. It contains stunning photographs of a woodland pond ecosystem. The sequence showing a tadpole developing over time into a frog totally captivates young children. Sharing of this type of literature during the field trip can greatly enhance the children's learning and understanding. Museum shops often carry related books and artwork that could be used in discussions before and after the museum visit. Large museums usually operate a children's shop that could become part of the field trip experience.

A visit to a museum does not have to be a one-time activity. Since many museums contain a large number of exhibits, trying to see everything in a single visit could make the trip too long and too tiring. It would be more productive to tie together the books, activities, and specific aspects of a museum to a single theme and then visit only the exhibits related to that theme. If the museum has a re-creation of some type of building or structure, for example, that might be a theme. An extension activity following such a visit would be to involve the children in the creation of their own museum. *Architecture Shapes*, *Architecture Colors*, and *Architecture Counts* by Michael Crosbie and Steve Rosenthal might be used as related literature. Activities might include creating buildings with blocks or cardboard. Colors for the structure could lead to a discussion about the need for the building to blend into its environment or to create a certain feeling. If the museum has an art gallery, the theme could be self-expression using an assortment of media such as paint, clay, play dough, and recycled materials. Related books include *Visiting the Art Museum* by Laurene and Marc Brown, *Katie's Picture Show* by James Mayhew, and *The Incredible Paintings of Felix Clousseau* by Jon Agee. Water, natural resources, sea life, or wetlands might be used as a theme if the museum has an aquarium. Books could include *Oceanarium* by Joanne Oppenheim and *Going on a Whale Watch* by Bruce McMillan. Activities could include creating a pictorial classroom aquarium or an actual aquarium.

Places Serving the Community

A community cannot exist without a variety of services. Some services, like fire and police protection, are an absolute necessity, while others, like stores, are more of a convenience. Still others, such as movie theaters, are there solely to entertain. Each place, however, can add to the quality of life in the community. The people working at these places have a variety of interesting jobs, and their work is important to the community. By understanding this, children can develop a better understanding of the community. The places serving the community can basically be divided into two groups: commercial and public service.

Commercial Locations. Places that exist to earn money for a profit constitute commercial locations. These include banks, stores, newspaper buildings, theaters, florists, some hospitals, and so forth. Children can understand the importance of these places to the community because they often know people who work at such places. Learning more about these places will help children to better comprehend the books they might read set in commercial locations.

Meeting some of the people who work at commercial locations and hearing them disucss the work they do is helpful. It might be possible to have one of the workers read a related story to the children as well. Books such as *Zoo Song* by Barbara Bottner and *Orchestranimals* by Vlasta van Kampen and Irene C. Eugen are appropriate not only at a zoo but at a symphony concert hall as well. Other books to share in conjunction with a zoo trip include *I Went to the Zoo* by Rita Gelman, *If Anything Ever Goes Wrong at the Zoo* by Mary Jean Hendrick, *When*

Re-creating the experience of a field trip through art transforms children into authors-illustrators of their own experiences.

We Went to the Zoo by Jan Ormerod, and *Alistair's Elephant* by Marilyn Sadler. Books that could be read in conjunction with a field trip to a store include *The Supermarket Mice* by Margaret Gordon, *George's Store at the Shore* by Francine Bassede, *The Storekeeper* by Tracy Campbell Pearson, and *The Pizza Monster* by Marjorie Sharmat and Mitchell Sharmat. Before (or after) taking children to visit

Alistair's Elephent *by Martin Sadler.*
Illustrations by Roger Bollen. © 1983; reprinted by permission of the publisher, Simon and Schuster Books for Young Readers.

transportation-related businesses, share books such as *Freight Train* by Donald Crews, *The Little Yellow School Bus* by Joe Ewers, *Trains* by Gail Gibbons, and Anne Rockwell's books: *Planes*, *Cars*, *Trains*, and *Trucks*.

Public Service Locations. In addition to the businesses found in the community, many services are provided through the work of public and private agencies. These services are often aimed at providing protection to residents, maintaining good health, and responding to the religious needs of the population. The places that provide these services are quite varied, making them fascinating field trip destinations. They include water filtration plants, firehouses, police stations, hospitals, clinics, weather stations, courthouses, churches, and so forth. The buildings often contain specialized equipment that performs important jobs related to the safety and health of the community. The people who work in these places are often quite willing to explain the importance of their work in the community.

A wide variety of books can be used in conjunction with a field trip to a public service location. When visiting a firehouse, one might read *Fire* by David Bennett or *Fire Engines* by Anne Rockwell. *Curious George Visits a Police Station*, one of a series of books by Margaret Rey and A.J. Shalleck, might be appropriate for use during a visit to the police station. Other books in this series follow Curious George as he visits an aquarium, restaurant, circus, hospital, and laundromat. A visit to a church or synagogue might include a reading of *Cathedral Mouse* by Kay Chorao. Books to read prior to visits to specific locations include *What's It Like to Be a Postal Worker* and *What's It Like to Be a Farmer*, both by Morgan Matthews; *What's It Like to Be a Firefighter* by Michael Pellowski; *What's It Like to Be a Chef* and *What's It like to Be a Sanitation Worker*, both by Susan Poskanzer; *What's It Like to Be a Veterinarian* by Judith Stamper; and *What's It Like to Be a Grocer* by Shelley Wilks.

Wherever a field trip has been scheduled, it is important to acknowledge and thank the people responsible for making it possible. Sharing a copy of an LEA story developed by the children after the trip is a thoughtful gesture. A thank you note might also be accompanied by photographs or children's drawings of the visit. Inviting radio, television, or newspaper reporters and photographers to accompany the children on these field trips is still another way of demonstrating the importance of the occasion.

PEOPLE TO SEE

It is impossible to arrange field trips to every place one would like children to visit, but many times a visit by a person with an interesting or specialized job may be even more meaningful. People are often flattered and quite willing to devote the time to such an activity. They can explain their jobs, demonstrate a piece or two of the equipment they use in the job, and perhaps read a story about their job to the children.

TIPS FOR TEACHERS

At program registration, survey parental occupations for possible future field trips and visitors.

Parents of children can be recruited for these activities. A meteorologist might demonstrate the use of a weather map, and read *Weather* by Rena Kirkpatrick. A boater, sailor, or shipyard worker might show how to make a paper boat, and read *Boats* by Ken Robbins. A florist or gardener might show how to display flowers, and read *Walkabout Flowers* by Henry Pluckrose. Each of these presentations could be followed by reenactments by the children. Parents may be the most overlooked group of people as positive contributors to learning within an educational program. Most likely, they will represent a number of different occupations and resources. It is critical to maintain frequent and effective communications with parents concerning the program. In this way, they will be better able to support it and contribute to it.

Other classroom visitors might include local artists or illustrators, teenagers, senior citizens, hockey players, and Santa Claus, to name a few possibilities.

Involving Parents

Parents often seek ways in which they can become actively involved in the education of their children. Parental involvement in both the literature and the content parts of the program can benefit parents, children, and the program. Parental inclusion in the program allows children to see various adults model the importance of books and helps them understand how books are related to life. In addition, children are usually delighted with and proud of the fact that their parents are visiting the classroom.

Classroom projects can involve many people. Courtesy Diana Comer.

Be sensitive to the fact that some parents cannot participate, usually because their jobs will not permit them to take the time off. When this occurs, other family members should be invited. Older siblings, aunts, uncles, and grandparents often represent a further source of people willing and eager to contribute to the education of children.

Careful planning of a parental visit will contribute to the success of the event. Inviting a parent to participate early or late in the day can help them fit the visit around their work schedule more easily. Day of the week, inclement weather, time of the year, and refreshments are all factors that need to be considered when planning parental participation. Notices and time schedules can aid both the parent, teacher, and the program. With careful planning, the program will not be overscheduled. Planning will also help to ensure that such things as notices and thank you notes are not overlooked. Developing a schedule for parental participation well in advance can help the planning for all involved. Keeping other parents informed about what is happening in advance can also be a benefit. They may be able to attend the program and even, in some cases, offer further discussion on ideas presented.

As with any effective part of the program, literature and books can be integrated with a parental visit. If parents are visiting the program to explain their jobs as bakers, lawyers, plumbers, or auto repair technicians, having them share a related story can enhance the visit. The story may be one selected by the teacher, parent, or child. Resources could be shared with parents beforehand to aid them in selecting an appropriate book. For example, a copy of one of the resource books by Jim Trelease[1] could be sent home two weeks before a planned visit by parents. In this way, parents could carefully consider a number of stories and choose the one they feel best supports the ideas they will talk about. Parents may also have children's books at home that were purchased because they were related to their employment.

Involving parents in education in this manner is a positive approach because it integrates them into their children's education. Parental involvement also makes use of a valuable resource: the work lives of the parents. Many parents are willing to help with the usual tasks of helping the school: baking cookies, supervising field trips, and helping at school parties. By including them in the actual educational program as well, one accords them additional respect.

Communicating with Parents

The key to an effective parental involvement program is communication. Parents must be aware of what is happening in the educational lives of their children. They need to know how they can help in the classroom, and what can be done at home with their children. This information goes beyond the usual notices about the topic being studied this month and the recommendation that parents read with their children. Those kinds of communications, while well intended, are too general to provide much guidance.

[1] Trelease, J. (1989). *The new read aloud handbook*. New York: Viking Penguin.

TIPS FOR TEACHERS

Ask parents what they would like to see in newsletters. Ask parents to contribute ideas for activities, book reviews, and projects to the newsletter.

This does not mean that a total home instructional program must be prepared to back up what is being done in the classroom. That would put an unhealthy amount of pressure on parents and children. But, if parents have a better idea of the topics being studied, why they are being studied, and the related books that they may wish to share at home, they will be in a better position to be involved. The idea is not to place pressure on anyone, parents or children, but to provide parents with enough information to be actively involved in making their children's educational life more meaningful.

TIPS FOR TEACHERS

Involve parents in the literacy development of their child.
* *Send home a weekly or monthly newsletter describing topics and activities being planned.*
* *Send home copies of books to be read with the children again, this time by the parents.*
* *Provide weekly suggestions for related activities to be done at home.*

Notes and Newsletters. Formal and informal parental communications are a primary source of information. They can be used to notify parents about more specific topics to be studied, the classroom visitor's schedule, meeting notices, and special projects for which supplies are needed. Newsletters can also be used to suggest books and stories related to the program. They can include home-based activities related to the literature and themes being used. These might include suggestions for repeated readings, museum visits, scavenger hunts, and local sightseeing opportunities.

Questionnaires and Surveys. Questionnaires and surveys can be distributed separately, or they can be part of a newsletter. Either way, they help to foster two-way communication. Requesting information and opinions gives parents an opportunity to provide input about their needs and potential contributions, such as classroom visits they would be willing to make, hobbies they could demonstrate, areas of concern, and activities in which they would like to be involved.

Community Representatives

In many cases, representatives of the community may be identified from the ranks of the parents of children in a program. When this is not the case, businesses, municipal departments, service organizations, and charitable foundations may be contacted as potential resources. The choices of whom to seek should be based upon the educational program and the learning goals for the children. Requesting a visit from an individual simply because he or she happens to be available may not be worthwhile. If the ensuing visit presents nothing to do with the program, it will be merely a diversion.

Individuals selected for classroom visits should represent the types of organizations one would visit on a field trip. The key is to include a diversity of visitors who can focus on specific areas of the program. They may be bankers, nurses, musicians, construction workers, office workers, or dentists. As such, the books that they may choose to share with the children will be equally diverse. A lawyer might use Peter Spier's *We the People*, while a nurse might use *All about Me* by Melanie Rice and Chris Rice. A meteorologist might read *The Stars Are Waiting* by Marjorie Murray, while an engineer could share *Cross a Bridge* by Ryan Hunter. A pilot or airline employee could share David Adler's *A Picture Book of Amelia Earhart*. A 4-H representative or farmer might choose to read Brenda Cook's *All about Farm Animals*. A baseball player could read *At the Ballgame* by S.A. Kramer, and a railroad worker could share *Shortcut* by Donald Crews.

Classroom visits require the same careful planning as a field trip. Making arrangements early helps all involved. A thank you note accompanied by illustrations or a copy of the LEA story developed by the children after the visit is usually appreciated by the guest. Including announcements in the parents' newsletter before and after a visitation is beneficial. It enables parents to extend the learning through discussion and by listening to their children tell about the experience.

SUMMARY

Most communities have a wealth of resources that can be useful to an early education program. The resources may be somewhat different from place to place, but such things as firehouses and restaurants are usually common to all. Since learning often depends on the development of background knowledge and an understanding of the world, it is beneficial to include the resources of a community in the educational program. Literature can be used to enhance this part of an integrated curriculum.

A community can be seen as including places and people. The places that make up a community are diverse, including everything from libraries to stores to churches. The people of the community reflect that diversity. In most communities one will encounter a variety of workers in such fields as banking, fire protection, music, and dentistry. Whether one takes the children to the place of work or brings the workers to the children, much will be learned.

Parents can be an outstanding source of support for field trip coordination and classroom visitations. A key component of tapping this resource is effective two-way communication. Such communication enables both parents and teachers to understand the concerns and needs of the children. Through this sharing, more effective instruction and learning can be planned.

QUESTIONS FOR THOUGHT AND DISCUSSION

1. What are some of the ways in which young children can learn about their community?
2. Why should field trips be planned as part of an integrated educational program?
3. Why is it important for young children to learn about their communities?
4. What are the two major areas to be considered in field trip planning?
5. When and why should literature be used in conjunction with a field trip?
6. What are some of the things children can learn from a field trip to a public library?
7. How should one select the books to be used in conjunction with a field trip?
8. Why can a class visitor sometimes provide an experience that is just as meaningful as a field trip?
9. How can parents as class visitors contribute to the educational programs of young children?
10. Why is effective communication important to successful parental involvement in the educational program?
11. How can parent/school communication be made more meaningful?

CHILDREN'S BOOKS CITED

Adler, D. (1998). *A picture book of Amelia Earhart*. New York: Holiday House.

Agee, J. (1988). *The incredible paintings of Felix Clousseau*. New York: Farrar, Straus, Giroux.

Babcock, C. (1993). *No moon*. New York: Crown.

Bassede, F. (1998). *George's store at the shore*. New York: Orchard.

Bennett, D. (1989). *Fire*. New York: Bantam.

Bottner, B. (1987). *Zoo song*. New York: Scholastic.

Boyd, L. (1998). *Lulu Crow's garden*. Boston: Little Brown.

Brown, L.K. & Brown, M. (1986). *Visiting the art museum*. New York: E.P. Dutton.

Chorao, K. (1988). *Cathedral mouse*. New York: E.P. Dutton.

Cohen, M. (1979). *Lost in the museum*. New York: Dell.

Cook, B. (1989). *All about farm animals*. New York: Doubleday.

Crews, D. (1989). *Freight train*. New York: Scholastic.

Crews, D. (1996). *Shortcut*. New York: Mulberry.

Crosbie, M. & Rosenthal, S. (1993). *Architecture colors*. New York: Preservation Press.

Crosbie, M. & Rosenthal, S. (1993). *Architecture counts*. New York: Preservation Press.

Crosbie, M. & Rosenthal, S. (1993). *Architecture shapes*. New York: Preservation Press.

Ewers, J. (1992). *The little yellow school bus*. New York: Random House.

Gelman, R. (1993). *I went to the zoo*. New York: Scholastic.

Gibbons, G. (1985). *Check it out*. New York: Harcourt Brace Jovanovich.

Gibbons, G. (1987). *Trains*. New York: Holiday House.

Gordon, M. (1984). *The supermarket mice*. New York: E.P. Dutton.

Hendrick, M.J. (1993). *If anything ever goes wrong at the zoo*. San Diego, CA: Harcourt Brace Jovanovich.

Hunter, R. (1998). *Cross a bridge*. New York: Holiday House.

Kirkpatrick, R. (1991). *Weather*. Austin, TX: Raintree.

Kramer, S.E. (1994). *At the ballgame*. New York: Random House.

Lavies, B. (1989). *Lily pad pond*. New York: E.P. Dutton.

Matthews, M. (1990). *What's it like to be a farmer*. Mahwah, NJ: Troll.

Matthews, M. (1990). *What's it like to be a postal worker*. Mahwah, NJ: Troll.

Mayhew, J. (1989). *Katie's picture show*. New York: Bantam.

McMillan, B. (1992). *Going on a whale watch*. New York: Scholastic.

Murray, M. (1998). *The stars are waiting*. Tarrytown, NY: Marshall Cavendish.

Oppenheim, J. (1994). *Oceanarium*. New York: Byron Press.

Ormerod, J. (1991). *When we went to the zoo*. New York: Lothrop, Lee, & Shepard.

Pearson, T.C. (1988). *The storekeeper*. New York: Dial.

Pellowski, M. (1990). *What's it like to be firefighter*. Mahwah, NJ: Troll.

Pluckrose, H. (1994). *Walkabout flowers*. Danbury, CT: Children's Press.

Poskanzer, S. (1990). *What's it like to be chef*. Mahwah, NJ: Troll.

Poskanzer, S. (1989). *What's it like to be a sanitation worker*. Mahwah, NJ: Troll.

Rey, M. & Shalleck, A.J. (1989). *Curious George visits a police station*. New York: Scholastic.

Rice, M. & Rice, C. (1987). *All about me*. New York: Doubleday.

Robbins, K. (1989). *Boats*. New York: Scholastic.

Rockwell, A. (1986). *Cars*. New York: E.P. Dutton.

Rockwell, A. (1993). *Fire engines*. New York: E.P. Dutton.

Rockwell, A. (1985). *Planes*. New York: E.P. Dutton.

Rockwell, A. (1992). *Trains*. New York: E.P. Dutton.

Rockwell, A. (1988). *Trucks*. New York: E.P. Dutton.

Rohmann, E. (1994). *Time flies*. New York: Crown.

Sadler, M. (1984). *Alistair in outer space*. Englewood Cliffs, NJ: Prentice Hall.

Sadler, M. (1983). *Alistair's elephant*. New York: Prentice Hall.

Sharmat, M. & Sharmat, M. (1989). *The pizza monster*. New York: Delacourt.

Smith, M. (1998). *This is your garden*. New York: Alfred A. Knopf.

Spier, P. (1987). *We the people*. New York: Doubleday.

Stamper, J. (1990). *What's it like to be a veterinarian*. Mahwah, NJ: Troll.

Van Kampen, V. & Eugen, I.C. (1989). *Orchestranimals*. New York: Scholastic.

Wilks, S. (1990). *What's it like to be a grocer*. Mahwah, NJ: Troll.

SELECTED REFERENCES

Berger, E. H. (1995). *Parents as partners in education: Families and schools working together*. Englewood Cliffs, NJ: Merrill.

Dunst, C.J., Trivette, C.M. & Deal, A.G. (1994). *Supporting and strengthening families*. Cambridge, MA: Brookline.

Gestwicki, C. (1992). *Home, school, and community relations: A guide to working with parents*. Albany, NY: Delmar Publishers.

Kohl, M.A. & Gainer, C. (1991). *Good earth art: Environmental art for kids*. Bellingham, WA: Bright Ring.

Moore, C. (1990). *A reader's guide for parents of children with mental, physical or emotional disabilities*. Rockville, MD: Woodbine.

Powell, D.R. (1989). *Families and early childhood programs*. Washington, DC: NAEYC.

Shockley, B., Michaelson, B. & Allen, J. (1995). *Engaging families*. Portsmouth, NH: Heineman.

Trelease, J. (1995). *The new read aloud handbook*. New York: Viking Penguin.

Vopat, J. (1995). *The parent project*. York, ME: Stenhouse.

... and they lived happily ever after.

Publishers and Suppliers

BOOKS

Companies identified with an asterisk (*) have a focus on one or more of the following: multiculturalism, disabilities, gender issues, social justice, self-esteem.

* Advocacy Press, P.O. Box 236, Santa Barbara, California 93102

* Africa World Press, P.O. Box 1892, Trenton, New Jersey 08607

Annick Press, P.O. Box 1338, Ellicot Station, Buffalo, New York 14205

Atheneum Books, 1230 Avenue of the Americas, New York, New York 10020

Bantam Doubleday Dell, 666 Fifth Avenue, New York, New York 10103

Boyds Mills Press, 910 Church Street, Honesdale, Pennsylvania 18431

Candlewick Press, 2067 Massachusetts Avenue, Cambridge, Massachusetts 02140

* Carolrhoda Books, 241 First Avenue North, Minneapolis, Minnesota 55401

Children's Book Council, 67 Irving Place, New York, New York 10003

Children's Television Workshop, 1 Lincoln Plaza, New York, New York 10023

Clarion Books, 222 Berkeley Street, Boston, Massachusetts 02116

Crowell, 10 East 53rd Street, New York, New York 10022

Crown Publishers, 400 Hahn Road, Westminster, Maryland 21157

Doubleday & Company, 245 Park Avenue, New York, New York 10167

Dutton Children's Books, 375 Hudson Street, New York, New York 10014

Farrar, Straus, Giroux, 19 Union Square West, New York, New York 10003

* Free Spirit Publishing, Suite 616, 400 First Avenue North, Minneapolis, Minnesota 55401

Greenwillow, 1350 Avenue of the Americas, New York, New York 10019

Grolier Publishing, 90 Sherman Turnpike, Danbury, Connecticut 06816

Harcourt Brace Jovanovich, 1250 Sixth Avenue, San Diego, California 92101

HarperCollins, 10 East 53rd Street, New York, New York 10022

Henry Holt, 115 West 18th Street, New York, New York 10011

Hill & Wang, 19 Union Square West, New York, New York 10003

Holiday House, 425 Madison Avenue, New York, New York 10017

Houghton Mifflin, 222 Berkeley Street, Boston, Massachusetts 02116

* Just Us Books, Suite 22-24, 301 Main Street, Orange, New Jersey 07050

* Kar-Ben Copies, 6800 Tildenwood Lane, Rockville, Maryland 20852

Alfred Knopf, 400 Han Road, Westminster, Maryland 21157

* Lee & Low Books, 95 Madison Avenue, New York, New York 10016

Little, Brown and Company, 34 Beacon Street, Boston Massachusetts 02106

Lothrop, Lee & Shepard, 105 Madison Avenue, New York, New York 10016

McGraw-Hill, 1221 Avenue of the Americas, New York, New York 10020

Macmillan Publishing Company, 866 Third Avenue, New York, New York 10022

William Morrow, 1350 Avenue of the Americas, New York, New York 10019

* North–South Books, Suite 800, 1123 Broadway, New York, New York 10010

* Open Hand Publishing, P.O. Box 22048, Seattle, Washington 98122

Orchard Books, 95 Madison Avenue, New York, New York 10016

* Our Child Press, 800 Maple Glen Lane, Wayne, Pennsylvania 19087

Prentice Hall, 1230 Avenue of the Americas, New York, New York 10020

Price/Stern/Sloan, 200 Madison Avenue, New York, New York 10016

Puffin, 375 Hudson Street, New York, New York 10014

G. P. Putnam's Sons, 200 Madison Avenue, New York, New York 10010

Raintree/Steck-Vaughn, P.O. Box 26015, Austin, Texas 78755

Random House, 400 Hahn Road, Westminster, Maryland 21157

Scholastic, 2931 East McCarty Street, Jefferson City, Missouri 65101

Scott Foresman, 1900 East Lake Avenue, Glenview, Illinois 60025

Simon and Schuster, 1230 Avenue of the Americas, New York, New York 10020

Troll Associates, 100 Corporate Drive, Mahwah, New Jersey 07430

* Victory Publishers, 3504 Oak Drive, Menlo Park, California 94025

Viking Penguin, 40 West 23rd Street, New York, New York 10010

Franklin Watts, Sherman Turnpike, Danbury, Connecticut 06816

Western Publishing, 850 Third Avenue, New York, New York 10022

* Albert Whitman, 6340 Oakton Street, Morton Grove, Illinois 60053

* Willowisp Press, 10100 SBF Drive, Pinellas Park, Florida 34666

Workman Publishing, 708 Broadway, New York, New York 10003

BOOK CLUBS

Walt Disney Music, Discovery Series, Department 5W5, 5959 Triumph Street, Commerce, California 90040

Firefly Book Club, Scholastic, 2931 East McCarty Street, P.O. Box 7503, Jefferson City, Missouri 65101

Golden Book Club, Western Publishing, 3650 Milwaukee Street, P.O. Box 7967, Madison, Wisconsin 53778

Parents Magazine Read-Aloud Book Club, 1 Parents Circle, P.O. Box 10264, Des Moines, Iowa 50336

Seesaw Book Club, Scholastic, 2931 East McCarty Street, P.O. Box 7503, Jefferson City, Missouri 65101

Sesame Street Book Club, Golden Press, 120 Brighton Road, Clifton, New Jersey 07012

Dr. Seuss and His Friends, The Beginner Readers Program, Department ZBU, Grolier Enterprises, P.O. Box 1797, Danbury, Connecticut 06816

Troll Book Club, 320 Route 17, Mahwah, New Jersey 07498

Trumpet Book Club, P.O. Box 604, Holmes, Pennsylvania 19043

Weekly Reader Children's Book Club, 4343 Equity Drive, P.O. Box 16613, Columbus, Ohio 43216

BIG BOOKS

Addison Wesley, 2725 Sand Hill Road, Menlo Park, California 94025

Harcourt Brace Jovanovich, 6277 Sea Harbor Drive, Orlando, Florida 32887

Houghton-Mifflin, 222 Berkeley Street, Boston, Massachusetts 02116

McGraw-Hill, 220 East Danieldale Road, DeSoto, Texas 75115

Random House, Department 436, 400 Hahn Street, Westminster, Maryland 21157

Rigby, P.O. Box 797, Crystal Lake, Illinois 60039

Scholastic, P.O. Box 7501, 2931 East McCarty Street, Jefferson City, Missouri 65101

Scott-Foresman, 1900 East Lake Avenue, Glenview, Illinois 60025

Sundance, P.O. Box 1326, Littleton, Massachusetts 01460

Troll Associates, 100 Corporate Drive, Mahwah, New Jersey 07430

Wright Group, 19201-120th Avenue NE, Bothell, Washington 98011

B Caldecott Medal Winners

DATE	TITLE	AUTHOR/ILLUSTRATOR
1938	*Animals of the Bible*	Helen Dean Fish/Dorothy P. Lathrop
1939	*Mei Li*	Thomas Handforth
1940	*Abraham Lincoln*	Ingri and Edgar Parin D'Aulaire
1941	*They Were Good and Strong*	Robert Lawson
1942	*Make Way for Ducklings*	Robert McCloskey
1943	*The Little House*	Virginia Lee Burton
1944	*Many Moons*	James Thurber/Louis Slobodkin
1945	*Prayer for a Child*	Rachel Field/Elizabeth Orton Jones
1946	*The Rooster Crows*	Traditional/Maud and Miska Petersham
1947	*The Little Island*	Golden MacDonald/Leonard Weisgard
1948	*White Snow, Bright Snow*	Alvin Tresselt/Roger Duvoisin
1949	*The Big Snow*	Berta & Elmer Hader
1950	*Song of the Swallows*	Leo Politi
1951	*The Egg Tree*	Katherine Milhous
1952	*Finders Keepers*	William Lipkind/Nicholas Mordvinoff
1953	*The Biggest Bear*	Lynd Ward
1954	*Madeline's Rescue*	Ludwig Bemelmans
1955	*Cinderella, or The Glass Slipper*	(Trad.) Charles Perrault/Marcia Brown
1956	*Frog Went A-Courtin*	ed. John Langstaff/Feodor Rojankovsky
1957	*A Tree Is Nice*	Janice May Undry/Marc Simont
1958	*Time of Wonder*	Robert McCloskey
1959	*Chanticleer and the Fox*	(Adaptation) Geoffrey Chaucer/ Barbara Cooney
1960	*Nine Days to Christmas*	Marie Hall Ets and Aurora Labastida/ Marie Hall Ets
1961	*Baboushka and the Three Kings*	Ruth Robbins/Nicolas Sidakov
1962	*Once a Mouse*	Marcia Brown
1963	*The Snowy Day*	Ezra Jack Keats
1964	*Where the Wild Things Are*	Maurice Sendak

1965	*May I Bring a Friend?*	Beatrice Schenk DeRegniers/ Beni Montresor
1966	*Always Room for One More*	Sorche Nic Leodhas/Nonny Hogrogian
1967	*Sam, Bangs & Moonshine*	Evaline Ness
1968	*Drummer Hoff*	Barbara Emberly/Ed Emberly
1969	*The Fool of the World*	Arthur Ransome/Uri
1970	*Sylvester and the Magic Pebble*	William Steig
1971	*A Story–A Story*	Gail E. Haley
1972	*One Fine Day*	Nonny Hogrogian
1973	*The Funny Little Woman*	(Retold) Arlene Mosel/Blair Lent
1974	*Duffy and the Devil*	Harve Zemach/Margot Zemach
1975	*Arrow to the Sun*	(Adaptation) Gerald McDermott
1976	*Why Mosquitoes Buzz in People's Ears*	(Retold) Verna Aardema/Leo and Diane Dillon
1977	*Ashanti to Zulu: African Traditions*	Margaret Musgrove/Leo and Diane Dillon
1978	*Noah's Ark*	Peter Spier
1979	*The Girl Who Loved Wild Horses*	Paul Goble
1980	*Ox-Cart Man*	Donald Hall/Barbara Cooney
1981	*Fables*	Arnold Lobel
1982	*Jumanji*	Chris Van Allsburg
1983	*Shadow*	(Translation) Blaise Cendrars/ Marcia Brown
1984	*The Glorious Flight: Across the Channel with Louis Bieriot*	Alice and Martin Provensen
1985	*St. George and the Dragon*	(Retold) Margaret Hodges/ Trina Schart Hyman
1986	*The Polar Express*	Chris Van Allsburg
1987	*Hey Al*	Arthur Yorinks/Richard Egielski
1988	*Owl Moon*	Jane Yolen/John Schoenherr
1989	*Song and Dance Man*	Karen Ackerman/Stephen Gammell
1990	*Lon Po Po/A Red-Riding Hood Story from China*	Ed Young (illustrator and translator)
1991	*Black and White*	David Macaulay
1992	*Tuesday*	David Weisner
1993	*Mirette on the High Wire*	Emily Arnold McCully
1994	*Grandfather's Journey*	Allen Say
1995	*Smoky Night*	David Diaz
1996	*Officer Buckle and Gloria*	Peggy Rathman
1997	*Golem*	David Wisniewski
1998	*Rapunzel*	Paul O. Zelinsky
1999	*Snowflake Bentley*	Jacqueline Briggs Martin/Mary Azarian

APPENDIX C
Thematic Unit Outline for Preschoolers: Bears

The purpose of a unit for three- and four-year-olds is to expand opportunities to use and acquire language. To do this, there should be an increased emphasis on stories with simple plots. Simple plots enable children to develop a sense of story while reinforcing their understanding of the power of language. Stories provide ideas for play. Children frequently re-create scenes from within the stories. Oral language skills grow rapidly during the early childhood years, and children may seek to retell parts of the stories. Encourage them to share some of their own background that is relevant to the story.

This thematic unit is adapted from one originally published in *Integrated Language Arts for Emerging Literacy* by Walter and Jean Sawyer, published by Delmar Publishers, Albany, NY, in 1991. The outline presented here includes objectives, activities, poems, songs, and parental activities related to the central theme of "bears." Although one objective is that children will learn information about bears from this unit, there are many more important language goals to be realized in the process.

OBJECTIVES

The purpose of the unit is to enable children to
- Develop an understanding of the concept of bears.
- Acquire information about kinds of bears (e.g. grizzly, teddy, polar) and where they might be found.
- Draw or write a scene from a book related to bears.
- Retell or re-create a concept or an idea from a story related to bears.
- Function in a developmentally appropriate way as a part of a group being read a story.

ACTIVITIES

To support the learning of children, adults might
1. Lead a discussion about bears. Elicit information from the children to help them see that they already have some knowledge about bears. Possible ideas for inclusion in the discussion include kinds of bears, homes, habits, hibernation, colors, and size.

2. Help children engage in a creative dramatics activity based on the story of "Goldilocks and the Three Bears."

3. Read aloud books related to bears on a regular basis during this period. Ask children to guess or predict what will happen at different points in the story.

4. Count the number of different kinds of bears discovered in the books read.

5. Make cookies in the shape of teddy bears. Eat the cookies at snack time. For an alternative use a recipe for a snack from the *Teddy Bear's Picnic Cookbook* (Darling and Day, 1991).

6. Have children bring in their favorite teddy bear from home. Give the children an opportunity to talk about their bears at circle time.

7. Engage children in a cooperative project (e.g. constructing a mobile or a chart) related to bears.

BOOKS

Asch, F. (1988). *Bear shadow*. Englewood Cliffs, NJ: Prentice-Hall.

Asch, F. (1988). *Bear's bargain*. New York: Simon and Schuster.

Asch, F. (1988). *Happy birthday, moon*. New York: Prentice-Hall.

Barton, B. (1997). *Where's the bear?* New York: Mulberry.

Berenstain, S. & Berenstain J. (1966). *The bears' picnic*. New York: Beginner Books.

Berenstain, S. & Berenstain, J. (1988). *The Berenstain bears: ready, get set, go!* New York: Random House.

Bohdal, S. (1986). *Bobby the bear*. Salt Lake City, UT: North-South Books.

Brett, J. (1987). *Goldilocks and the three bears*. New York: Dodd, Mead.

Butler, D. (1989). *My brown bear Barney*. New York: Greenwillow.

Carlstrom, N. W. (1990). *It's about time, Jesse Bear*. New York: Macmillan.

Dagliesh, A. (1992). *The bears on Hemlock Mountain*. New York: Simon and Schuster.

Darling, A., & Day, A. (1991). *Teddy bears' picnic cookbook*. New York: Viking-Penguin.

De Beer, H. (1997). *Little Polar Bear mini pop-up book*. New York: North-South.

Dunbar, J. (1987). *A cake for Barney*. Danbury, CT: Orchard.

Freeman, D. (1976). *Bearymore*. New York: Penguin.

Freeman, D. (1968). *Corduroy*. New York: Viking.

Glen, M. (1991). *Ruby*. New York: G. P. Putnam's Sons.

Graham, T. (1987). *Mr. Bear's chair*. New York: E. P. Dutton.

Graham, T. (1988). *Mr. Bear's boat*. New York: E. P. Dutton.

Hall, D. (1985). *Polar Bear leaps*. New York: Alfred A. Knopf.

Hayes, S. (1986). *This is the bear*. New York: J. P. Lippincott.

Hofmann, G. (1986). *The runaway teddy bear*. New York: Random House.

Hofmann, G. (1978). *Who wants an old teddy bear?* New York: Random House.

Hissey, J. (1990). *Jolly tall*. New York: Philomel.

Inkpen, M. (1998). *Nothing*. New York: Orchard.

Johnston, T. (1991). *Little Bear sleeping*. New York: G. P. Putnam's Sons.

Maris, R. (1984). *Are you there, Bear?* New York: Viking Penguin.

Marshall, J. (1988). *Goldilocks and the three bears*. New York: Dial.

Martin, Jr., B. (1967). *Brown Bear, Brown Bear, what do you see?* New York: Holt, Rinehart, and Winston.

McCue, L. (1987). *Corduroy on the go*. New York: Viking-Kestral.

Minarik, E. H. (1957). *Little Bear*. New York: Harper and Row.

Morgan, M. (1988). *Edward loses his teddy bear*. New York: E. P. Dutton.

Morris, Jackie. (1995). *Bears, bears, and more bears* . Hauppague, NY: Barrows.

Muntean, M. (1983). *Bicycle Bear*. New York: Parents Magazine.

Murphy, J. (1984). *What next, Baby Bear!* New York: Dial

Penny, M. (1991). *Bears*. New York: Franklin Watts.

Rylands, L. (1989). *Teddy Bear's friend*. New York: E. P. Dutton.

Stoddard, S. (1985). *Bedtime for bears*. Boston: Houghton Mifflin.

Tolhurst, M. (1990). *Somebody and the three blairs*. New York: Orchard.

Waber, B. (1997). *Bearsie Bear and the surprise sleepover party*. Boston: Houghton Mifflin.

Wahl, J. (1987). *Humphrey's bear*. New York: Henry Holt.

Yeoman, J. (1987). *The bear's water picnic*. New York: Atheneum.

Yektai, N. (1991). *Bears in pairs*. New York: Simon & Schuster.

Zalben, J. B. (1988). *Beni's first Chanukah*. New York: Henry Holt.

Ziefert, H. (1986). *Bear all year: a guessing game book*. New York: Harper and Row.

POEMS

Alexander, R. (1983). "Bear Weather." In *Poetry place anthology*. New York: Scholastic.

Carlson, N. (1990). *It's about time, Jesse Bear*. New York: Scholastic.

Goldstein, B. (1989). *Bear in mind: A book of bear poems*. New York: Viking-Kestral.

Johnston, T. (1991). *Little Bear sleeping*. New York: G. P. Putnam's Sons.

Kredenser, G. (1983). "Polar Bear." In J. Prelutsky (Ed.), *The Random House book of poetry for children*. New York: Random House.

Martin, Jr., B. (1983). *Brown Bear, Brown Bear, what do you see?* New York: Henry Holt.

Prelutsky, J. (1986). "Grandma Bear." In *Ride a purple pelican*. New York: Greenwillow.

Yolen, J. (1983). "Grandma Bear." In J. Prelutsky, (Ed.), *The Random House book of poetry for children*. New York: Random House.

SONGS

Blankenship, J. (1984). *Teddy beddy bears*. New York: Random House.

Charette, R. (1983). "Baxter The Bear." In *Where do my sneakers go at night?* (record). Windham, ME: Pine Point Records.

Grayson, M. (1962). "The Bear Went Over The Mountain." In *Let's do finger plays*. Washington, DC: Robert B. Luce.

Nelson, E. L. (1984). "The Bear Song" and "Fuzzy Wuzzy (Was A Bear)." In *The funny song book*. New York: Sterling.

Recker, P., & Packard, R. (1984). "Lullaby For Teddy-o." In *Peanutbutterjam* (record). Hartford, CT: Peanutbutterjam Records.

Rosen, G., & Shontz, B. (1984). "One Shoe Bear" and "House At Pooh Corner." In *Rosenshontz: It's the truth* (record). Brattleboro, VT: RS Records.

Rosen, B., & Shontz, B. (1986). "Rock 'n' Roll Teddy Bear." In *Rosenshontz: Rock 'n' roll teddy bear* (record). Brattleboro, VT: RS Records.

Rosen, G., & Shontz, B. (1988). "Party Teddy Bears." In *Rosenshontz: Family vacation* (record). Brattleboro, VT: RS Records.

Wirth, M., Stassevitch, V., Shotwell, R., & Stemmler, P. (1983). "Teddy Bear Chant." In *Musical games, finger plays, and rhythmic activities for early childhood*. West Nyack, NY: Parker.

HANDS-ON ACTIVITIES

1. "Bear String Block Printing"—Children create a block print in the shape of a bear. If string is used, thick, flexible string is best for younger children. Complete instructions are found in *Storybook Stew* by Suzanne Barchers and Peter Rauen, published in 1996 by Fulcrum Publishing, Golden. CO.
2. "Teddy's Refrigerator Cookies"—A smaller group of children can make refrigerator cookies using this recipe. Plastic utensils should be used for slicing. The complete directions are available in the *Storybook Stew* publication.
3. Go outdoors for a teddy bear picnic. If the weather permits, do it on October 25, Teddy Roosevelt's birthday.

PARENT ACTIVITIES

Teachers should

1. Remind parents of the benefits of reading aloud books with bear characters and bear themes during this time.

2. Encourage parents to reread, at home, the books that were read aloud at school.

3. Suggest that parents listen to the child retell a story that was read in school.

4. Help parents to locate a toy store in order to look at the teddy bears on display. Talk about the different teddy bears (e.g. colors, size, attractiveness, similarities).

5. Encourage parents to make up a story about a teddy bear.

6. Suggest that the family visit a zoo to see live bears.

7. Share the benefits of a visit a library to take out books about bears.

8. Share songs about bears and teddy bears.

9. Ask parents to visit a museum to view an exhibit about bears.

10. Encourage playing with teddy bears with the child. Talk about the play, and encourage the child to talk about what is happening.

11. Suggest that families make cookies with a teddy bear cookie cutter.

12. Share activities such as making a sculpture of a bear using clay or play-dough.

13. Suggest that parents invite other children to have a teddy bear picnic in the park. Bring bear-shaped cookies, juice, and teddy bears.

Subject Grouping of Selected Books

The groupings of books in this section were selected because of their proven value with children. They are seen as truly exceptional pieces of literature containing important concepts and ideas that many young children will find motivating and interesting. The list does not contain every title found in this book. It is intended as a quick reference to be used on a regular basis as a starting point for locating high-quality books for children. Only the titles and authors are listed here. Full bibliographical information can be located using the author index and end-of-chapter references in this book.

ANIMALS AND ANIMAL CHARACTERS

Betty Birney, *Tyrannosaurus Tex*

Eric Carle, *The Grouchy Ladybug*

Eric Carle, *The Very Hungry Caterpillar*

Pamela Edwards, *Four Famished Foxes and Fosdyke*

Wanda Gag, *Millions of Cats*

Maggie Glen, *Ruby*

Bob Kolar, *Stomp, Stomp*

Dorothy Kunhardt, *Pat the Bunny*

Marcus Pfister, *The Rainbow Fish*

H. A. and Margaret Rey, *Curious George*

Serena Romanelli, *Little Bobo Saves the Day*

Douglas Wood, *Old Turtle*

BASIC SKILLS (ABC, COUNTING)

Catherine and Laurence Anholt, *One, Two, Three, Count with Me*

Michael Bond, *Paddington's 123*

Norman Bridwell, *Clifford's ABC*

Eric Carle, *1, 2, 3 to the Zoo*
Doyle Dodds, *The Shape of Things*
Ed Emberly, *First Words: Animals*
Paul Giganti, *Each Orange Had Eight Slices*
Tana Hoban, *26 Letters and 99 Cents*
Angela Johnson, *One of Three*
Steven Kellogg, *Aster Aardvark's Alphabet Adventures*
Bill Martin, Jr., and John Archambault, *Chicka Chicka Boom Boom*
Patricia McKissack, *A Million Fish . . . More or Less*
Cynthia Rylant, *Everyday Town*
Steven Schnur, *Autumn, an Alphabetic Acrostic*
Jenny Williams, *Everyday ABC*

COMMUNITY

Barbara Bottner, *Zoo Song*
Laurene Brown and Marc Brown, *Visiting the Art Museum*
Kay Chorao, *Cathedral Mouse*
Miriam Cohen, *Lost in the Museum*
Brenda Cook, *All about Farm Animals*
Donald Crews, *Freight Train*
Gail Gibbons, *Trains*
Margaret Gordon, *The Supermarket Mice*
S. A. Kramer, *At the Ballgame*
Tracy Pearson, *The Storekeeper*
Margaret Rey and A. J. Shalleck, *Curious George Visits a Police Station*

DISABILITIES

Charles Amenta, *Russell Is Extra Special*
Barbara Booth, *Mandy*
Miriam Cohen, *See You Tomorrow, Charles*
Barbara Dugan, *Loop the Loop*
Maggie Glen, *Ruby*
Debra Hess, *Wilson Sat Alone*
Robert Kraus, *Leo the Late Bloomer*
Margaret Mahy, *The Three-Legged Cat*
Daniel Pinkwater, *Uncle Melvin*

ELDERLY PERSONS

Tomie dePaola, *Nana Upstairs, Nana Downstairs*

Berlie Doherty, *Willa and Old Miss Annie*

Gloria Houston, *My Great Aunt Arizona*

Robert Munsch, *Love You Forever*

Douglas Wood, *Old Turtle*

Jill Paton Walsh, *When Grandma Came*

FAMILY AND FRIENDS

Aliki, *We Are Best Friends*

Tom Birdseye, *Waiting for Baby*

Anthony Browne, *Willy and Hugh*

Eve Bunting, *The Wall*

Nancy Carlson, *How to Lose All Your Friends*

Peter Catalanotto, *The Painter*

Teresa Celsi, *The Fourth Little Pig*

Trish Cooke, *So Much*

Judy Cox, *Now We Can Have a Wedding*

Jane Cutler, *Darcy and Gran Don't Like Babies*

Dorothy Corey, *Will There Be a Lap For Me?*

Rebecca Emberly, *My Mother's Secret Life*

Kevin Henkes, *A Weekend with Wendell*

Angela Johnson, *Joshua by the Sea*

Holly Keller, *Lizzy's Invitation*

Arnold Lobel, *Frog and Toad Are Friends*

George Ella Lyon, *Mama Is a Miner*

James Marshall, *George and Martha*

Sally Mavor, *You and Me*

Megan McDonald, *Beezy Magic*

Else Holmelund Minarik, *Little Bear's Friend*

Barbara Shook Hazen, *Tight Times*

Dav Pilkey, *A Friend for Dragon*

Chris Soentpiet, *Around Town*

Jill Paton Walsh, *When Grandma Came*

Elizabeth Winthrop, *As the Crow Flies*

FEARS AND CONCERNS

Marc Brown, *Arthur Goes to Camp* (imaginary fears)

Debbie Harter, *Walking Through the Jungle* (fear of the unknown)

Libby Hathorn, *Grandma's Shoes* (death of a grandparent)

Virginia Kroll, *Faraway Drums* (moving)

Susan Kuklin, *When I See My Dentist* (visit to a doctor or dentist)

Jonathan London, *Gray Fox* (illness)

Sheila MacGill-Callahan, *And Still the Turtle Watched* (pollution)

Vaunda Micheaux Nelson, *Always Gramma* (Alzheimer's disease)

Leslea Newman, *Too Far Away to Touch* (HIV/AIDS)

Sally Noll, *That Bothered Kate* (jealousy and guilt)

Matt Novak, *The Pillow War* (war)

Shulamith Oppenheim, *The Lilly Cupboard* (prejudice)

Dr. Seuss, *The Butter Battle Book* (war)

Tres Seymour, *We Played Marbles* (war)

Yukio Tsuchiya, *Faithful Elephants* (war)

Judith Viorst, *Mama Says There Aren't Any Zombies, Ghosts, Vampires, Creatures, Demons, Monsters, Fiends, Goblins or Things* (monsters)

Judith Viorst, *The Tenth Good Thing about Barney* (death)

Bernard Waber, *Ira Sleeps Over* (sleeping at a friend's house)

Elizabeth Winthrop, *As the Crow Flies* (divorce/separation)

HOLIDAYS AND SEASONS

Alan Benjamin, *Hanukkah Chubby Board Book And Dreidels*

Stan and Jan Berenstain, *Comic Valentine*

Margaret Wise Brown, *The Runaway Bunny*

Eve Bunting, *A Turkey for Thanksgiving*

Deborah Lattimore, *Cinderhazel* (Halloween)

Kim Lewis, *First Snow*

Robert Maass, *When Winter Comes*

Bill Martin, Jr., *Old Devil Wind* (Halloween)

Leslea Newman, *Matzo Ball Moon* (Passover)

Marcus Pfister, *The Christmas Star*

Janet Riehecky, *Christmas in Other Lands*

Allen Say, *Tree of Cranes* (Japan, Christmas)

Ben Schecter, *When Will the Snow Trees Grow?*

Lynne Schwartz, *The Four Questions* (Passover)

James Stevenson, *The Great Big Especially Beautiful Easter Egg*

Caroline Stutson, *By the Light of the Halloween Moon*

Martin Waddell, *Little Mo* (winter)

Charlotte Zolotow, *The Bunny Who Found Easter*

MULTICULTURAL

Asun Balzola, *Por Los Aires*

Omar Castaneda, *Abuela's Weave*

Veronika Charles, *The Crane Girl*

Debbie Chocolate, *The Piano Man*

Lucille Clifton, *The Boy Who Didn't Believe in Spring*

Juanita Havil, *Treasure Nap*

Yumi Heo, *One Afternoon*

Elizabeth Howard, *Aunt Flossie's Hats (and Crab Cakes Later)*

Linda Jacobs, *Amelia's Road*

Angela Johnson, *Daddy Calls Me Man*

Angela Johnson, *Joshua by the Sea*

Ryerson Johnson, *Kenji and the Magic Geese*

Ezra Jack Keats, *The Snowy Day*

Alejandro Cruz Martinez, *The Woman Who Outshone the Sun/La Mujer Que Brillaba Aun Mas Que el Sol*

Ann Morris, *Houses and Homes*

Chris Raschka, *Yo! Yes!*

Maxine Rosenberg, *Brothers and Sisters*

Cecile Schoberle, *Morning Sounds, Evening Sounds*

Catherine Stock, *Where Are You Going, Manyoni?*

Ashley Wolff, *Stella and Roy*

NATURE AND SCIENCE

Aliki, *My Visit to the Aquarium*

Chris Babcock, *No Moon*

Joanna Cole and Bruce Degen, *The Magic School Bus Inside the Human Body*

Susi Fowler, *I'll See You When The Moon Is Full*

Jean Craighead George, *Dear Rebecca, Winter Is Here*
Michelle Koch, *World Water Watch*
Reeve Lindbergh, *What Is the Sun?*
David Macaulay, *The Way Things Work*
Hana Machotka, *Terrific Tails*
Bruce McMillan, *Going on a Whale Watch*
Christopher Lynne Myers, *McCrephy's Field*
Daniel San Souci, *North Country Night*
Robert Yagelski, *The Day the Lift Bridge Stuck*
Charlotte Zolotow, *The Seashore Book*

SELF-ESTEEM

Tomie dePaola, *Oliver Button Is a Sissy*
Richard Edwards, *Moles Can Dance*
Helen Lester, *Three Cheers For Tacky*
Libba Moore Gray, *Fenton's Leap*
Kevin Henkes, *Chrysanthemum*
Holly Keller, *Lizzy's Invitation*
Pili Mandelbaum, *You Be Me, I'll Be You*
Margaret Miller, *Now I'm Big*
Watty Piper, *The Little Engine That Could*
Jane Yolen, *Sleeping Ugly*

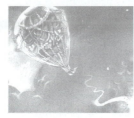

Author Index

Subject Index